Agile Technical Practices Distilled

A learning journey in technical practices and principles of software design

Pedro M. Santos

Marco Consolaro

Alessandro Di Gioia

Agile Technical Practices Distilled

Authors: Pedro M. Santos, Marco Consolaro, and Alessandro Di Gioia

Course Managing Editor: Vishal Kamal Mewada

Acquisitions Editor: Bridget Neale

Production Editor: Shantanu Zagade

Editorial Board: David Barnes, Mayank Bhardwaj, Ewan Buckingham, Simon Cox, Mahesh Dhyani, Taabish Khan, Manasa Kumar, Alex Mazonowicz, Douglas Paterson, Dominic Pereira, Shiny Poojary, Erol Staveley, Ankita Thakur, and Jonathan Wray

First Published: June 2019

Production Reference: 2030919

ISBN: 978-1-83898-084-9

Published by Packt Publishing Ltd.

Livery Place, 35 Livery Street

Birmingham B3 2PB, UK

Table of Contents

Testing Legacy Code   123

Design IV –Design Patterns 135

Design VIII –The Four Elementsof Simple Design   219

Preface

About

This section briefly introduces the authors and what is covered in this book.

About the Book

The number of popular technical practices has grown exponentially in the last few years. Learning the common fundamental software development practices can help you become a better programmer. This book uses the term agile as a wide umbrella and covers agile principles and practices, as well as most methodologies associated with it.

You'll begin by discovering how driver navigator, chess clock, and other techniques used in the pair programming approach introduce discipline while writing code. You'll then learn how to safely change the design of your code using refactoring. While learning these techniques, you'll also explore various best practices to write efficient tests. The concluding lessons of the book delve deep into the SOLID principles – the five design principles that you can use to make your software more understandable, flexible, and maintainable.

By the end of the book, you will have discovered new ideas for improving your software design skills, the relationship within your team, and the way your business works.

About the Authors

Pedro M. Santos has over 25 years of experience in the software industry. He has worked in the finance, aviation, consultancy, media, and retail industries and has built a wide range of software, ranging from embedded systems to cloud-based distributed applications. He has lived in Portugal (Lisbon), Brazil (São Paulo), Spain (Madrid, Barcelona), Netherlands (Hilversum), and Belgium (Gent), and, currently, he is based in the UK (London), where he focuses on educating and inspiring other developers. He has spent hundreds of hours in pairing sessions as well as coaching and mentoring developers at all levels of proficiency. His tutoring experience covers almost every aspect of software development: programming basics, object-oriented and functional design principles, refactoring legacy applications, pragmatic testing practices, architectural decisions, and career development choices. Follow Pedro on Twitter at *@pedromsantos*.

Marco Consolaro is a software craftsman, systems thinker, agile technical coach, entrepreneur, philosopher, and restless traveler – all blended with Venetian humor. Marco learned to code in Basic on a Commodore when he was 9 years old. He graduated from Venice University in 2001 with a degree in Computer Science. Since then, Marco has worked in Italy and the UK and is always looking to learn something new. When his journey led him to the agile principles, he quickly realized the effectiveness of such an approach for both technical and organizational areas. He now strongly believes that an iterative approach based on trust, transparency, self-organization, and quick feedback loops is the key to success for any team in any discipline. His dream is to see these principles based on systems thinking understood and implemented at every level in businesses and public administrations. Follow Marco on Twitter at *@consolondon*.

Alessandro Di Gioia has helped a variety of companies (from small startups to large enterprises for the past 18 years) embrace agile technical practices. He has worked in Italy and Norway. For the past few years, he has resided in London. His professional life changed when he came across agile methodologies, especially Extreme Programming. He likes concise, expressive, and readable code as well as making existing solutions better when needed. He is always trying to learn better ways of designing asynchronous distributed architectures and crafting software, in either an object-oriented or functional style. Although Alessandro considers himself a forever learner, he is also a coach and a mentor because he loves to share his experiences with others. Follow Alessandro on Twitter at *@Parajao*.

Learning Objectives

- Apply the red, green, and refactor cycle of TDD to solve procedural problems
- Implement the various techniques used in the pair programming approach
- Use code smells as feedback
- Test your production code using mocks and stubs
- Refactor legacy code to bring it in line with modern agile standards
- Apply the object calisthenics ruleset to enhance your software design

Approach

The content in this book is presented as a journey. Each concept is introduced gradually. New concepts are added on top of the previous materials. Several exercises are available for you to spend some time practicing the new material.

Audience

This book is designed for software developers looking to improve their technical practices. Software coaches may also find it helpful as a teaching reference manual. This is not a beginner's book on how to program. You must be comfortable with at least one programming language and must be able to write unit tests using any unit testing framework.

Acknowledgements

Pedro

This book is for my love and life companion, Nucha. Without her, I would not be what I am.

I dedicate this book to my sons – Diogo, Vasco, and André.

I also dedicate this book to my mother, Odete Pinto, for her love and all she sacrificed to allow me to become what I am today.

Finally, I dedicate this book to my brother, João Moreira Santos – a brother, a friend, and an example.

I would like to thank many others that also helped shape me. I'm only standing on the shoulders of giants. First, to my grandparents – Eduardo Ferreira dos Santos, Maria Augusta Moreira, Rosa Pinto, and Pedro Pinto; my uncles – Antonio Moreira and Fernando Moreira; my friends – Sergio Antunes, Fernando Silva, Pedro Pinto, António (Tó) Nunes, Nuno Joaquinito, Jorge Silva, Pedro Friezas, Edin Kapic, Ger Mán, Samir Talwar, Sandro Mancuso, Guillem Fernandez, Marcos Grau, and Robert Firek; my high school teachers – Maria Barroso, Carlos, Daniel, and Franco; my coauthors and friends, Marco Consolaro and Alessandro Di Gioia, and, finally, to my very dear and missed friend, Nelson dos Santos Costa.

"Se a vida fosse curta todos os homens seriam poetas."

Marco

Firstly, I want to dedicate this book to my family. My wife, Joanna Kathlyn, for the support and the patience of dealing with me in everyday life; my mum, Mariuccia, for always believing in me; and my cousin, Devis Cracco, who let me play with his Commodore when we were kids. This book couldn't be possible without you.

A special mention goes to my dear and still missed father, Stefano, who passed away almost two decades ago, even before my graduation – his greatest wish. His example has been the main cornerstone of my education and I am proud of always being the one defending the Truth, free critical thinking, and respect for others – no matter what.

I am sure you would be proud of who I am and of the achievement of writing this book. I hope to be able to do the same good job with your grandson, Jaden Stefano, the latest, greatest joy of our family. And thanks to you, Jaden, for taking out the best of us all!

Next, I want to thank here my high school's informatics teacher, Paola Trappolin, for the patience she had with me in those years. She was very disappointed with my lack of discipline, but never let that jeopardize my motivation, recognizing and honestly appreciating my talent.

The same was also true for my math teacher, Paolo Quadri, who recently passed to a better life. Thank you for leading and teaching by example, not just with words. The world needs more teachers like you!

Ultimately, I want to mention a few top quality professionals I met during my career who share the same values and, with time, became inevitably great friends. They have always been very supportive and genuinely excited about this work. People such as Nick Tune, Joao Fernandes, Eldon Ferran De Pol, Michele Leonetti, Claudio Perrone, and, obviously, Pedro and Alex, the other four hands on this book. Thanks for never making me feel alone in the holistic, everyday battle for improving the general quality of software development. We are still a minority, but this book might help the cause!

A special final mention to Sandro Mancuso and the fantastic Codurance's gang where Pedro, Alex, and me initially met: the seed of this book has been planted there. Thank you for being the great environment where our destiny crossed and changed!

Alessandro

Not even in my prayers and my dreams, I was hoping for you to achieve all of this. Your accomplishments are proof that I did well as a father. This is what my father told me just some months ago after 5 years since I moved from Italy. The truth is without my parents, their support, their trust and faith in what I and my sister could do I wouldn't have done much. So I want to dedicate this book to my parents Gianpaolo and Rosaria, and to my lovely little sister Eleonora. Thinking of you all makes me feel at home anywhere. I also want to dedicate this book to one special person in my life, my love, friend and sparring partner Giulia. 13 years and not feeling them. This book is also dedicated to my Kung Fu teacher, Master Yang Lin Sheng and his family. He accepted me as one of his students almost twenty years ago and showed me the real meaning of Kung Fu. It is a lifelong lesson to learn but I am enjoying every single step in this journey. Finally, I want to dedicate this book to a special person that since I was a child represented the symbol of intelligence, competence, hard work and success. My cousin Antonio Magrì which saw all of this more than 30 years ago. I will never forget you. There are many people that helped me improve, grow and keep up in hard times. My friend and mentor Pedro Moreira dos Santos, my apprentice Halima Koundi, my friends: Mike J. Sullivan you'll go far, a software designer talent Marco Consolaro, friends and real rock star developers Frode Hus, Jarle Nigård, Anders Østhus, Jith Ponrasa, Lorenzo Tandin and Andrea Germani, my reality check Ed Pollit, Steve Lydford I'll never forget our long talks coaching each other, the two master craftsmen Sandro Mancuso and Mashooq Badar, my "brothers" Stefano Nava, Luca Recalcati, Antonello Italiano, Giorgio Banfi, Riccardo Oriani and "sisters" Sara Leva, Alessandra Dell'Orco, Marzia Palladino and all the amazing people I had the pleasure to meet at Codurance.

Conventions

Code words in text, database table names, folder names, filenames, file extensions, pathnames, dummy URLs, user input, and Twitter handles are shown as follows: "The `GetTask` method returns the next task to execute on the instrument."

A block of code is set as follows:

```
var username = new Random().Next(1, 11) % 2 == 0
                ? "Pedro"
                : string.Empty;
```

New terms and important words are shown in bold. Words that you see on the screen, for example, in menus or dialog boxes, appear in the text like this: "This has the consequence of testing the test infrastructure rather than the **Subject Under Test**."

Agile Technical Practices

The most difficult step ever is the first step. It comes with doubts, uncertainties, and all sort of fears. If you defy all odds and take it, your confidence will replicate very fast and you'll become a master!

– Israelmore Ayivor

Is This Book for Me?

This book is about technical practices in the context of agile software development. It is aimed at software developers looking to improve their technical practices. Software coaches may also find it helpful as a teaching reference manual.

This is not a beginner's book on how to program. We expect readers to be comfortable with at least one programming language and to be able to write unit tests using any unit testing framework.

Why We Wrote This Book?

The principal driving forces that pushed us to craft this book are the passion for what we do and the wish to provide a straightforward path to other fellow developers. We have been working for the last 20 years in the software world as developers, coaches, and mentors. The content of this book has been distilled over those years of daily practicing, experimenting, and sharing.

We have been teaching and coaching others on this material for years with such amazing results that we felt that writing this book was something we owed to the community. We independently came to the conclusion that the very important matters about software development are the principles driving every line of code, not the technical knowledge of one specific vendor's product or another. Astonishingly, when discussing this, we discovered that we all share the very same principles (with some personal flavors).

We have identified a journey that could take the most diligent readers to mastery in a matter of weeks. If you are prepared to spend some time and effort going through the material, you will improve as a software developer.

We are what we repeatedly do. Hence, excellence is not an act, but a habit.

– Will Durant, paraphrasing Aristotle's Nicomachean Ethics

Why Distilled?

Distillation is the purification or concentration of a substance, obtaining the essence or volatile properties contained in it. It is also the separation of one substance from another. In this book, we will try to do the same, extracting and sharing the essence of all the best practices we have come across in our careers. We are concentrating here on the best of the best of what has worked, enriched by our own principles and values.

We want this book to be a single reference for what we think are the essential practices a developer should master. We have learned our lessons the hard way, but you don't have to. If you learn even one thing from it, you are already a better professional than yesterday. If you are better, the world of software development is better: **transcendental Kaizen**.

The idea for the book's title arose when the plan was born on a rare snowy night in London. After discussing the idea together over pizza (and a few Peronis), we ordered a couple of rounds of digestive grappa. It was then that we started joking about the title and soon we had fallen in love with it, so here it is!

> **Caution**
>
> In Vicenza (Veneto, Italy), there are several instances per year of addiction to grappa.

What are Agile Technical Practices?

During the last decade, the number of popular technical practices has grown exponentially. So, coming up with a list of core ones can be a daunting task. Every single programmer will have core beliefs, and a consensus can be challenging to achieve. However, the authors feel that among all those techniques there are a number of essential principles to grasp from many of them.

We use the agile term as a wide umbrella covering agile principles and practices as well as most methodologies associated with it. As for technical practices within agile, we will need to explore a bit.

The Agile Manifesto does not mention any technical practices. Scrum And Kanban do not specify any either. Can we use the software craftsmanship manifesto? There are no specific technical practices are discussed there either. What about **Extreme Programming (XP)**?

XP does have a set of technical practices, namely:

- Feedback:
    - Pair programming
    - Planning games
    - Test-driven development (TDD)
    - Whole teams

- Continuous process:
    - Continuous integration
    - Design improvements/refactoring
    - Small releases

- Shared understanding:
    - Coding standards
    - Collective code ownership
    - Simple designs
    - System metaphors

- Programmer welfare:
    - A sustainable pace

Which of the previously mentioned fundamental technical practices can be trained and studied individually?

In this book, we decided to focus our attention mainly on these four:

- TDD
- Pair programming
- Refactoring
- Simple designs

Now, another question arises: do we really need a core of technical practices in agile? Let's try to answer this with two more questions:

1. *How often do projects stagnate under their own weight?*

2. *Why does this happen over and over again?*

One of the main causes is probably technical debt. This is one of the reasons why technical practices are so crucial to the success of an agile project. They allow us to continue delivering value by addressing the accidental complexity or tech debt as it emerges.

So, is the subset of XP practices (TDD, pair programming, refactoring, and simple design) our core practices? Could these practices help prevent tech debt from accumulating? Simple design and refactoring look promising. Let's label them as *technical design practices*. What about pair programming and TDD? They belong in a slightly different category. Let's label them as technical feedback practices.

Working with practices related to design and feedback empowers experimentation. Consider a design change: first you get feedback from the pair, then change the design, and get feedback from the tests. Quick, continuous experimentation using feedback loops is how all kinds of systems can evolve and our programs make no exceptions. That's why you should aim to build a structure that gives quick feedback you can trust, so you can try new things without the worry of breaking the existing ones. Remember: "Inertia is your enemy!"

Optimism is an occupational hazard of programming: feedback is the treatment.

– Kent Beck, Extreme Programming Explained

TDD, pair programming, refactoring, and simple design are still reasonably big boxes we must open. So, let's see what we might find inside of each one.

Pair Programming

When we are more granular on pair programming, we find the following concepts and practices:

- Driver-navigator
- Ping-Pong/Popcorn
- Chess clock
- Pomodoro
- Pair rotation

Test-Driven Development TDD

There are two big TDD schools: the Classic/Classicist/Chicago school and the Outside-In/Mockist/London school. Let's add both to the TDD box. Outside-In TDD relies heavily on Mocks and Stubs, referred more generically as **test doubles**, so let's add test doubles as well. The transformation priority premise is a great way to evolve code without adding complexity too soon, so it can be seen as part of TDD or simple design. We choose to add it to TDD.

We end up with the following technical practices:

- Classic TDD
- Outside-In TDD
- Test doubles
- Transformation Priority Premise

Design Improvements/Refactoring

Doing the same exercise for refactoring, we end up with this:

- IDE productivity
- Refactoring smells
- Refactoring legacy code
- Design patterns

Simple Design

Design is a much more controversial subject, but XP advocates simple design. So, let's stay with high-level, generally accepted design principles and practices, such as:

- Object calisthenics
- Code smells
- The four elements of simple design
- Coupling and cohesion
- Connascence
- SOLID

These are the main technical subjects you will encounter during the journey we have organized for you. If you follow the planned schedule, you should find the learning path quite smooth, always building upon the previous steps. Feel free to wander away from the path and use the book as a quick reference manual for a particular subject.

Beyond Design

All our technical knowledge is not enough if we are not working with the business helping to achieve its goals. The great professional must be able to understand the business and have the principles to make the right choices in terms of understanding and clarifying requirements and being a positive team member. That's why the last section of the book changes the focus from building the thing right to building the right thing. We touch on outside-in development, behavior-driven design principles, domain-driven design, principles derived from lean and system thinking, and our take on working as a member of a team.

We have used some big words in the previous paragraphs. Don't worry if you are unfamiliar with them. That is what this book is for. We hope you find it inspiring – or at least interesting. Explore and enjoy!

Rules, Principles, and Values

To do your best is not enough. First you must know what to do, and then do your best.

– W. Edwards Deming

What is the difference between rules, principles, and values?

Here is what the dictionary says:

- **Rule**: One of a set of explicit or understood regulations or principles governing conduct or a procedure within a particular area of activity. A principle that operates within a particular sphere of knowledge, describing or prescribing what is possible or allowable. A code of practice and discipline for a religious order or community.

- **Principle**: A fundamental truth or proposition that serves as the foundation for a system of belief or behavior or for a chain of reasoning. A general scientific theorem or law that has numerous special applications across a wide field. A fundamental source or basis of something.

- **Value**: The regard that something is held to deserve; the importance, worth, or usefulness of something. Principles or standards of behavior; one's judgment of what is important in life.

We live in a world with rules everywhere. On the road, at work, at school, or at the movies: we have to respect the rules of the environment we are in.

Sometimes, we are overwhelmed by the number of rules. Most of the time, we don't really even know the exact rules, yet we are able to behave correctly in (almost) any situation. That's because when rules follow common *principles* and *values* (which together make up common sense), it's pretty easy to work out the most important ones.

For example, you don't need to memorize the rules of the cinema to understand that if your phone rings in the middle of the show, it would annoy those around you. Or, you don't need to consciously remember the rule of the road that requires you to stop at the red light; you just know it's a very wise thing to do. That's because sensible rules are expressions of principles and values valid in a specific context. In the cinema, we want to be nice and let everybody enjoy the show, so we try not to be noisy. On the street, we want everybody to travel safely, so we respect the convention of traffic lights at crossing points.

How Rules Can Lead to Intellectual Laziness

We are so used to having rules to observe that many of us seem to be lost without them. Rules are obviously useful, but can unfortunately lead to a dangerous habit for a software developer: switching off *critical thinking*.

The main problem is that there are very few rules valid in any situation (the infamous *silver bullet*). Most rules are tightly bound to a context and, if the context changes, the rules might not be relevant anymore. Furthermore, the habit of following rules without questioning the context can lead in the long run to *intellectual laziness*. In this case, it seems easier to blindly follow some rules instead of working them out (based on principles and values) for the particular context.

Our profession is about instructing a machine to follow rules written in the form of coding. Critical thinking is one of the most relevant and hard-to-emulate qualities that define the difference between human beings and the artificial intelligence way of thinking. Switching off critical thinking only moves you steadily down the path of uselessness. If it were just about following rules, since robots are much better then us in doing that, they would have already filled all the programming jobs available.

Use Rules as a Shortcut to Internalize Principles

Nevertheless, we use rules as shortcut in order to practice and learn how to behave in a particular scenario. The final goal should never be an exercise of the mere memorization of rules. The ultimate achievement of practicing a ruleset is the internalization of the basic principles underlying them.

In the following lessons, we will introduce several rulesets for different contexts. Please don't force yourself to memorize them. If you don't remember something, open the page and consult the book as a reference. Try to work out the rules in your mind, starting from the principles. Experiment with different variations and evaluate the pros and cons of each outcome. Exercise until you understand and remember the principles, not the rules.

Once you master most of the principles we discuss here, something very cool might happen: you will find yourself more naturally predisposed to think about software design using a particular subset of those principles. Or, even more cool, you might want to find your very own principles, those that work and make sense for you, driving every single line of your code.

Either way, congratulations. That means you have started to build your own set of software design values.

In the first lessons of the book, we focus mostly on rules and then slowly move into principles and values. Be patient. Just imagine you are a young driver: in the beginning, you focus on following the rules, but once you are an experienced driver, you are able to extract your own rules from internalized principles and your core values.

Learn the rules like a pro, so you can break them like an artist.

– Pablo Picasso

How This Book Is Organized

The content we present is structured like a journey. As with every journey into a new environment, the beginning is slow and safe, but it is crucial for setting the stage for what comes next. The adventure then gains momentum as confidence grows, learning new subjects that introduce new techniques and principles to advance more steadily. Finally, in the final lessons, we demonstrate how the learned principles can be applied in several contexts, converging to allow the best solutions.

This is why we have divided the journey in four main sections:

- **First steps**
- **Walking**
- **Running**
- **Flying**

Each part is divided into several lessons with a common structure:

- New principles: New concepts are added on top of the previous materials.

- Katas: Exercises for you to spend some time practicing the new material.

- Great habits: We build up a collection of good practices step by step.

- Where we are in the big picture of OO software design?

  A bird's eye view of where the lesson practices belong in the world of software design. It relates lesson practices with other practices, rules, and principles.

- When I should move to the next lesson?

  A few questions to help you decide whether you are ready to move on.

- Resources: In case you want to go deeper into the material presented, the *Resources* sections provide web links and recommended books.

How to Get the Most out of This Book

To perform the katas, you will need access to a computer with your favorite development environment configured.

This book does not focus on any languages or tools in particular. We firmly believe that habits, principles, and values are the most crucial part of a developer's knowledge and that they are technologically agnostic. Hence, you are welcome to choose the ones that best suit you.

We have organized and presented the information in this book in a logical sequence. We strongly feel that practice and exercise are the fundamental resources needed for this journey. That's why you will find code challenges and katas at every lesson. They were selected to stimulate critical thinking about the subjects, leading you on a fun and pragmatic step-by-step learning path.

Mastery is applied knowledge, and even the most talented person can't skip practicing to reach it. Spend time going through the exercises to master the concepts and practices presented.

> **Caution**
>
> Our brain is addicted to information. Resist the urge to read this book without performing the exercises. Information **per se** is not very useful.

Programming is a skill best acquired by practice and example rather than from books.

– Alan Turing

Asking for Help or Feedback

If you want to get feedback or help from the community about the topics presented in this book, go to the book's community page at http://community.agiletechpraxis.com/.

Helping Others

Ideally, you should work on the exercises as a pair. Even better, have a journey companion. Either working on your own or with a pair, we strongly encourage you to join the community.

As soon as you feel confident, you can help others along the path. Help by answering questions and sharing your experience. Helping others is a great way to challenge your knowledge and internalize what you have learned!

Feedback about This Book

We would love to hear your feedback about this book:

- What you liked?
- What inspired you?
- What you learned?
- What we missed?

- What we could have explained better?

- What you disagree with?

We value your opinions and feelings about this work, and we will be always thankful if you decide to share them with us. You can go to Our Quick Feedback Form at http://www.agiletechpraxis.com/feedback or send us an email at info@agiletechpraxis.com.

Resources

Web

- Extreme Programming: A Gentle Introduction: http://www.extremeprogramming.org/.

- What is extreme programming, Ron Jeffries: http://ronjeffries.com/xprog/what-is-extreme-programming/.

Books

- Apprenticeship Patterns: Guidance for the Aspiring Software Craftsman, Dave Hoover, Adewale Oshineye: https://www.goodreads.com/book/show/5608045-apprenticeship-patterns.

- The Clean Coder: A Code of Conduct for Professional Programmers, Robert C. Martin: https://www.goodreads.com/book/show/10284614-the-clean-coder.

- Extreme Programming Explained: Embrace Change, Kent Beck: https://www.goodreads.com/book/show/67833.Extreme_Programming_Explained.

- The Passionate Programmer: Creating a Remarkable Career in Software Development, Chad Fowler: https://www.goodreads.com/book/show/8393116-the-passionate-programmer.

- The Pragmatic Programmer: From Journeyman to Master, Andy Hunt and David Thomas: https://www.goodreads.com/book/show/4099.The_Pragmatic_Programmer.

- Pragmatic Thinking and Learning: Refactor Your Wetware, Andy Hunt: https://www.goodreads.com/book/show/3063393-pragmatic-thinking-and-learning.

- The Software Craftsman: Professionalism, Pragmatism, Pride, Sandro Mancuso: https://www.goodreads.com/book/show/23215733-the-software-craftsman.

- Software Craftsmanship: The New Imperative, Pete McBreen: https://www.goodreads.com/book/show/1035377.Software_Craftsmanship.

First Steps

A journey of a thousand miles begins with a single step.

— Lao Tzu

1

Pair Programming

Pair programmers: Keep each other on task. Brainstorm refinements to the system. Clarify ideas. Take the initiative when their partner is stuck thus lowering frustration. Hold each other accountable to the team's practices.

– Kent Beck

When I started my career, I worked on software for television broadcast, mainly developing computer graphics for sports, news, and so on. Unknowingly, I was up for a stressful challenge as I could never be late.

No matter what, the TV broadcast would go on air at the scheduled time, so software had to be ready. When deadlines were approaching, I remember drinking too many coffees over long nights, pairing with my friend Rui to deliver in time. When we were too exhausted to continue, we would take turns, having a nap under the desks.

The first time I read about pairing, I skipped the lesson, as it was nothing new to me. I had been doing it for many years. What could I possibly learn?

It turns out I missed a lot. My pairing with Rui had little resemblance to the discipline of pair programming. Although I had spent many hours pairing with him, I had never paired with anyone else. We naturally found our balance by organizing ourselves, so we did not need to add any structure to our work. In hindsight, it was the pressure of the deadline that kept us going.

Approaching pairing with someone you've never worked with before requires a bit more structure for it to succeed. Actually, pairing has nothing to do with rushing for meeting a specific deadline!

A few years later, I moved to a bigger organization. Everything was more structured, and we were not expected to work through the night.

This organization had a strict code review policy. Once a developer finished their task, they would call someone senior to walk through all the code they had written with. Inevitably, the reviewer would find flaws, things they did not agree with, and the developer was required to make all the changes to comply.

This was very frustrating, as I would only get feedback *after* completing a task. I did not know it at the time, but this is a symptom of a broken feedback loop. Pair programming brings in the feedback as early as possible, thus allowing us to react to it faster.

What is Pair Programming?

Pair programming is a disciplined approach to writing software. It assigns specific roles and responsibilities to each pair member, defines strategies to switch positions, and promotes breaks to avoid pairs exhausting themselves.

Pair programming is about shortening the feedback loop when writing code. It is easier to change software as we write it. To validate our ideas, we can discuss design choices in real time with an unbiased peer. If we have an extra person reviewing while we write code, we reduce the feedback loop to a few seconds. And the faster the feedback, the faster we converge on a quality-rich solution. Lean thinking applied!

> **Caution**
> Pair programming requires a high level of maturity from peers.

> **Important**
> Pair programming should be a choice, not an enforced practice.

Roles

In pair programming, each person takes a turn assuming one of these roles:

- **Driver**: Responsible for the coding work, such as typing, moving the mouse, and so on.

- **Navigator**: Responsible for reviewing the driver's work, looking at the code from a strategic level and continuously posing questions, such as:

  How will this fit with the rest of the code?

  Will this implementation require changes elsewhere?

  Could we design this program better?

  Are there any accidental mistakes?

> **Caution**
>
> If you are in a position of power, authority, or seniority, it's on you to make sure your pair enjoys a good experience when pairing with you. Avoid using your power to impose decisions or making your pair feel uncomfortable while pairing with you.

Driver/Navigator Switch Techniques

Pair programming encourages participants to switch roles often. These procedures make sure everyone has a chance to drive and navigate. It is crucial that both partners spend an equal amount of time performing each role. There are a few techniques you can use to encourage this.

Chess Clock

Using a chess clock, the pair assigns a time period for performing each role. When the clock rings or a natural breaking point occurs, the pair switches roles.

Ping Pong/Popcorn

1. **A Driver (B Navigator)**: Writes a new test and sees that it fails for the right reason.
2. **B Driver (A Navigator)**: Implements the code needed to pass the test.
3. **B Driver (A Navigator)**: Writes the next test and sees that it fails for the right reason.
4. **A Driver (B Navigator)**: Implements the code needed to pass the test.

5. **A Driver (B Navigator)**: Writes the next test and sees that it fails for the right reason.

6. Rinse and repeat.

> ## Caution
> If you do not use ping pong/popcorn or the chess clock, use something else to remind you to switch roles. Do not just rely on your partner pointing out that you need to change roles, as he or she may not feel comfortable requesting it.

> ## Strong-Style Pairing
> *For an idea to go from your head into the computer, it MUST go through someone else's hands.*
>
> *– Llewellyn Falco*

Let's look at Llewellyn Falco's strong-style pairing: https://llewellynfalco.blogspot.com/2014/06/llewellyns-strong-style-pairing.html.

We find this style of pairing very interesting from the point of view of **Mob Programming** because of the high level of trust and maturity required. Once this technique is learned, mob programming would follow smoothly.

In this style, the driver has to *trust the navigator* while *becoming comfortable with incomplete understanding*. The driver will follow the directions expressed by the navigator and is allowed to ask questions when *what* has been said is not clear. Discussing *why* should be deferred until the idea is fully coded; this is when ideas can be discussed, or the navigator can take hints on how to proceed.

This style is very effective when the navigator has the whole picture and the roadmap to implement a functionality. The driver can focus on writing the code and learn the ideas while they unfold in the code. The navigator will have to *give the next instruction to the driver the instant they are ready to implement it* and *talk in the highest level of abstraction that the driver can understand*.

Sometimes the navigator and the driver will butt heads. I have often made the mistake of trying to argue the merits of my ideas when the actual problem is that the driver does not trust me. If you don't trust someone, all the logic in the world isn't going to help. A simple solution to this is simply to ask for a temporary window of trust.

Breaks

Spending significant amounts of time pairing can be very exhausting. Keeping the communication channel open while coding is an extra activity that pairs have to do all the time. Things that are trivial for someone may not be as trivial for someone else at that point. After a few pairing iterations, people involved in pair programming are usually tired, and this leads to decreased clarity and/or pair dysfunction.

Never forget we are human beings doing an intellectually intensive task. As humans, our potential is extraordinary, but we are not immune to failures, especially when tired. If you want to give your best when programming, avoid pushing your mental stamina beyond its boundaries. A *sustainable pace* is key.

> **Important**
>
> Remember to have breaks when you are working and especially when pairing.

Pomodoro

The Pomodoro Technique was proposed in late 1980s by Italian consultant *Francesco Cirillo*. It is an excellent way to balance short sprints of work with regular breaks. The name *Pomodoro* comes from the mechanical timers people used in kitchens to track cooking time for pasta. When Francesco started experimenting with the technique, he used the timer he found at home, which was in the shape of a tomato (*pomodoro* in Italian).

Figure 1.1: Pomodoro clock

There are five steps to this technique:

1. Decide on the task to be done.

2. Set the (pomodoro) timer to n minutes (traditionally 25 minutes).

3. Work on the task until the timer rings.

4. Take a short break (3-5 minutes).

5. After four (pomodoro) cycles, take a more extended break (15-30 minutes).

> **Caution**
>
> If you do not use the Pomodoro Technique, use something else to remind you to take regular breaks. Do not just rely on your partner pointing out that you need to change roles, as he or she may not feel comfortable requesting it.

The adjustment period from solo programming to collaborative programming was like eating a hot pepper. The first time you try it, you may not like it because you are not used to it. However, the more you eat it, the more you like it.

– Anonymous XP practitioner

Katas

No exercises yet. Enjoy life! When you are ready to return, we will be here waiting for you.

When Should I Move to the Next Lesson?

Whenever you feel ready.

Resources

Web

- **Llewellyn's strong-style pairing**: Llewellyn Falco (https://llewellynfalco.blogspot.com/2014/06/llewellyns-strong-style-pairing.html).

- **Mob programming and strong-style pairing**: Emily Bache (http://coding-is-like-cooking.info/2016/09/mob-programming-strong-style-pairing/).

- **Pair programming**: Marek Kusmin (http://www.kusmin.eu/wiki/index.php/Pair_Programming).

- **Pairing techniques**: Roger Almeida (http://roger-almeida.blogspot.co.uk/2010/04/pairing-techniques.html).

- **The Pomodoro Technique**: Francesco Cirillo (http://baomee.info/pdf/technique/1.pdf).

- **Rethinking pair programming**: Sandro Manusco (http://codurance.com/2015/03/15/rethinking-pair-programming/).

- **Teddy bear pair programming**: Adrian Bolboacă (http://blog.adrianbolboaca.ro/2012/12/teddy-bear-pair-programming/).

- **What is pair programming?**: Adrian Bolboacă (http://blog.adrianbolboaca.ro/2013/09/what-is-pair-programming/).

Classic TDD I – Test-Driven Development

Any fool can write code that a computer can understand. Good programmers write code that humans can understand.

– Martin Fowler

When I was developing software for automated cash machines, we created a simple **Graphical User Interface (GUI)** to test our code. The GUI was a plain window full of small buttons, each performing a specific operation.

To perform a test, an operator would press the buttons on the GUI. The granularity of the operations was so fine that to run a test, an operator had to press several buttons in a specific sequence.

We did not have automated sequences, nor were we generating any reports. Nevertheless, we were very proud of our test GUIs. The quality assurance engineers loved them, and they were a lifesaver on many occasions.

This had little resemblance to **Test-Driven Development (TDD)**, but at that time, TDD had not been *invented* yet. However, the high value provided by that mechanism made me aware of the importance of tests.

When I first read about TDD, I was surprised. We should write the test before the implementation, and the tests should be testing behavior instead of performing atomic operations; running all tests would be automated and a report generated. I was immediately sold.

Don't let the apparent simplicity of TDD deceive you. I have spent many years believing I was doing TDD. At one point, I had the opportunity to pair with a seasoned TDD practitioner; that's when I realized I had been missing a lot.

Classic TDD

Classic TDD is the original approach to TDD created by *Kent Beck*. It is also known as the Detroit/Chicago school of TDD. This practice allows you to:

- Spend less time debugging code to prove that it works: Tests will show that your code works correctly and implements the expected behavior.

- Reduce the fear of changing code: Tests act as a safety net. Would you walk on a rope several hundred feet high? What if you had a safety net? TDD is your safety net.

- Use tests as living documentation: Well-crafted tests describe the behavior in your code, and above all, serve as up-to-date documentation.

- Use tests as a feedback loop for design decisions: If tests are difficult to write, your design can probably be improved.

The Three Laws of TDD

Follow these rules until you gain enough experience in TDD or until you feel confident enough to break them (like Picasso).

Robert C. Martin (Uncle Bob) formalized the TDD rules: The three rules of TDD are detailed at http://butunclebob.com/ArticleS.UncleBob.TheThreeRulesOfTdd.

1. You Are Not Allowed to Write Any More of a Unit Test That Is Sufficient to Fail, and Compilation Failures Are Failures

Start by writing **one** failing unit test. We don't want to write all the tests beforehand as sometimes the implementation will *suggest* a test we had not envisioned before. If we write all tests beforehand, we may miss some important test scenarios. TDD is a feedback loop that works both ways. We not only get feedback from failing and passing tests, production code also gives feedback on needed tests.

Make sure the test is failing for the right reason. An unexpected fail is not a valid failure (such failures could include unexpected exceptions thrown, missing libraries, or missing imports). Missing implementation can actually be a valid failure scenario. If we start by writing our test, we will not have any implementation of the subject we are testing, thus the compiler should error. Create enough production code to allow our code to compile, and then recheck that the test is failing for the right reason (that is, the test assertion is not valid for the time being).

2. You Are Not Allowed to Write Any Production Code Unless It Is to Make a Failing Unit Test Pass

This rule ensures that production code is only produced as a consequence of the need to implement a specific behavior, represented by one or more unit tests. If we follow this rule, we should end up with all production code covered by tests, thus increasing our confidence in the production code. This rule also helps to ensure all design decisions are made as a response to a behavior that our production code needs to implement.

3. You Are Not Allowed to Write Any More Production Code That Is Sufficient to Pass the One Failing Unit Test

Once we have a passing test, we do not write any more production code until we have a failing test. See the previous rule for the reasons why.

These rules define the red-green-refactor cycle of TDD shown in the following figure:

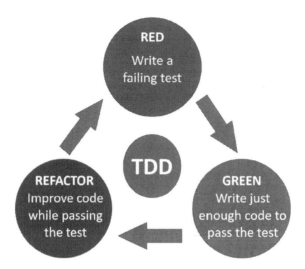

Figure 2.1: The red-green-refactor cycle of TDD

Refactoring and the Rule of Three – Baby Steps

Refactoring is missing from the previous rules. We feel that TDD without refactoring is just half of the game. For the time being, in the refactoring phase, just look for duplication. But wait until you are sure you have a duplication pattern. Avoid removing duplication too soon, as this may lead you to extract the wrong abstractions.

> **Important**
>
> Extract duplication only when you see it for the third time.

The **Rule of Three** defers duplication minimization until there is enough evidence of duplication. Code that does not contain duplication is often referred to as abiding by the **Do not Repeat Yourself (DRY)** principle.

> **Important**
>
> Duplication is far easier to refactor than the wrong abstraction. Use the Rule of Three if you are not sure what the correct abstraction would look like.

Three Methods of Moving Forward in TDD

So, you have written your first test, and it is failing for the right reason. Now what? How do you make it pass (make it green)? There are a few simple ways to achieve this.

From Red to Green

1. **Fake it**

   Just return the exact value you need. If your test expects a zero from a method, simply do it. Usually, you use this when you are unsure about how to implement a specific functionality, or your previous steps were too significant, and you cannot figure out what went wrong. Something that works is better than something that doesn't work!

2. **Obvious implementation**

   When you are sure of the code you need to write, write it, and see the test go green! Most of the time, you will use this method to move forward with TDD quickly.

3. **Triangulation**

   When you want to introduce new behavior, write a new and more specific test that forces the code to be more generic (triangulation equals using tests as pivot points).

Degrees of Freedom

We borrow this concept from physics, chemistry, and mechanics. In mechanics, degrees of freedom refers to the six degrees of freedom:

Six degrees of freedom (6DoF) refers to the freedom of movement of a rigid body in three-dimensional space. Specifically, the body is free to change position as forward/backward (surge), up/down (heave), left/right (sway) translation in three perpendicular axes, combined with changes in orientation through rotation about three perpendicular axes, often termed yaw (normal axis), pitch (transverse axis), and roll (longitudinal axis).

– Wikipedia

Wikipedia (Six degrees of freedom): https://en.wikipedia.org/wiki/Six_degrees_of_freedom.

Six degrees of freedom in a three-dimensional space:

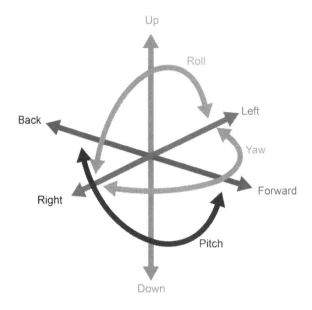

Figure 2.2: Six degrees of freedom
Source: Wikimedia Commons (https://commons.wikimedia.org/wiki/File:6DOF_en.jpg)

The concept of six degrees of freedom can be used as a metaphor for code behaviors and can be very useful when writing tests. The idea is that we stay in one behavior until we are sure that that behavior is completed.

So, to extend the metaphor, if you are testing a particular degree of freedom (**roll**, for example), stay on it until you are convinced it is working as expected, then move on to surge, heave, and sway. Avoid jumping from behavior to behavior before one is completed. Staying on a behavior means testing that behavior for happy and sad paths and for the average and extremes values it could expose. Take special care to not start implementing a combination of distinct behaviors before they are tested independently.

Naming Tests

Tests should have names that describe a business feature or behavior. When naming tests, avoid:

- Using technical names for tests (as in `myMethodNameReturnsSomething`)

- Leaking implementation details in test names (as in `myTestReturnsFalse` or `CommandPatternTest`)

If your test names express business behaviors, when you change the technical implementation or refactor code, your test names should remain unchanged.

We have seen many developers using a test name strategy similar to **ClassName_MethodName_ShouldDoSomething**. However, this can cause problems; if you rename your class or method, it confuses the meaning of your test name.

A Test Name Pattern

```csharp
class MyClassShould
{
  [Test]
  void DoSomething()
  {}
}
```

We read the test name as a full sentence starting with the test class name: *My class should do something.*

For example:

```csharp
class CarShould
{
  [Test]
  void decrease_speed_when_brakes_are_applied()
  {}

  [Test]
  void increase_speed_when_accelerator_is_applied()
  {}
}
```

Katas

Fizz Buzz by cyber-dojo

Cyber-dojo foundation (See license): http://www.cyber-dojo.org/.

Write a function that takes numbers from 1 to 100 and outputs them as a string, but for multiples of 3, it returns `Fizz` instead of the number, and for multiples of 5, it returns `Buzz`. For numbers that are multiples of both 3 and 5, it returns `FizzBuzz`.

> **Tip**
>
> Start by writing a failing test. Think about what behaviors your code should implement.

Fizz Buzz – partial walkthrough

Let's first pick the behavior where numbers not divisible by 3 or 5 are returned as a string. Let's start with number 1.

Write a new failing test.

```
When I fizzbuzz number 1, I get back a string representing it
```

Use **fake it** as an implementation strategy.

```
return "1"
```

Run the test and make sure it's green.

Write a new failing test since we do not have enough examples to prove the behavior we are implementing yet.

```
When I fizzbuzz number 2, I get back a string representing it
```

Use **obvious implementation** as an implementation strategy.

```
if number == 1 then return "1" else return "2"
```

Run the tests and make sure they are all green.

Write a new failing test.

```
When I fizzbuzz number 4, I get back a string representing it
```

Why did we not write the test for number 3 after the test for number 2? The reason is that number 3 would add new behavior to the code base, and we haven't finished implementing the behavior we are working on yet.

Use **obvious implementation** as an implementation strategy.

```
if number == 1 then return "1"
else if number == 2 then return "2"
else return "4"
```

Run the tests and make sure they are all green.

We now have duplication in our code, so it is time to refactor to remove it.

```
return str(number)
```

After the refactor, run the tests and make sure they are all green.

Now that we have tests to prove the behavior for numbers not divisible by 3 or 5, we can start testing numbers divisible by 3.

Use **triangulation** to force a change to a new behavior.

Write a new failing test.

```
When I fizzbuzz number 3, I get back "fizz"
```

Use **obvious implementation** as an implementation strategy.

```
if number == 3 then return "fizz"
else return str(number)
```

Run the tests and make sure they are all green.

The implementation now has a pivot point. The **if** statement pivots execution in two different directions.

Fizz Buzz Kata Summary

Input	Expected output	Strategy	Implementation
1	"1"	fake it	return "1"
2	"2"	obvious implementation	if number == 1 then return "1" else return "2"
4	"4"	obvious implementation	if number == 1 then return "1" else if number == 2 then return "2" else return "4"
4	"4"	refactor (because of duplicated if's)	return str(number)
3	"fizz"	triangulation + obvious implementation	if number == 3 then return "fizz" else return str(number)

Figure 2.3: Table showing fizz buzz kata summary

Take over from this point on and finish the Fizz Buzz kata on your own.

> **Note**
>
> The solution for this can be found at page 367.

More Katas

Leap Year by cyber-dojo

Write a function that returns true or false depending on whether its input integer is a leap year or not. A leap year is defined as one that is divisible by 4, but is not otherwise divisible by 100 unless it is also divisible by 400. For example, 2001 is a typical common year and 1996 is a typical leap year, whereas 1900 is an atypical common year and 2000 is an atypical leap year.

Cyber-dojo foundation (See license): http://www.cyber-dojo.org/.

Nth Fibonacci by cyber-dojo

Write some code to generate the Fibonacci number for the nth position. For example: `int Fibonacci(int position)`. The first Fibonacci numbers in the sequence are 0, 1, 1, 2, 3, 5, 8, 13, 21, 34.

Cyber-dojo foundation (See license): http://www.cyber-dojo.org/.

> **Note**
> The solution for this can be found at page 368.

Great Habits

There is a set of good habits you should aim to internalize. In the following lessons, we will add more to this list.

Considerations when Writing a New Test

- Tests should test one thing only.

  Imagine you have 1,000 tests and a failing test. Can you spot a single failing behavior? This does not mean you should write a single assertion. It is fine to have multiple assertions as long as they are testing the same behavior.

- Create more specific tests to drive a more generic solution (**triangulate**) by adding new tests that force your code to pivot.

- Give your tests meaningful names (behavior/goal-oriented names) expressing your business domain.

  – Avoid technical names for tests. For example: `myMethodNameReturnsSomething`.

  – Avoid leaking implementation details in test names: For example: `myTestReturnsFalse` or `CommandPatternTest`.

  – Avoid writing technical tests; you should test behaviors, not the technicality of components.

- Always see that the test fails for the right reason.

  An unexpected failure is not a valid failure. Examples of such failures include unexpected exceptions being thrown, missing libraries, and missing imports.

- Ensure that you have meaningful feedback from the failing test.

  Make sure your test name, examples, and assertion provide good feedback when a test fails. When a test fails, you should be able to intuitively pinpoint the broken behavior.

- Keep your tests and production code separate.

  Do not mix test code with production code. You do not want to deploy test code with your production code.

- Organize your unit tests to reflect your production code.

  Test projects should follow a structure similar to the production code structure.

Considerations When Making a Failing Test Pass

Write the simplest code to pass the test. Fake it or use obvious implementation. It is okay to write any code that makes you get to the refactor phase more quickly. It is okay to write any code that you might improve at a later stage. Don't be embarrassed by writing simple code. Trying to write smart code too early is often not the best choice.

Considerations After the Test Passes

Use the Rule of Three to tackle duplication. If you need something once, build it. If you need something twice, pay attention. If you need it a third time, abstract it. Keep in mind that duplication is easier to tackle than the wrong abstractions. This is the reason why we want to see duplication three times.

Classic TDD Flow

The test-driven programming workflow shown here was inspired by a tweet from our good friend, *Rachel M. Carmena*:

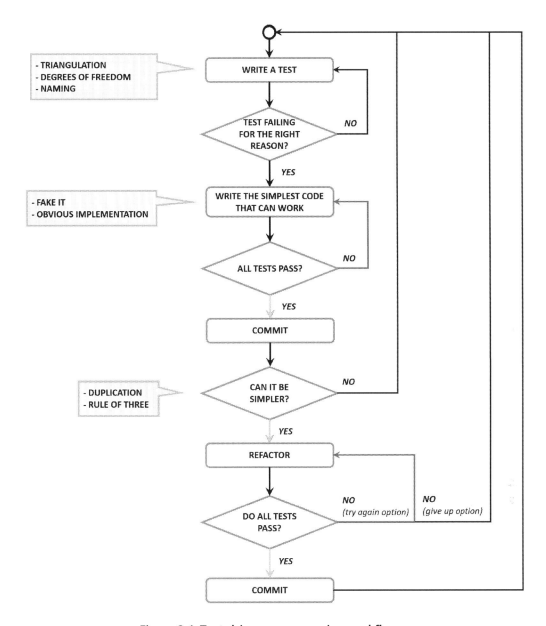

Figure 2.4: Test-driven programming workflow

The preceding diagram is inspired by a tweet from *Rachel M. Carmena* (**@bberrycarmen**, https://twitter.com/bberrycarmen/status/1062670041416716289).

Where are We in the Big Picture of Object-Oriented (OO) Software Design?

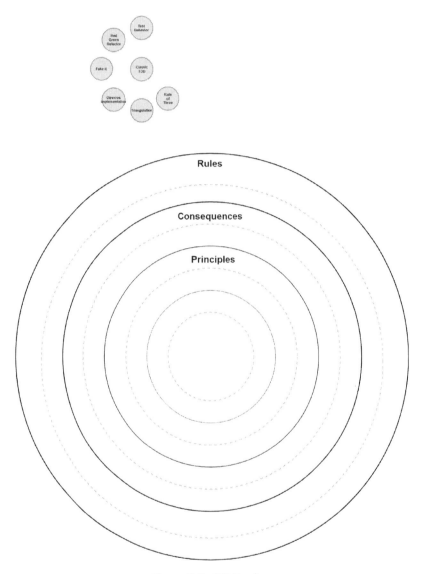

Figure 2.5: OO Design

When Should I Move to the Next Lesson?

As soon as you can apply TDD's red-green-refactor practice to solve procedural problems:

- Can you write a test before any code?
- Are your tests and test names behavior-related?

- Are you able to stay in the same behavior until you finish it?

- Can you write the simplest implementation that makes the test pass?

- Can you spot duplication and refactor it, including duplication in test code?

Whenever you can, apply the three methods of moving forward in TDD:

- Fake it

- Obvious implementation

- Triangulation

Bonus

Can you use TDD to write any of the katas from scratch in under 20 minutes?

If you need to review something to answer any of the preceding questions, review the **Great Habits** section, where we summarize most of the new material in this lesson.

When you can answer "yes" to all of the preceding questions, you are ready to move on.

Resources

Web

- **The Mysterious Art Of Triangulation**, *Jason Gorman*: http://codemanship.co.uk/parlezuml/blog/?postid=1157.

- **Test-driven development**, *Wikipedia*: https://en.wikipedia.org/wiki/Test-driven_development.

- **Test-driven programming workflow**, *Rachel M. Carmena*: https://twitter.com/bberrycarmen/status/1062670041416716289.

- **The three rules of TDD**, *Robert C. Martin*: http://butunclebob.com/ArticleS.UncleBob.TheThreeRulesOfTdd.

Books

Test-Driven Development: By Example, Kent Beck: https://www.goodreads.com/book/show/387190.Test_Driven_Development.

3

Classic TDD II

I'm not a great programmer; I'm just a good programmer with great habits.

– Kent Beck

Like most developers starting TDD, I encountered a common blocker: coming up with good test names. With experience and a little help from other programmers, I learned to not reach for the test name too soon. I give the test a temporary name; **foo** is a fine name. Then I concentrate on what the assertion should look like for the behavior I'm testing. Once I get the assertion right, I need to think how I get there. Once I have all this, naming the test becomes so much easier.

Writing the Assertion First and Working Backward

In this lesson, we will write our tests in a slightly different way. When creating a new test, we will go straight to the assertion we are trying to prove. This will ensure that test code exists solely to support the assertion, thus minimizing any code written for the tests.

Once we have the assertion, we will code backward, writing the code we need to perform the assertion. Only then will we define the test name.

For example, let's look at **fizzbuzz**:

In order of writing:

```
assert fizzBuzzed == "1"

var fizzBuzzed = fizzBuzzer.FizzBuzz(1)

var fizzBuzzer = new FizzBuzzer()
```

Final code:

```
var fizzBuzzer = new FizzBuzzer() +

var fizzBuzzed = fizzBuzzer.FizzBuzz(1) +

assert fizzBuzzed == "1"
```

Organizing Your Test in Arrange, Act, and Assert Blocks

Tests are about **assertions** (ASSERT). For an assertion to be possible, we need to take an action on the code we are asserting (ACT). Sometimes, to take an action, we need to create the context to enable the action (ARRANGE). Organizing tests in arrange, act, and assert blocks helps keep the tests clean and easy to read.

For example, let's look at **fizzbuzz**:

```
//Arrange block (aka Given) - create all necessary preconditions
var fizzBuzzer = new FizzBuzzer()


//Act block (aka When) - execute the subject under test
var fizzBuzzed = fizzBuzzer.FizzBuzz(1)


//Assert block (aka Then) - assert the expected results have occurred
assert fizzBuzzed == "1"
```

However, we think that *less is more* when we are trying to understand the meaning of some code. We are not fans of inline comments in code, especially if they quickly come to repeat themselves. You do not need to add them to your blocks. Once you start using this convention for all tests, a simple separation using blank lines should be enough. If you are disciplined, it will sink in very quickly.

The ideal unit test should have only three statements:

1. Create an object.

2. Call a method.

3. Assert.

Although it is not always possible to keep things so minimal, you can use private methods and test setup snippets to minimize the number of lines in each of the sections.

Keeping the code to a minimum on tests optimizes clarity and readability. When a test fails, you do not want to spend too much time understanding it.

```
var fizzBuzzer = new FizzBuzzer()

var fizzBuzzed = fizzBuzzer.FizzBuzz(1)

assert fizzBuzzed == "1"
```

Benefits of Organizing Tests in Arrange, Act, and Assert Blocks

- Clearly separates what is being tested from the setup and verification steps

- Clarifies and focuses attention on specific test responsibilities

- Makes some test smells more obvious, such as assertions intermixed with **Act** code or tests that test too many things at once

Unit Test Principles

- **Fast**: Unit tests have to be fast in order to be executed often. Fast means tests should execute in milliseconds.

- **Isolated**: There should be no dependency between tests. Ideally, we should be able to execute them in a random order.

- **Repeatable**: There should be no assumed initial state, nothing left behind, and no dependency on external services that might be unavailable, such as databases or filesystems.

- **Self-validating**: There should be no manual test interpretation or intervention. Red or green!

- **Timely**: Tests are written at the right time.

Katas

Use your new habits when solving the katas. Start from the assertion and work backward. Organize your tests into arrange, act, and assert blocks. Follow the unit test principles we just looked at.

Stats Calculator by cyber-dojo

Your task is to process a sequence of integer numbers to determine the following statistics:

- Minimum value

- Maximum value

- Number of elements in the sequence

- Average value

Cyber-dojo foundation (See license): http://www.cyber-dojo.org/.

For example: [6, 9, 15, -2, 92, 11]

- Minimum value = -2

- Maximum value = 92

- Number of elements in the sequence = 6

- Average value = 21.833333

Anagrams by cyber-dojo

Write a program to generate all potential anagrams of an input string.

Cyber-dojo foundation (See license): http://www.cyber-dojo.org/.

For example, the potential anagrams of biro are:

- biro bior brio broi boir bori

- ibro ibor irbo irob iobr iorb

- rbio rboi ribo riob roib robi

- obir obri oibr oirb orbi orib

Bonus! Practicing TDD at an Extreme – Baby Steps

Allot a maximum of two minutes to complete each of the following tasks. If you get stuck and exceed two minutes, reset your work and start from scratch.

Write a failing test (this is the only task where a failing test is allowed):

- Make the failing test pass.
- Refactor.
- Think (you cannot repeat this task).

Important

If you cannot make progress in two minutes, it is usually due to:

- Trying to achieve too much. Break your work into smaller steps.
- The code base is in bad shape. You probably need to refactor.

Great Habits

In this lesson, we introduced a few new TDD habits. Check them out in the following list.

Considerations when Writing a New Test

- Tests should test one thing only.
- Create more specific tests to drive a more generic solution (triangulate).
- Give your tests meaningful names (behavior/goal-oriented names) that reflect your business domain.
- See that the test fails for the right reason.
- Ensure you have meaningful feedback from failing tests.
- Keep your tests and production code separate.
- Organize your unit tests to reflect your production code (similar project structure).

- Organize your test in arrange, act, and assert blocks (**new habit**).

  – Arrange (also known as **Given**) all necessary preconditions.

  – Act (also known as **When**) on the subject under test.

  – Assert (also known as **Then**) that the expected results have occurred.

- Write the assertion first and work backward (**new habit**).

  – Write your test by first writing the assertion; don't worry yet about naming the test properly.

  – Write the act section of your test.

  – Write the arrange block, if required.

  – Finally, name the test.

- Write fast, isolated, repeatable, and self-validating tests (**new habit**).

Considerations when Making a Failing Test Pass

- Write the simplest code to pass the test.

- Write any code that makes you get to the refactor phase more quickly.

Considerations after the Test Passes

- Use the *Rule of Three* to tackle duplication.

Classic TDD Flow | 33

Classic TDD Flow

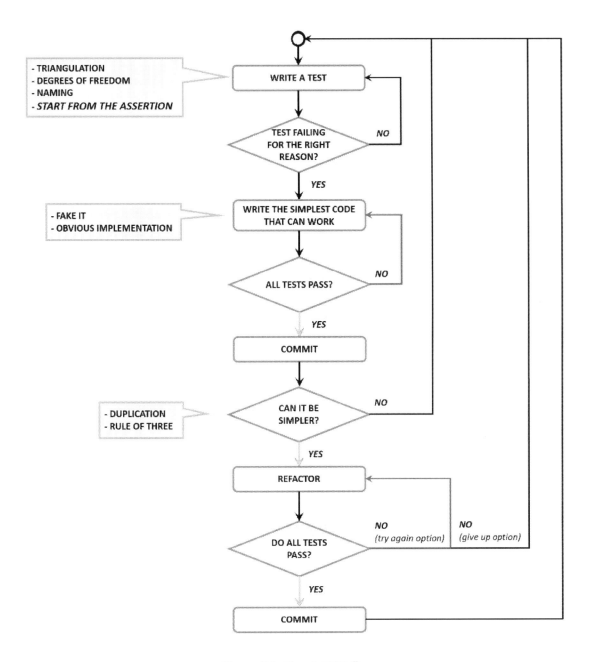

Figure 3.1: Classic TDD flow

Where are we in the Big Picture of Object-Oriented (OO) Software Design?

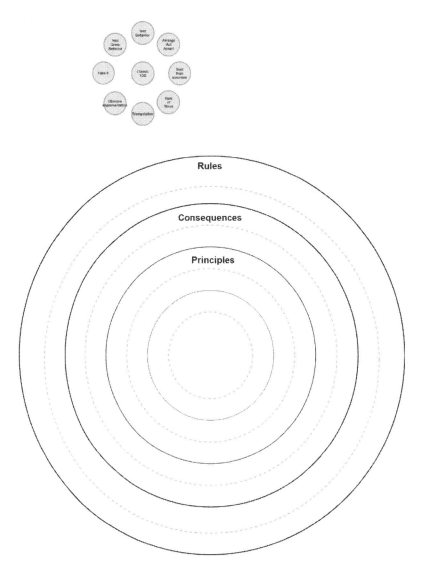

Figure 3.2: OO Design

When Should I Move to the Next Lesson?

- When you can apply the new **great habits**

- When you can write the assertion first and work backward on the test

- When you are able to give your tests meaningful names (behavior/goal-oriented names) that reflect your business domain

- When you are able to write any code that makes you get to the refactor phase more quickly

- When you make effective use of the Rule of Three to tackle duplication, including test code

There is a lot more information on **great habits**, but if you nail down just the ones mentioned here, you are prepared to move on.

Resources

Web

- Naming Test Classes and Methods, Sandro Mancuso: http://codurance. com/2014/12/13/naming-test-classes-and-methods/.

Books

- Test-Driven Development: By Example, Kent Beck: https://www.goodreads.com/ book/show/387190.Test_Driven_Development.

Classic TDD III – Transformation Priority Premise

As tests get more specific, code gets more generic.

– *Robert C. Martin*

When a friend mentioned the **Transformation Priority Premise (TPP)** in a mob session we were doing in the Arctic region of Finland, I was baffled. I had been practicing Test-Driven Development (TDD) for many years and considered myself an above-average practitioner, yet I had never heard of TPP. As soon as I had a moment with my friend, I grilled him with questions and then spent the night in my cabin learning it.

TPP is quite important in the context of TDD as it defines **obvious implementation**. Before finding out about TPP, I had been using instinct/intuition, experience, and feedback. TPP brings a bit of process and rationale to evolving code.

Kata

In this lesson, we start with a kata before we introduce the new material. With TPP, we found out that it is better to do the kata twice.

We will first work only with the material we have covered so far. We will then use the new concepts introduced in this lesson. This way, you get a chance to compare the two implementations and witness the effect of using TPP on your code.

Roman Numerals by cyber-dojo

Write a function to convert Arabic numbers to Roman numerals as best as you can, following the TDD practices we have been using.

Cyber-dojo foundation (See license): http://www.cyber-dojo.org/.

Given a positive integer number (for example, **42**), determine its Roman numeral representation as a string (for example, **XLII**). You cannot write numerals like IM for 999.

Examples of Roman numerals by cyber-dojo are as follows:

Arabic	Roman	Arabic	Roman
1	I	60	LX
2	II	70	LXX
3	III	80	LXXX
4	IV	90	XC
5	V	100	C
6	VI	200	CC
7	VII	300	CCC
8	VIII	400	CD
9	IX	500	D
10	X	600	DC
20	XX	700	DCC
30	XXX	800	DCCC
40	XL	900	CM
50	L	1000	M

Figure 4.1: Roman numbers by cyber-dojo (1-1000)

Arabic	Roman	Thousands	Cents	Tenths	Units
846	DCCCXLVI	—	DCC	XL	VI
1999	MCMXCIX	M	CM	XC	IX
2008	MMVIII	MM	—	—	VIII

Figure 4.2: Roman numbers by cyber-dojo (846, 1999, and 2008)

Important

Resist the temptation to read ahead until you have finished implementing the Roman numerals kata.

TPP – Defining Obvious Implementation

If we go back to how we evolve code in TDD, we follow these three methods:

- Fake it
- Obvious implementation
- Triangulation

Faking it is a well-defined method; we just return a value that works, and this passes the test.

Triangulation is also well-defined; we just write a new failing test that forces the code to change.

However, obvious implementation is ambiguous. It may mean one thing for one developer and something else for another developer. The transformations in the following table are a way to clarify this ambiguity.

As far as we know, Robert C. Martin was the first to present the idea of evolving code in a sequence of transformations: The Transformation Priority Premise, https://8thlight. com/blog/uncle-bob/2013/05/27/TheTransformationPriorityPremise.html.

TPP Table

#	Transformation	Start code	End code
1	{} -> nil	{}	[return] nil
2	Nil -> constant	[return] nil	[return] "1"
3	Constant -> constant+	[return] "1"	[return] "1" + "2"
4	Constant -> scalar	[return] "1" + "2"	[return] argument
5	Statement -> statements	[return] argument	[return] min(max(0, argument), 10)
6	Unconditional -> conditional	[return] argument	if(condition) [return] 1 else [return] 0
7	Scalar -> array	dog	[dog, cat]
8	Array -> container	[dog, cat]	
9	Statement -> tail recursion	a + b	a + recursion
10	If -> loop	if(condition)	loop(condition)
11	Statement -> recursion	a + recursion	recursion
12	Expression -> function	today – birth	CalculateBirthDate()
13	Variable -> mutation	day	var Day = 10; Day = 11;

Figure 4.3: TPP table

Transformations at the top of the list are preferred to those at the bottom. It is better (or simpler) to change a constant into a variable than it is to add an **if** statement. So, when making a test pass, favor the transformations that are simpler (top of the list) to those that are more complex (bottom of the list).

Another way to use the **TPP** is to keep writing new code using obvious implementation. Whenever duplication is detected, refactor to a simpler or more complex transformation to remove it. When refactoring, first try to go to a simpler transformation. This does not work all the time; often you need to move to a more complex transformation to avoid duplication.

The Transformations

When you have a failing test, follow the TPP table previously illustrated to evolve your production code, starting with transformation 1, `{} -> nil`. Stop when your test passes.

Write another failing test and (ideally) stay on the same transformation, or, if required, move to the next one on the table. Most of the time, we do not need to reach the end of the TPP table to solve a problem. This is a good sign. It means we solved a problem using only simple transformations.

Transformation 1 – {} -> Nil

This is the simplest transformation. If we have no implementation, the simplest transformation is returning nil, null, or nothing. For example, `return nil`.

Transformation 2 – Nil -> Constant

The next transformation is to evolve `return nil` to return a constant. For example, `return 0`.

Transformation 3 – Constant -> Constant+

This transformation uses a more complex constant or a combination of constants.

Transformation 4 – Constant -> Scalar

In this transformation, we can use any input arguments on our method, and we can also transform a constant into a variable.

Transformation 5 – Statement -> Statements

So far, the only statement we have used is `return`. Now we are free to use any unconditional statements.

Transformation 6 – Unconditional -> Conditional

Until now, we have avoided splitting the path of execution since it adds quite a bit of complexity. This is the first transformation that allows the use of an `if` statement or other conditional statements or operators. Usually, we get to this transformation quickly. Once we reach it, we tend to stay on it until we spot duplication, or the code becomes too complex. This is a gear-changing transformation because we are introducing the concept of selection.

Sequencing, selection, and iteration: http://www.101computing.net/sequencing-selection-iteration/.

Transformation 7 – Scalar -> Array

If we end up with too many **if** statements, one option is to refactor them into a lookup table.

Transformation 8 – Array -> Container

Sometimes the array is not the best data structure or not the most descriptive. In this transformation, we can refactor the data structure from an array to a more complex one, if required.

Transformation 9 – Statement -> Tail Recursion

As with the **unconditional -> conditional** transformation, this is another gear-shifting transformation. We introduce the concept of iteration by using recursion. We want to use tail recursion even if our language compiler does not optimize for it. Grossly oversimplifying, the recursive function call should be the last thing we execute in an expression.

Sequencing, selection, and iteration: http://www.101computing.net/sequencing-selection-iteration/.

Explanation of what tail recursion is: https://stackoverflow.com/questions/33923/what-is-tail-recursion.

Transformation 10 – If -> Loop

In this transformation, we are now allowed to use any iteration our language provides. We can refactor code to use loops.

Transformation 11 – Statement -> Recursion

We can make use of full recursion without worrying about whether it is tail recursive or not.

Transformation 12 – Expression -> Function

We can extract complex logic into simpler functions.

Transformation 13 – Variable -> Mutation

This last transformation introduces the concept of mutation. We should not mutate any variables until we reach this transformation. This is why previous transformations favored recursion over loops. Traditional loops in imperative languages tend to rely on variable mutation. Immutability is a very important concept and property of code, and we should strive to keep everything as immutable as possible, even when not using a functional language.

> **Important**
>
> Please do not take the TPP table literally. This is a starting point. Adapt this table to your style, your programming language, and your environment. For the moment, we ask you to take it as is, but once you feel comfortable with it, we encourage you to shape it to your context.

Example Using the TPP on the Fibonacci Sequence

Input	Expected output	Transformation	Implementation
0	0	{} -> nil	Does not work
0	0	Nil -> constant	return 0
1	1	Constant -> scalar	return index
2	1	Unconditional -> conditional	if number < 2 then return index else return index - 1
3	2	Unconditional -> conditional	No change
4	3	Unconditional -> conditional	No change
5	5	Scalar -> array	var fibs = [0, 1, 1, 2, 3, 5]; return fibs[index]
6	8	Scalar -> array	var fibs = [0, 1, 1, 2, 3, 5, 8]; return fibs[index]
7	13	Scalar -> array(duplication)	var fibs = [0, 1, 1, 2, 3, 5, 8, 13]; return fibs[index]
8	21	Statement -> tail recursion	if index < 2 return index else return fib(index - 1) + fib(index - 2)

Figure 4.4: The TPP on the Fibonacci sequence

The idea of the TPP is to evolve code while keeping complexity under control.

Katas

Roman Numerals by cyber-dojo

Restart the Roman numerals kata, but this time apply all **great habits** we have looked at so far, plus TPP. Try to evolve your code using only the TPP table. Don't think about how to implement a test. Just keep moving down the TPP table. If you do this, the problem should solve itself. If you find yourself jumping steps, pause and consider whether there is a simpler way to move forward with a simpler transformation.

> **Note**
>
> The solution for this section can be found on page 369.

Prime Factors by cyber-dojo

Factorize a positive integer number into its prime factors using TDD and the TPP table.

Cyber-dojo foundation (See license): http://www.cyber-dojo.org/.

The examples of prime factors by cyber-dojo are as follows:

Number	Prime factors
2	[2]
3	[3]
4	[2,2]
6	[2,3]
9	[3,3]
12	[2,2,3]
15	[3,5]

Figure 4.5: Prime factors by cyber-dojo

Boolean Calculator by Alessandro Di Gioia

Implement a Boolean calculator that gets a string as input and evaluates it to the Boolean result.

These are the specifications:

Supports single values:

```
"TRUE" -> true
"FALSE" -> false
```

Supports the **NOT** operator:

```
"NOT TRUE" -> false
```

Supports the **AND** operator:

```
"TRUE AND FALSE" -> false
"TRUE AND TRUE" -> true
```

Supports the **OR** operator:

```
"TRUE OR FALSE" -> true
"FALSE OR FALSE" -> false
```

Supports any number of **AND** and **OR**, giving precedence to **NOT** then **AND** and, eventually, the **OR** operation:

```
"TRUE OR TRUE OR TRUE AND FALSE" -> true
"TRUE OR FALSE AND NOT FALSE" -> true
```

Supports parentheses:

```
"(TRUE OR TRUE OR TRUE) AND FALSE" -> false
"NOT (TRUE AND TRUE)" -> false
```

Bonus:

Prints the **Abstract Syntax Tree** representing the calculation:

```
"(TRUE OR TRUE OR TRUE) AND FALSE"


AND
|_ OR
|  |_ TRUE
|  |_ OR
|        |_ TRUE
```

```
|         |_ TRUE
|_ FALSE
```

"TRUE OR TRUE OR TRUE AND FALSE"

```
OR
|_ TRUE
|_ OR
   |_ TRUE
   |_ AND
      |_ TRUE
      |_ FALSE
```

"NOT ((TRUE OR TRUE) OR (TRUE AND FALSE))"

```
NOT
|_ OR
   |_ OR
   |  |_ TRUE
   |  |_ TRUE
   |_ AND
      |_ TRUE
      |_ FALSE
```

"TRUE OR TRUE OR NOT TRUE AND FALSE"

This, because of precedence, is equivalent to:

"(TRUE OR (TRUE OR ((NOT TRUE) AND FALSE)))"

```
OR
|_ TRUE
|_ OR
   |_ TRUE
```

```
|_ AND
    |_ NOT
    |   |_ TRUE
    |_ FALSE
```

Great Habits

In this lesson, we introduced a new great habit. Check it out in the following list.

Considerations when Writing a New Test

- Tests should test one thing only.

- Create more specific tests to drive a more generic solution (triangulate).

- Give your tests meaningful names (behavior/goal-oriented names) that reflect your business domain.

- See that the test fails for the right reason.

- Ensure you have meaningful feedback from failing tests.

- Keep your tests and production code separate.

- Organize your unit tests to reflect your production code (similar project structure).

- Organize your test in arrange, act, and assert blocks.

- Write the assertion first and work backward.

- Write fast, isolated, repeatable, and self-validating tests.

Considerations when Making a Failing Test Pass

- Write the simplest code to pass the test.

- Write any code that makes you get to the refactor phase quicker.

- Use transformation priority premise (**new habit**).

Considerations after the Test Passes

- Use the **Rule of Three** to tackle duplication.

Classic TDD flow

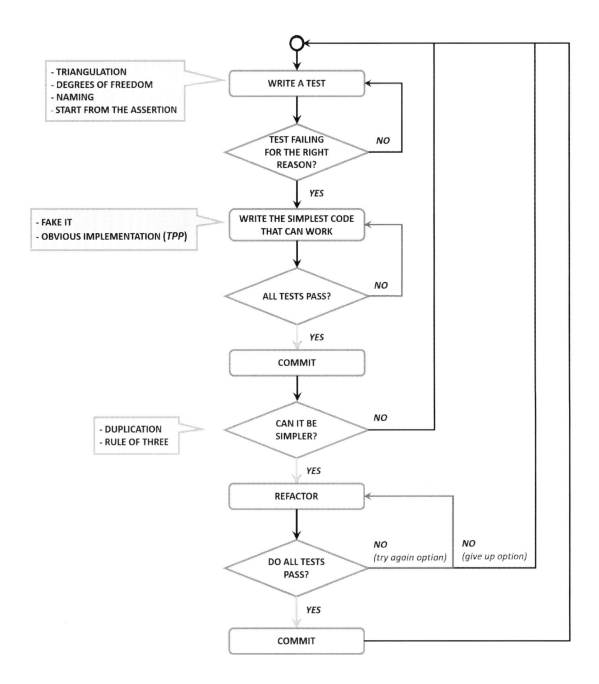

Figure 4.6: Classic TDD flow

Where are We in the Big Picture of Object-Oriented (OO) Software Design?

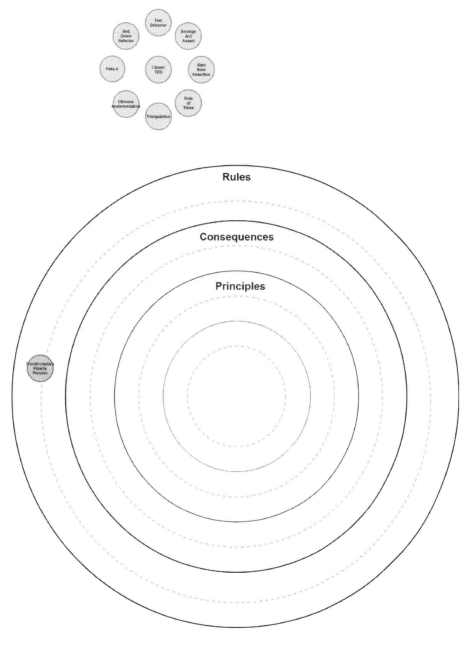

Figure 4.7: OO Design

When Should I Move to the Next Lesson?

- When you can apply the TPP table to evolve your code.

- When you are proficient with TDD practices. In the next lesson, we move to design, so make sure you have TDD practices under your belt.

Resources

Web

- **Functional Calisthenics**, Jorge Gueorguiev Garcia: https://codurance. com/2017/10/12/functional-calisthenics/.

- **The Transformation Priority Premise**, Robert C. Martin: https://8thlight.com/ blog/uncle-bob/2013/05/27/TheTransformationPriorityPremise.html.

- **The Transformation Priority Premise Applied**, Micah Martin: https://8thlight. com/blog/micah-martin/2012/11/17/transformation-priority-premise-applied. html.

- **The Transformation Priority Premise with JavaScript**, Carlos Blé: https://youtu. be/D2gFmSUeA3w.

5
Design 1 – Object Calisthenics

Perfection (in design) is achieved not when there is nothing more to add, but rather when there is nothing more to take away.

– Antoine de Saint-Exupery

The first time I came into contact with object calisthenics was at a meetup in London with my friend Ger Mán. We were so overwhelmed that we decided not to write any tests in order to focus on understanding this concept.

Big mistake!

Without the tests for feedback, we started making small errors that accumulated into a messy code base. The next day, without the pressure of the meetup, we paired up again and calmly worked on the exercise using object calisthenics as best as we could. Finally, it started to make some sense.

When I am coaching software developers, the *Object Calisthenics* session is usually the first big challenge. Object calisthenics forces people to think differently about software design, not by adding anything, but by removing. Object calisthenics is about constraining software design decisions; it is about what you cannot do.

In the beginning, this can cause some frustration, like the frustration I felt on my first encounter with object calisthenics. However, this is a very powerful design tool. In my humble opinion, the benefits outweigh the pain by a large margin.

It's the Design...

After spending a few lessons on test-driven development, we'll now turn our attention to simple design. Why do we need to consider design?

- **TDD is not enough**: TDD will have a positive side effect on design, but simply doing TDD will not take care of design by itself.

- **DRY (Do not Repeat Yourself) is not enough**: So far, our refactoring efforts have been focused on removing duplication. This is crucial to write maintainable code, but it is not enough.

- **TDD will punish you if you don't understand design**: When we find ourselves writing very complex test code, we should consider changing the design of the implementation.

We'll also move from using TDD to solve simple algorithmical problems to problems that require more design decisions.

Kata

In this lesson, as in the previous, we'll start a kata before we introduce new material.

Tic-Tac-Toe

Try to implement the game of Tic-Tac-Toe as best as you can by following the TDD practices we have been using so far.

Tic-Tac-Toe rules:

- X always goes first

- Players alternate placing X's and O's on the board

- Players cannot play on a played position

- A player with three X's or O's in a row (horizontally, vertically, or diagonally) wins

- If all nine squares are filled and neither player achieves three in a row, the game is a draw

> **Important**
>
> Resist the temptation to read ahead until you have finished implementing the Tic-Tac-Toe kata.

Object Calisthenics – 10 Steps to Better Software Design

Object calisthenics is a simple ruleset that, if applied correctly, should have a big effect on your designs. For the time being, follow these rules; we will discuss the principles behind them later on:

- Only one level of indentation per method
- Don't use the **ELSE** keyword
- Wrap all primitives and strings (wrap primitive types in classes)
- First-class collections (wrap collections in classes)
- One dot per line
- Don't abbreviate
- Keep all entities small
- No classes with more than two instance variables
- No getters/setters/properties
- All classes must have state

Object calisthenics does not give you anything new; on the contrary, it takes stuff away. Expect these rules/constraints to be challenging/frustrating if you have never used them before. Be strict for now – no exceptions! The time to bend the rules has not yet come.

> **Important**
>
> Pay extra attention to **not** break the following rules.

Only One Level of Indentation per Method

Why?

- It helps to ensure that a method focuses on doing only one thing

- It reduces the size of your units, enabling easier reuse

Don't Use the ELSE Keyword

Why?

- It promotes a main execution lane, with a few special cases

- It suggests polymorphism to handle complex conditional cases, making the code more explicit (for example, using the **State Pattern**)

- We are trying to use the **Null Object** pattern to express that a result has no value

Wrap All Primitives and Strings

- You cannot have method arguments (except in constructors) that are primitive types (`int`, `float`, `double`, `bool`, `string`, and `char`).

- You cannot have method return values that are primitive types (`int`, `float`, `double`, `bool`, `string`, and `char`).

- For every primitive type that you need to pass around, create a class to act as home for related behaviors.

- It is okay to have primitive types in the private member variables of the class.

Why?

- Primitives are super-types that have only contextual meaning. They can express anything, so we tend to use them for everything.

- Make the code more explicit by expressing intent through types that become behavior attractors.

- Objects will have inherent meaning.

- It's the cure for **primitive obsession** code smell.

First-Class Collections

- You cannot have method arguments (except in constructors) that are collections (`array`, `hash table`, `set`, and `list`...).

- Create a class for all collections, even if a collection is just a private member variable in a class. This gives collection behaviors a home.

- Any class that contains a collection should contain no other member variables.

Why?

- Consider collections as primitives; that way, any behavior specific to your collection will be attracted to a single place.

- Filters will become part of the class.

- Joins or special rules applied to collection elements will be contained within the class.

- Changing the internal representation won't affect the clients that improve decoupling.

Example

If we want to model a classic invoice domain, we can approach it as shown in the following sample:

```
public class InvoiceLine
{
}


public class Invoice
{
    private List<InvoiceLine> lines;
}
```

Using first-class collections, we could design the model as follows:

```
class InvoiceLine
{
}


// First-class collection
```

```
class InvoiceDetails
{
    private List<InvoiceLine> lines;
}


class Invoice
{
    InvoiceDetails details;
}
```

With the latter approach, we have a home for all behaviors that belong in the collection instead of adding those behaviors to the **Invoice** class. That way, we achieve a better separation of concerns.

No Getters/Setters/Properties

- Especially if used only for unit test assertions, do not add public getters/setters/properties just for the purpose of making tests easier to write.

- Consider overriding equality to overcome this constraint.

Why?

- Aligns with the idea of **object-oriented programming (OOP)** as a network of entities that collaborate by passing messages (calling methods) on each other.

- Instead of asking an object for its data and then acting on it, tell the object what it should do for you.

- Data structures and objects are both represented by the **class** keyword in Java and C#, but they have different responsibilities.

Example

If we want to test a **Person** instance, we can approach it as shown in the following sample:

```
public class Person
{
    string getFirstName()
    string getLastName()
```

```
    }


    public void A_Test_That_Verifies_We_Get_The_Expected_Person()
    {
      // we get a person instance from somewhere
      assert.equal("Bart", person.getFirstName)
      assert.equal("Simpson", person.getLastName)
    }
```

If we apply the constraint of no getters/setters/properties, especially if used only for tests, we can approach it as shown in the following sample:

```
    public class Person
    {
        firstName
        lastName


        // Override equality
        boolean equals(Object o) {
          // implement equality for person
        }
    }


    public void A_Test_That_Verifies_We_Get_The_Expected_Person()
    {
      var bart = new Person("Bart", "Simpson")
      // we get a person instance from somewhere
      assert.equal(bart, person)
    }
```

With this approach, we do not add getters/properties to our class and expand the class interface just for the purpose of testing. There are other benefits as well, but we will discuss those later in the book.

Wrap All Primitives and Strings

Primitives are super-types that have only contextual meaning. They can express anything, so we tend to use them for everything.

Why?

They make the code more explicit, expressing intent through types that become behavior attractors so that these objects will have inherent meaning.

Example

Keeping with the classic invoice domain, we can approach calculating the total and apply discount as shown in the following sample code:

```
class Invoice

{

    void ApplyDiscount(decimal discount)

    decimal CalculateTotal()

}
```

If we wrap all primitives and strings, we could design the total and apply discount methods as follows:

```
class Discount

{
}


class Money

{
}


class Invoice

{

    void ApplyDiscount(Discount discount)

    Money CalculateTotal()

}
```

With this approach, we have a home for all behaviors that belong to money (currency exchange, for example) and discount (types of discounts, for example) instead of adding those behaviors to the `Invoice` class. That way, we achieve a better separation of concerns.

One Dot per Line

This code, `dog.Body.Tail.Wag()`, looks innocuous at first glance, but in reality we are *coupling* our code with classes that are far away from us. We only know about **dogs** and its public interface. The interface of **dog body** is an alien concept and we are creating a coupling issue with it. In order to fix this coupling issue, we can create a method in **dog** that hides its dependencies from us; for example, `dog.ExpressHappiness()`.

Why?

- It exposes the intent hides implementation, telling an object to do something for you instead of asking for its internal representation.

- It reduces the amount of knowledge you should have to enable a behavior.

- This doesn't apply to **LINQ (Language Integrated Query)** and fluent interfaces.

Don't Abbreviate

If we need a long name, it's likely we are missing a concept. Make it explicit.

Why?

- Abbreviations can be confusing, so it's better to be clear.

- If we are repeating the name over and over, maybe we are missing an opportunity to remove duplication.

Keep All Entities Small

- 10 files per package
- 50 lines per class
- 5 lines per method
- 2 arguments per method

Why?

- Small classes tend to be focused on doing just one thing, making them easier to reuse.

- It makes classes easier to understand.

- Use packages (namespaces) to cluster related classes.

- Small packages force them to have a clear purpose and identity.

No Classes with More Than Two Instance Variables

Why?

- The more instance variables, the lower the cohesion within the class.

- Usually, classes with more than one instance variable are orchestrators, and classes with one instance variable are actuators. Separate the responsibilities.

All Classes Must Have State

No static methods and no utility classes.

Why?

- Sometimes, we really don't have state, but usually, if we have a static method, it means it could be anywhere.

- Try to create classes that have clear responsibilities and require state maintenance. This forces us to create a network of collaborators that expose behavior and hide state.

Heuristics

- **Tell don't ask**: Tell objects to perform actions instead of asking them for data and processing it elsewhere – similar to no getters/setters.

- **Law of Demeter**: Each component should only talk to its friends; don't talk to strangers – similar to one dot per line.

Katas

Tic-Tac-Toe

Implement the game of Tic-Tac-Toe again, following all TDD practices plus object calisthenics rules. When you are finished, compare the solution you came up with first and the one using object calisthenics.

> **Tip**
>
> Try to make invalid state unrepresentable. Make the compiler work for you. If client code tries to pass invalid state to your code, the compiler should signal an error.

Game of Life

Implement *Game of Life* using object calisthenics plus everything we covered before.

For those not familiar with this game, here is a description adapted from Wikipedia: Conway's Game of Life, https://en.wikipedia.org/wiki/Conway%27s_Game_of_Life.

The universe of Game of Life is an infinite, two-dimensional orthogonal grid of square cells, each of which is in one of two possible states: alive or dead (or populated and unpopulated, respectively). Every cell interacts with its eight neighbors, which are the cells that are horizontally, vertically, or diagonally adjacent. At each step in time, the following transitions occur:

- Any live cell with fewer than two live neighbors dies, as if by under population
- Any live cell with two or three live neighbors lives on to the next generation
- Any live cell with more than three live neighbors dies, as if by overpopulation
- Any dead cell with exactly three live neighbors becomes a live cell, as if by reproduction

The initial pattern constitutes the seed of the system. The first generation is created by applying the previously mentioned rules simultaneously to every cell in the seed; births and deaths occur simultaneously, and the discrete moment at which this happens is sometimes called a **tick**. Each generation is a pure function of the preceding one. The rules continue to be applied repeatedly to create further generations.

Great Habits

In this lesson, we introduced object calisthenics. Check them out in the following list.

Considerations When Writing a New Test

- Tests should test one thing only
- Create more specific tests to drive a more generic solution (triangulate)
- Give your tests meaningful names (behavior/goal-oriented) that reflect your business domain
- See tests fail for the right reason
- Ensure you have meaningful feedback from failing tests
- Keep your tests and production code separate
- Organize your unit tests to reflect your production code (similar project structure)
- Organize your tests in arrange, act, and assert blocks
- Write the assertion first and work backward
- Write fast, isolated, repeatable, and self-validating tests

Considerations When Making a Failing Test Pass

- Write the simplest code to pass the test
- Write any code that makes you get to the refactor phase quicker
- Use **Transformation Priority Premise**
- Consider using object calisthenics to drive design decisions (**New habit**)

Considerations after the Test Passes

- Use the Rule of Three to tackle duplication
- Refactor design constantly (**New habit**)
- Apply object calisthenics to improve your design (**New habit**)

Classic TDD flow

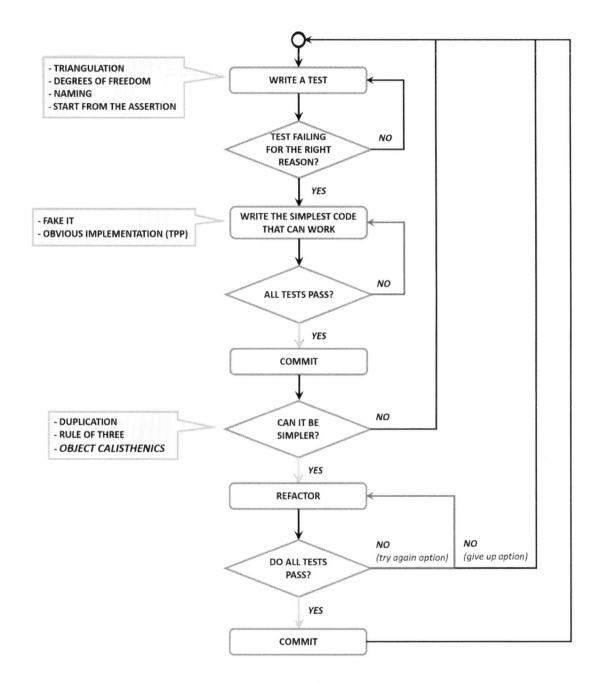

Figure 5.1: Classic TDD flow

Where Are We in the Big Picture of OO Software Design?

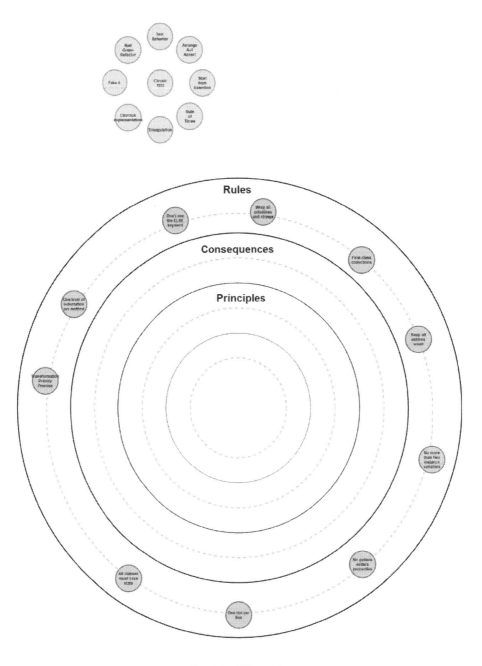

Figure 5.2: OO Design

When Should I Move on to the Next Lesson?

We have now covered most of the rules. In the next lessons, we will be covering higher-level concepts. Make sure you can apply TDD effectively, including:

- Red, green, refactor
- Writing the test starting from the assertion
- Using the transformation priority premise to keep your code simple
- Using object calisthenics to help you with design

You should feel ready to walk now. :)

Resources

Web

- Does TDD really lead to good design? Sandro Mancuso: http://codurance.com/2015/05/12/does-tdd-lead-to-good-design/.
- Improving code quality with Object Calisthenics, Diego Mariani: https://medium.com/web-engineering-vox/improving-code-quality-with-object-calisthenics-aa4ad67a61f1.
- Object Calisthenics, William Durand: https://williamdurand.fr/2013/06/03/object-calisthenics/.
- Object calisthenics paper: http://www.xpteam.com/jeff/writings/objectcalisthenics.rtf.
- Object calisthenics: write better object oriented code, Fran Dieguez: http://www.frandieguez.com/blog/2012/12/object-calisthenics-write-better-object-oriented-code/.
- Wikipedia, Conway's Game of Life: https://en.wikipedia.org/wiki/Conway%27s_Game_of_Life.

Walking

My grandmother started walking five miles a day when she was sixty. She's ninety-seven now, and we don't know where the heck she is.

– Ellen DeGeneres

6

Design 2 – Refactoring

Refactor: not because you know the abstraction, but because you want to find it.

– Martin Fowler

Refactoring, for me, used to mean something like, "*Let me bring the bulldozer and fix all this code.*" I remember spending nights breaking everything apart, changing the design, and then bringing it all together again. In this process, I would easily have hundreds of tests failing while I was changing the design. This was what I called **refactoring**. Then, one day, I read a tweet saying something like, "*Refactoring is about changing the design without changing the behavior, and it can only happen if tests are passing all the time.*"

After digesting the message of that tweet, I started to practice refactoring that way. I tried to use it on projects, but it led to frustration as I was too inexperienced to use it in *real* code. With time and more practice, I finally got to a point where I could do it. I could change the design while my tests were all passing, thus assuring me I had not changed the behavior of the code I was refactoring. It takes patience and perseverance, but anybody can do it.

The idea of refactoring is to change the design without changing the behavior of code. We should refactor both production code and tests, because having solid and well-designed tests is as important as production code. We should leave no broken windows in our code base, as this encourages other windows to be broken.

> **Note**
>
> Broken windows theory: https://en.wikipedia.org/wiki/Broken_windows_theory

So far, our refactoring phase of the TDD cycle has been concerned with removing duplication. However, refactoring is much more than that. Removing duplication is only the first step of refactoring. Refactoring is mainly about finding abstractions and shaping them; duplication is just a symptom.

> **Note**
>
> There is a saying in software development: all problems can be solved with another layer of abstraction. Refactoring is the choreography we use to move code from design A to design B in a safe and efficient way.

When to Refactor (For Now)

Refactor in these circumstances:

- When we find duplication in our code. (Don't forget the *Rule of Three*.) DRY violation.

- When we break any object calisthenics rule.

We will extend these concepts in upcoming lessons.

Main Refactors

There are five atomic refactors that can be applied to methods, functions, classes, variables, and so on:

- **Rename**: Change the name of classes, methods, variables....

- **Extract**: Extract a class (or methods or variables...) to create a new abstraction

- **Inline**: The inverse of extract–inline a method (or variable), deconstructing an abstraction

- **Move**: Move a class (or methods or variables...) to some other place in the code base
- **Safe delete**: Delete code and its usages in the code base

IDE Agility (Know Your Shortcuts)

Although you can perform refactors manually, most development environments already automate a lot of them. The five atomic refactors are widely supported, and some of the higher-level refactors are as well. Using an IDE, if we trust it, allows for very safe and efficient automated refactors, thus avoiding manual mistakes.

We should invest some time into becoming proficient with our IDE refactors and refactoring shortcuts. This enables us to experiment more with refactoring since we can quickly do, and undo, refactors. It also allows us to chain several refactors to move code from A to Z in a safe and efficient way.

Kata

The idea behind refactoring golf exercises is to practice refactoring from a starting point to the desired endpoint while minimizing the number of movements needed to perform the change code.

In these katas, we are given an initial code base and a desired final result. The objective is to apply the minimal refactoring moves to take us from the initial code base to the final one, using as few movements as possible.

Refactoring Golf

The original idea for the refactoring golf exercise has been hard to find; giving credit to one person alone is not possible. Different versions have been created by several people, such as Ivan Moore, Dave Cleal, Mike Hill, Jason Gorman, Robert Chatley, and David Denton.

Refactoring Golf is a game designed to stretch your refactoring muscles and get you to explore your IDE to see what's really possible using shortcuts and automation.

These repos contain several source trees, or numbered *Holes* based on several different exercises with different subjects. The idea behind all these exercises, however, is the same.

Each hole carries on from the last, like in a golf game. Your goal is to (as safely and efficiently as possible) refactor the Hole-X code to look like the Hole X+1 code. You must aim to do it in as few *strokes* as possible. A stroke is essentially a change made to the code, and every stroke costs you points.

Your pairing partner should carefully score you as follows:

- One point for every change made to the code using a shortcut or automated IDE feature; for example, automated refactoring, using a code template, or performing a find/replace operation.

- Two points for every manual edit. Note that a single *edit* could cover multiple lines of code.

- Double points for every change made while the code cannot pass the tests after the previous change.

- Zero points for code formatting; for example, deleting whitespace or optimizing imports.

- Allow yourselves a maximum of two attempts in each round to determine your best score.

> **Hints**
>
> You may find that customizing your IDE is useful; for example, custom code templates or even custom refactorings.
>
> You can find several public repositories with different subjects for refactoring golf: https://github.com/search?utf8=%E2%9C%93&q=refactoring+golf&type=.

Refactor 80-20 Rule

From our experience, we've learned that 80% of the value in refactoring comes from improving the readability and understandability of code. The remaining 20% comes from design changes. We will thus focus on the first 80%.

Once we are comfortable with basic refactoring movements and choreographies, it is time to apply this new practice to code. In the refactoring golf exercise, we were given a starting point and an end point. In a real refactoring session, the endpoint is an imaginary point.

We created a checklist to help you approach refactoring code. It includes rules, tips, and a sequence we can follow. As always, once we get more proficient with our refactoring and design skills, we can leave this list behind us.

Refactoring Guidelines

Stay in the Green While Refactoring

Tests should test behavior, so there is no reason why we should break any tests during refactoring. If you break any tests while refactoring, undo, go back to green, and start over.

Don't change production code that is not covered by tests. If we need to refactor some code that has no tests, then start by adding behavior tests. We will cover this point in more detail in the next lesson, which deals with legacy code.

It may be that we have tests, but they are coupled with the implementation in a way that it is not possible to change the implementation without breaking the tests. In this case, we start refactoring by the tests, and once we have tests that are not coupled with the implementation, we can start refactoring the implementation.

Use IDE-automated refactoring to minimize text editing and risk—provided you trust your IDE automated refactors. Most IDEs try to keep your code compiling, and if they cannot achieve this, they warn you before you make the refactor move. Also, usually, IDEs provide the **Undo** feature for refactors, so if you break something, just undo.

Be strict about staying on green. We learned that, in refactoring, it is more effective to let go of something as soon as tests break, rather than stubbornly trying to fix things to make tests pass.

Remember to execute tests after each refactor to make sure we are still in the green.

Commit as Often as Possible

A source control tool enables us to safely and quickly revert to a known good point, provided we took small steps and committed frequently. If, by any chance, we find ourselves in a bad spot, we can revert back to a safe point and start over. Refactoring should be a series of small experiments that we can easily roll back from.

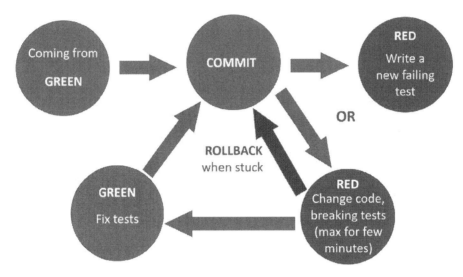

Figure 6.1: Extended TDD cycle: the refactor cycle

Refactor Readability before Design

If we cannot fully understand what the code we are refactoring does, then what are the chances of succeeding? Small improvements in code readability can drastically improve code understandability.

To improve readability, you should start with better names for variables, methods, and classes. The idea is to express intent rather than implementation details. We recommend Arlo Belshee's approach to naming.

Arlo Belshee, Good naming is a process, not a single step: http://arlobelshee.com/good-naming-is-a-process-not-a-single-step/.

Format

Format the code – a simple but very effective technique. Format consistently and don't force the reader to waste time due to inconsistent formatting.

Example:

Before

```
if (i == 1) tempScore = m_score1;
else { score += "-"; tempScore = m_score2; }
```

After

A simple change can make the code much more obvious for the reader:

```
if (i == 1)
{
  tempScore = m_score1;
}
else
{
  score += "-";
  tempScore = m_score2;
}
```

Rename

- Rename bad names, variables, arguments, instance variables, methods, and classes
- Make abbreviations explicit

Example:

Before

```
class TennisGame1 : ITennisGame
{
    private int m_score1 = 0;
    private int m_score2 = 0;
}
```

After

In this example, the meaning of **m_score1** is confusing, so we renamed it to the more obvious name of **player1Score**:

```
class TennisGame1 : ITennisGame

{

    private int player1Score = 0;

    private int player2Score = 0;

}
```

Remove

- Delete unnecessary comments.

- Delete dead code. Don't make the reader waste time trying to figure out code that is not in use anymore.

Example:

Before

```
class TennisGame : ITennisGame

{

    private int player1Score = 0;

    private int player2Score = 0;

    private string player1Name;

    private string player2Name;


    public TennisGame1(string player1Name, string player2Name)

    {

        this.player1Name = player1Name;

        this.player2Name = player2Name;

    }

}
```

After

Player name fields are assigned in the constructor, but are not used anywhere, so we should remove them and the constructor.

```
class TennisGame : ITennisGame

{

    private int player1Score = 0;

    private int player2Score = 0;

}
```

Extract

- Constants from magic numbers and strings

- Conditionals

Example:

Before

```
if (number % 3 == 0 && number % 5 == 0)

{



 . . .



}
```

After

```
if (isDivisibleByThreeAndFive(number))

{



 . . .



}
```

Reorder

Refine the scope for improper variable scoping, and make sure variables are declared close to where they are used.

Change Design (Simple Changes)

- Extract private methods from deep conditionals
- Extract smaller private methods from long methods, and encapsulate cryptic code in private methods
- Return from methods as soon as possible
- Encapsulate where we find missing encapsulation
- Remove duplication

Example

Before

```
string score = "";
if (player1Score == player1Score)
{
  switch (player1Score)
  {
      case 0:
          score = "Love-All";
          break;
      case 1:
          score = "Fifteen-All";
          break;
      case 2:
          score = "Thirty-All";
          break;
      default:
          score = "Deuce";
          break;
  }
  ...
}
```

After

```
string score = "";

if (player1Score == player2Score)

{

  score = formatScoreWhenPlayersAreTied();

  ...

}


string formatScoreWhenPlayersAreTied()

{

  switch (player1Score)

  {

      case 0:

          return "Love-All";

      case 1:

          return "Fifteen-All";

      case 2:

          return "Thirty-All";

      default:

          return "Deuce";

  }

}
```

Kata

Tennis Refactoring by Emily Bache

We have used the Tennis Game kata over and over in our coaching sessions. Its effectiveness comes from the fact that it does not require major design changes to vastly improve the code base. The code has tests, so we can focus on refactoring the implementation, starting with `TennisGame1`. Clean up the code to a point where someone can read it and understand it with ease. You can find the repository of Tennis refactoring kata by Emily Bache here: https://github.com/emilybache/Tennis-Refactoring-Kata).

Parallel Change (Or Expand, Migrate, and Contract)

The technique of Parallel Change was an original idea of Joshua Kerievsky. It was explained in 2010, in a talk called **The Limited Red Society**. InfoQ, Joshua Kerievsky, The Limited Red Society: https://www.infoq.com/presentations/The-Limited-Red-Society.

Parallel Change, also known as **expand**, **migrate**, and **contract**, is a refactor pattern to implement breaking changes safely (staying in the green). It consists of three steps: expand, migrate, and contract.

Expand

Introduce new functionality by adding new code instead of changing existing code. If you are expanding a class or an interface, introduce new methods instead of changing existing ones. If the behavior from the outside is similar and only the implementation changes, duplicate existing tests and point them to the new code, leaving the existing tests untouched. Make sure tests for existing code are still working.

Implement new functionality starting from the tests, either by writing new tests or by adapting duplicated old tests. Make sure to write new code using TDD practices. Once all new functionality is implemented, move to the migration step.

Migrate

Deprecate old code and allow clients to migrate to new expanded code, or change client code to point to new code.

Contract

Once all client code is migrated to new code, remove old functionality by removing deprecated code and its tests.

Kata

Parallel Change Kata by Pawel Duda and Carlos Blé

Change the `ShoppingCart` class. The class should be able to handle multiple items instead of the single one it currently supports. Run the tests every time you make a change. The tests must not be red at any time. No compile errors, no failures. Commit. Refer to the Parallel Change code by Pawel Duda and Carlos Blé at https://github.com/unclejamal/parallel-change.

Great Habits

In this lesson, we introduced a few new habits. Check them out in the following list.

Considerations When Writing a New Test

- Tests should test one thing only
- Create more specific tests to drive a more generic solution (triangulate)
- Give your tests meaningful names (behavior/goal-oriented) that reflect your business domain
- See tests fail for the right reason
- Ensure you have meaningful feedback from failing tests
- Keep your tests and production code separate
- Organize your unit tests to reflect your production code (similar project structure)
- Organize your tests in arrange, act, and assert blocks
- Write the assertion first and work backward
- Write fast, isolated, repeatable, and self-validating tests

Considerations When Making a Failing Test Pass

- Write the simplest code to pass the test
- Write any code that makes you get to the refactor phase quicker
- Use **Transformation Priority Premise**
- Consider using object calisthenics to drive design decisions

Considerations after the Test Passes

- Use the **Rule of Three** to tackle duplication
- Refactor design constantly
- Apply object calisthenics to improve your design
- Stay in the green while refactoring (**New habit**)
- Use the IDE to refactor quickly and safely (**New habit**)
- Refactor code for readability/understandability first (**New habit**)

When Should I Move on to the Next Lesson?

- When you feel comfortable using your IDE to refactor efficiently

- When you can perform the atomic refactors confidently while staying in the green

We have now covered most of the rules. In the next lessons, we will cover higher-level concepts. Make sure you can apply TDD effectively.

Resources

Web

- Good naming is a process, not a single step, Arlo Belshee: http://arlobelshee.com/good-naming-is-a-process-not-a-single-step/.

- The Limited Red Society, Joshua Kerievsky: https://www.infoq.com/presentations/The-Limited-Red-Society.

- Parallel Change Code, Pawel Duda and Carlos Blé: https://github.com/unclejamal/parallel-change.

- Refactoring Sequences: Safe Unwrap, Carlos Blé: https://youtu.be/DpGk34Lqo-A.

- Refactoring Techniques, SoureMaking.com: https://sourcemaking.com/refactoring/refactorings.

- Replace String Constants With Type–Variation II, Carlos Blé: https://youtu.be/o8PVNrfl1p8.

- Smells to Refactorings Cheatsheet, Industrial Logic: https://www.industriallogic.com/blog/smells-to-refactorings-cheatsheet/.

- What To Tidy, Kent Beck: https://medium.com/@kentbeck_7670/what-to-tidy-28cb46e55009.

Books

- **Refactoring: Improving the Design of Existing Code**, Martin Fowler, Kent Beck, Don Roberts, Erich Gamma: https://www.goodreads.com/book/show/44936.Refactoring.

- **Refactoring Workbook**, William C. Wake: https://www.goodreads.com/book/show/337298.Refactoring_Workbook.

7
Design 3 – Code Smells

Design is choosing how you will fail.

– Ron Fein

When I started my career, I spent most of my learning efforts going after specific technologies, trying to understand them in as much depth as I could. As years went by, I started realizing that this was a fruitless path in the long run. Technologies are constantly being hyped and doomed. Part of the game for me used to be guessing what the next thing would be. Sometimes I got it right, sometimes not. Eventually, I stopped chasing specific technologies and started learning more about things that have been relevant and fundamental for many years.

Object-oriented design has not changed much in the past 20 to 30 years - perhaps even longer. What I did not know is there is a price to pay for following this path. Suddenly, I was no longer the one that knew the most about a specific technology on the team. Sometimes, I felt frustrated for not knowing some detail in a framework, but eventually I just accepted it, as this was no longer my path.

Code smells are one of the most important concepts in object-oriented design. Once I was able to spot them, my internal feedback loop improved dramatically.

Design is about compromises. I don't believe in perfect design; there is always a compromise somewhere. Code smells for me are about making conscious compromises on design.

We started our journey on object-oriented software design by discussing object calisthenics. These are a very powerful set of rules that, if applied correctly, can have an enormous effect on designs. Following rules has advantages and disadvantages. The main advantage is an immediate effect as soon as you start applying them. The biggest disadvantage is that they usually don't provide a clear reason as to why they work. In this lesson, by looking at code smells, we'll delve into the first level of why object calisthenics rules work. (In subsequent lessons, we will dig deeper into these *whys*.)

The name **smell** is significant. Smells are *not* called **mistakes** for important reasons:

*   Smells are the symptoms of a problem rather than the problem itself, just like the symptoms of a disease are not the disease itself.

*   Smells provide feedback on our decisions, and we should pay attention to them, as they may indicate deeper problems.

*   Designing software is a constant compromise, and sometimes we have to accept code smells as a compromise as long as it's a conscious compromise. As software developers, we should be very conscious of our design and code decisions and have an opinion on every decision we make.

Smells are not yet the principles or values behind the rules; they are somewhere in between. If we break rules, we end up with design and code issues. Code smells are the *visible symptoms* of those problems.

In this lesson, we'll cover the two main categories of smells in software: **design smells** and **code smells**.

Design Smells

These are high-level smells – the tip of the iceberg. We should treat these smells as flashing warning signs. They definitely alert us about big problems, though they provide little information on the real cause of those problems.

If we find a design smell, it's probably time to stop, reflect upon our past design decisions, and decide whether we need to revisit those decisions. The problem with design smells is that they tend to take time to manifest, and sometimes it's too late.

The following is a list of design smells:

- **Rigidity**: The system is hard to change because every change forces many other changes to other parts of the system.

- **Fragility**: Changes cause the system to break in places that have no conceptual relationship to the part that was changed.

- **Immobility**: It is hard to disentangle the system into components that can be reused in the other systems.

- **Viscosity**: Doing things right is harder than doing things wrong.

- **Needless Complexity**: The design contains infrastructure that adds no direct benefit.

- **Needless Repetition**: The design contains repeating structures that could be unified under a single abstraction.

- **Opacity**: It is hard to read and understand. It does not express its intent well.

Code Smells

Code smells are more granular smells that are usually easier and less costly to fix than design smells. There are four categories of code smells:

Bloaters

Something that has grown so large that it cannot be effectively handled:

- **Long Method**: Methods should do only one thing. **Single Responsibility Principle (SRP)** violation. One level of abstraction. "*Keep all entities small*" object calisthenics rule violation.

- **Large Class**: Classes should have only one responsibility. Possible SRP violation. No more than 50 lines per class. "*Keep all entities small*" object calisthenics rule violation.

- **Primitive Obsession**: Don't use primitive types as substitutes for classes. If the data type is sufficiently complex, use a class to represent it. "*Wrap all primitives and strings*" object calisthenics rule violation.

- **Long Parameter List**: "*Keep all entities small*" object calisthenics rule violation.

    – **Ideal**: 0 parameters–niladic method

    – **Okay**: 1 parameter–monadic method

    – **Acceptable**: 2 parameters–dyadic method

    – **Debatable**: 3 parameters–triadic method

    – **Avoid Special Justification**: More than 3 parameters–polyadic method

- **Data Clumps**: The same data items appearing together in lots of places (that is, parameters, DTOs, sets of variables, and so on). Special case of **duplicated code**. DRY violation. There is a missing concept that could be expressed as a class introducing a level of abstraction.

Couplers

Something that causes excessive coupling of different modules:

- **Feature Envy**: A class that uses methods or properties of another class excessively. "*All classes must have state*" object calisthenics rule violation.

- **Inappropriate Intimacy**: A class that has dependencies on implementation details of another class. Special case of **Feature Envy**.

- **Message Chains**: Too many dots: `Dog.Body.Tail.Wag()` should be: `Dog.ExpressHappiness()`. "*One dot per line*" object calisthenics rule violation.

- **Middleman**: If a class is delegating all its work, cut out the middleman. Beware of classes that are wrappers over other classes or existing functionality. Special case of Lazy Class. "*All classes must have state*" object calisthenics rule violation.

Object-Orientation Abusers

Cases where the solution does not fully exploit the possibilities of object-oriented design:

- **Switch Statements**: Can lead to the same switch statement scattered about a program in different places. Can lead to DRY violation.

- **Temporary Field**: A class contains an instance variable set only in certain circumstances. Possible "*no classes with more than two instance variables*" object calisthenics rule violation.

- **Refused Bequest**: A throw has not been implemented. Usually means the hierarchy is wrong. **Liskov Substitution Principle (LSP)** violation.

- **Alternative Classes with Different Interfaces**: If two classes are similar on the inside, but different on the outside, perhaps they can be modified to share a common interface.

Change Preventers

Something that hinders changing or further developing the software:

- **Divergent Change**: One class is commonly changed in different ways for different reasons. **Open/Closed Principle (OCP)** and/or SRP violation. God class. Can be caused by *Primitive Obsession* and/or *Feature Envy*.

- **Shotgun Surgery**: Opposite of *Divergent Change*. One change forces lots of little changes in different classes. DRY violation. Can be caused by *Primitive Obsession*, *Feature Envy*, or *copy pasting driven development*.

- **Parallel Inheritance Hierarchies**: Special case of *Shotgun Surgery*. Creating a subclass of one class forces the subclass of another.

Dispensables

Something unnecessary that should be removed from the source code:

- **Lazy Class**: A class that does too little. May be acting only as middleman or a data class, or can be caused by *speculative generality*.

- **Data Class**: Classes that have fields, properties, and nothing else. Anemic classes that contain no behavior. Special case of *Lazy Class*. Can be "*all classes must have state*" object calisthenics rule violation or "*no classes with more than two instance variables*" object calisthenics rule violation.

- **Duplicated Code**: Identical or very similar code (or duplicated knowledge) exists in more than one location. DRY violation.

- **Dead Code**: Code that has no references to it. Commented or unreachable code.

- **Speculative Generality**: **YAGNI (You Aren't Going to Need It)** violation or only users of method or class are test cases.

- **Comments**: Make an effort to create code that expresses intent instead of adding comments.

Highlighted Code Smells

In our experience, we have found that the most dangerous code smells are: *Duplication*, *Primitive Obsession*, *Feature Envy*, and *Message Chains*. For that reason, we decided to highlight them, especially the last three, as we have already paid enough attention to duplication in previous lessons.

Code Smells Hierarchy

Primitive obsession, feature envy, and message chains lead to many other code smells and should thus be dealt with as soon as possible.

Primitive obsession

- Duplicated code
- Shotgun surgery
- Divergent change
- Long parameter list

Feature Envy / Inappropriate Intimacy

- Lazy class
- Data class
- Middleman
- Data clumps
- Long method
- Large class
- Duplicated code
- Shotgun surgery
- Divergent change
- Long parameter list

Message Chains

- Data clumps
- Duplicated code

Primitive Obsession

Don't use primitive types as substitutes for classes. If a data type is sufficiently complex, use a class to represent it.

For example, if we need to represent money, it's very tempting to use an `int`, a `float`, or a `decimal` primitive type. This looks very benign. When we need to refer to money, we represent it with a primitive type. But now the business needs money to be in multiple currencies. How many places do we need to change? What if we pass an exchange rate instead of the money value to a method? If we had a type for it, the code wouldn't even compile, making wrong state unrepresentable!

Another consequence of primitive obsession is the excessive need for validation. Again, if money is represented by a primitive type, what do we do with negative values?

This code smell leads to the *Shotgun Surgery* code smell because behavior tends to be spread in many places, causing a cascade of changes.

Feature Envy

A class that uses methods or properties of another class excessively. An example is class **A** only contains state and class **B** uses the state from class **A** to perform some operation(s) with it. We say that class **B** has *Feature Envy* of class **A** because class **B** contains the behavior that should be in class **A**. As a general rule, behavior should be close to the state it uses.

Feature ENVY usually implies that the envied class is a **Lazy Class**. This smell may also lead to Shotgun Surgery, as behavior can be scattered in many places or may also lead to Divergent Change as a class may become a **God Class** (knowing too much).

Example

`PositionUpdater` uses data from `Coordinate`, causing the *Feature Envy* smell, and `Coordinate` is a data class:

```
public class Coordinate
{
  public int X {get; set}
  public int Y {get; set}
}


public class PositionUpdater
{
  public Coordinate MoveUp(Coordinate coordinate)
```

```
    {
        return new Coordinate{X = coordinate.X, Y = coordinate.Y + 1};
    }
}
```

After removing the *Feature Envy* code smell, **Coordinate** looks like this:

```
public class Coordinate
{
    public int X {get; private set}
    public int Y {get; private set}

    public void MoveUp()
    {
        coordinate.Y += 1;
    }
}
```

Message Chains

The **Message Chains** code smell represents *coupling* (covered later in this book) and also leads to the Shotgun Surgery code smell or Divergent Change code smell. We must avoid this code smell like the plague. In our coaching sessions, we use a checklist to help avoid this smell. This code smell is also known as the **Law of Demeter**.

A More Formal Checklist

Messages should be sent only to an object (methods should only be invoked on objects) in the following conditions:

- Itself
- Objects contained in attributes of itself or a super class
- An object that is passed as a parameter to the method
- An object that is created by the method
- An object that is stored in global variables. We don't use global variables, do we?

A More Informal Checklist

We can only play with toys that:

- We own
- We build
- We are given

Object Calisthenics Preventing Code Smells

Object calisthenics is a set of rules that help us avoid some code smells. If we decide to break the rules, we'll have consequences that materialize as code smells. In design, following rules is not always the best path; sometimes we need to bend or break rules. This is fine as long as we are conscious about it; namely, the consequences and the benefits. Software design should be a series of decisions. Our worst enemy is accidental complexity due to unconscious design decisions.

Quora: https://www.quora.com/What-are-essential-and-accidental-complexity.

Object calisthenics violation	Code smells consequence
Only one level of indentation per method	Long Method
Don't use the ELSE keyword	Long Method/Duplicated Code
Wrap all primitives and strings	Primitive Obsession/Duplicated Code/Shotgun Surgery
First class collections	Divergent Change/Large Class
One dot per line	Message Chains
Don't abbreviate	NA
Keep all entities small	Large Class/Long Method/Long Parameter List
No classes with more than two instance variables	Large Class
No geers/seers/properties	NA
All classes must have state, no static methods, no utility classes	Lazy Class/Middle Man/Feature Envy

Figure 7.1: Object calisthenics violation and code smells consequence

When to Refactor (Extended for Code Smells)

Refactor in these circumstances:

- When we find duplication in our code. (Don't forget the *Rule of Three*.) DRY violation.

- When we break any object calisthenics rules.

- When code exhibits code smells that we did not expect.

Refactor Code Smells

Martin Fowler, in his excellent and groundbreaking book, *Refactoring: Improving the Design of Existing Code*, creates a categorization and terminology for many refactors. We will not dive into this too much since it's covered in his book. Terminology is often disregarded, but it plays an important role in communicating effectively. In the following table, we list the most common refactors we can use to remove particular code smells. The refactors in this table are also taken from Fowler's book:

Switch Statements OOA	Inappropriate Intimacy COU	Large Class BLO
Replace Conditional with Polymorphism	Move Method	Extract Class
Replace Type Code with Subclasses	Move Field	Extract Subclass
Replace Type Code with State/Strategy	Extract Class	Extract Interface
Move Accumulation to Visitor	Hide Delegate	Replace Data Value with Object
Replace Conditional Dispatcher with Command	Replace Inheritance with Delegation	Replace Conditional Dispatcher with Command
Replace Parameter with Explicit Methods		Replace Implicit Language with Interpreter
Introduce Null Object		Replace State-Altering Conditionals with State
Primitive Obsession BLO	**Duplicated Code** DIS	**Long Method** BLO
Replace Data Value with Object	Chain Constructors	Extract Method
Encapsulate Composite with Builder	Extract Composite	Compose Method
Introduce Parameter Object	Extract Method	Introduce Parameter Object
Extract Class	Extract Class	Move Accumulation to Collecting Parameter
Move Embellishment to Decorator	Form Template Method	Move Accumulation to Visitor
Replace Conditional Logic with Strategy	Introduce Null Object	Decompose Conditional
Replace Implicit Language with Interpreter	Factory Method	Preserve Whole Object
Replace Implicit Tree with Composite	Pull Up Method	Replace Conditional Dispatcher with Command
Replace State-Altering Conditionals with State	Pull Up Field	Replace Conditional Logic with Strategy
Replace Type Code with Class	Substitute Algorithm	Replace Method with Method Object
Replace Type Code with State/Strategy	Adapter	Replace Temp with Query
Replace Type Code with Subclasses		
Replace Array With Object		
Divergent Change CHP	**Shotgun Surgery** CHP	**Feature Envy** COU
Extract Class	Move Method	Extract Method
	Move Field	Move Method
	Inline Class	Move Field
Long Parameter List BLO	**Data Clumps** BLO	**Parallel Inheritance** Hierarchies CHP
Replace Parameter with Method	Extract Class	Move Method
Introduce Parameter Object	Preserve Whole Object	Move Field
Preserve Whole Object	Introduce Parameter Object	
Middle Man COU	**Data Class** DIS	**Message Chains** COU
Remove Middle Man	Move Method	Hide Delegate
Inline Method	Encapsulate Field	Extract Method
Replace Delegation with Inheritance	Encapsulate Collection	Move Method
Speculative Generality DIS	**Temporary Field** OOA	**Lazy Class** DIS
Collapse Hierarchy	Extract Class	Collapse Hierarchy
Rename Method	Introduce Null Object	Inline Class
Remove Parameter		
Inline Class		
Refused Bequest OOA	**Alternative Classes with Different Interfaces** OOA	**Incomplete Library Class** COU
Push Down Field	Unify Interfaces with Adapter	Introduce Foreign Method
Push Down Method	Rename Method	Introduce Local Extension
Replace Inheritance with Delegation	Move Method	
Comments DIS	**Dead Code** DIS	
Rename Method		
Method		
Introduce Extract Assertion		

Figure 7.2: Refactor code smells

BLO – Bloater, CHP – Change preventer, COU – Coupler, DIS – Dispensable, OOA – Object Orientation Abuser

For those interested in a deeper dive into the world of refactoring, see the web links and books in the *Resources* section of this lesson.

Kata

Smelly Tic-Tac-Toe

We created a very smelly implementation of Tic-Tac-Toe in our Code Smells: https://github.com/AgileTechPraxis/CodeSmells open source repository. There are quite a few code smells in the implementation:

- Comments
- Data class
- Data clumps
- Divergent change
- Duplicated code
- Feature envy
- Large class
- Lazy class
- Long method
- Long parameter list
- Message chain
- Primitive obsession
- Shotgun surgery

Start by identifying the smells, then slowly refactor the code. Remember to keep the tests passing at all times during the refactor. It's okay to revert back to a previous working state at any moment.

> **Note**
>
> For a sample (partial) solution, see the *Appendices* section on the page 385.

Great Habits

In this lesson, we introduced new habits. Check it out in the following list.

Considerations When Writing a New Test

- Tests should test one thing only

- Create more specific tests to drive a more generic solution (triangulate)

- Give your tests meaningful names (behavior/goal-oriented) that reflect your business domain

- See tests fail for the right reason

- Ensure you have meaningful feedback from failing tests

- Keep your tests and production code separate

- Organize your unit tests to reflect your production code (similar project structure)

- Organize your tests in arrange, act, and assert blocks

- Write the assertion first and work backward

- Write fast, isolated, repeatable, and self-validating tests

Considerations When Making a Failing Test Pass

- Write the simplest code to pass the test

- Write any code that makes you get to the refactor phase quicker

- Use the transformation priority premise

- Consider using object calisthenics to drive design decisions

Considerations After the Test Passes

- Use the *Rule of Three* to tackle duplication

- Refactor design constantly

- Apply object calisthenics to improve your design

- Stay in the green while refactoring

- Use the IDE to refactor quickly and safely

- Refactor code for readability/understandability first

- Look out for code smells and refactor your code accordingly (**New habit**)

Classic TDD Flow

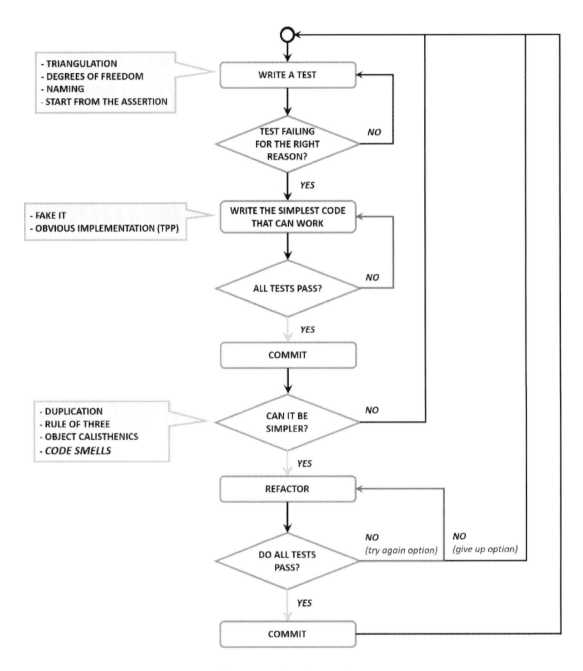

Figure 7.3: Classic TDD flow

The Big Picture

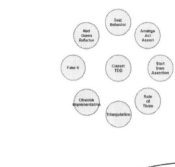

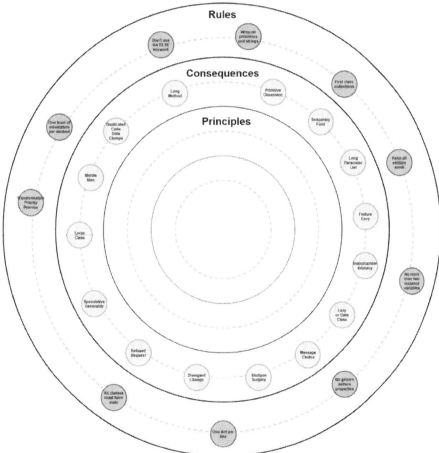

Figure 7.4: OO design—Has fewer elements

When Should I Move on to the Next Lesson?

- When you understand the connection between calisthenics and code smells

- When you can design code using smells as feedback

Resources

Web

- Code Smells, SourceMaking.com: http://sourcemaking.com/refactoring/bad-smells-in-code.

- No Silver Bullet – Essence and Accident in Software Engineering, Fredrick P. Brooks Jr.: http://worrydream.com/refs/Brooks-NoSilverBullet.pdf.

- Out of the tar pit, Ben Mosley and Peter Marks: https://github.com/papers-we-love/papers-we-love/blob/master/design/out-of-the-tar-pit.pdf.

- Simple Made Easy, Rich Hickey: https://www.infoq.com/presentations/Simple-Made-Easy.

- Software Development Anti-Patterns, SourceMaking.com: https://sourcemaking.com/antipatterns/software-development-antipatterns.

Books

- Refactoring: Improving the Design of Existing Code, Martin Fowler, et al.: https://www.goodreads.com/book/show/44936.Refactoring.

8

Test Doubles

Functions that change state should not return values and functions that return values should not change state.

– Bertrand Meyer, *Object-Oriented Software Construction*

I still remember when I joined the first hardcore XP team. It was still experimental at that company, and we didn't have the funds for tools in the beginning, aside from an IDE refactoring helper. We couldn't introduce frameworks without a bureaucratic request – a troublesome authorization process lasting weeks. Nevertheless, our backlog needed to be delivered in time. That's where I had to learn to inject dependencies manually and to manually develop all test doubles. We called it "*poor man dependency injection*" and "*poor man mocking*," underscoring the fact that we were forced to re-invent the wheel for budgetary reasons.

Despite that little drag, we succeeded in delivering the backlog in time and with very few bugs. The company finally allowed us to introduce the frameworks we needed to optimize the amount of work not done.

However, I always remember those days of the "*poor man way*" as the most interesting; I have learned so much from implementing *Test Doubles* manually! If you have never tried it yourself, I suggest giving it a try. It's a very interesting exercise!

Marco

If you have read the **gang of four** (**GOF**) book *Design Patterns*, one of the guiding principles mentioned in the introduction is "*program to an interface, not an implementation.*" One advantage is that it opens the doors for using *Test Doubles*.

A *Test Double* borrows from the name and use of stunt doubles in movies. Gerard Meszaros introduced the term in his book *xUnit Test Patterns*. A Test Double is any kind of object used in place of a real object for testing purposes.

Martin Fowler mentions Test Doubles in his blog post, too.

Principles

In the beginning, Test Doubles became popular as an instrument for isolating tests from third-party libraries. Despite that being one of its use cases, and still very useful, it is not the only one and perhaps not the most important.

To attain good object-oriented design, the Test Doubles technique leverages **Test-Driven Development** by guiding the composition of a coherent, well-encapsulated system of types within a code base. By focusing on behavior instead of data, Test Doubles leads developers to think about object interactions early, identifying the public interfaces first. This focal point switch in the way tests are created is crucial in finding optimal object compositions.

Command-Query Separation

Command-Query Separation or **CQS** is a principle that states that a software interface abstraction is designed with two types of methods. One method type is known as a **Command method**, and the other method type is known as a **Query method**:

> **Note**
>
> Vaughn Vernon, Really Simple CQRS, Kalele blog: https://kalele.io/blog-posts/really-simple-cqrs/.

- A **Command** method modifies or mutates the state underneath the interface but does not answer any portion of that state.

- A **Query** method answers the current state beneath the interface but must not modify that state before answering it.

Keeping this principle in mind, we can describe a usage pattern for Test Doubles.

Queries

A *query* is a method call that returns data and shouldn't have any effect on the state of an object. (It should be *idempotent*.)

> Information
>
> **Use Stubs for Queries in the Arrange section**
>
> Stubs' main task is about "*making happy noises*." A way to achieve this is, when return data is required, to return canned data from dependencies – perfect for queries.

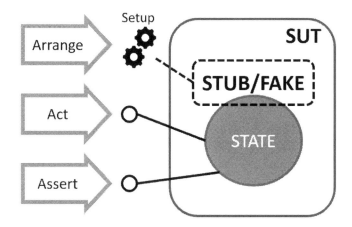

Figure 8.1: Use stubs for queries

Commands

A *command* is a method call that changes the state of the system; hence, it has a side effect, and it should return **void**.

> Information
>
> **Use Mocks for Commands in the Assert section**
>
> Commands are all about side effects on other parts of the system, and Mocks are all about verifying the occurrence of a behavior (that is, that the side effects' trigger occurred).

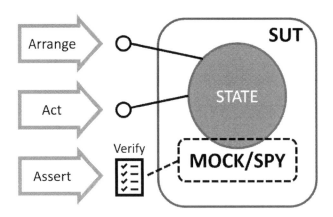

Figure 8.2: Use mocks for commands

Different Types of Test Doubles

Dummy Objects

Dummy objects are needed only to complete the parameters' list of a method but are never actually used. They are not very common in well-designed systems since they are often an indication of room for design improvements.

Stubs

Stubs respond to calls made during a test with some pre-programmed output specific for each test. This implies that they need to be specifically set up for every test.

Stubs are used to provide synthetic replacements for *queries* called on collaborators of the **Subject Under Test**.

Fake Objects

Fake objects are handmade stubs (sometimes called **poor man Stubs**).

Mocks

Mocks are set up with expectations of the calls they are expected to receive. They can throw an exception if they receive a call they don't expect and/or are queried during the assertion phase to verify that they received all the calls they were expecting.

Mocks are used to provide a way of confirming that *commands* have been triggered correctly by the **Subject Under Test**.

Spies

Spies are handmade Mocks (sometimes called **poor man Mocks**).

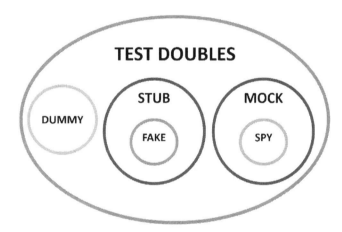

Figure 8.3: Venn diagram of Test Doubles

Test Doubles Guidelines

Only Use Test Doubles for Classes That You Own

Using Test Doubles is a technique for software design. That's why it is important to only mock/stub types that belong to the team's code base. The key concept here is that if the Test Doubles are coupled with an external interface, they cannot change the design to respond to requirements that arise from the process.

The same is valid for fixed types, such as those defined by the runtime or external libraries. So, how do we test the interaction with an external library? The trick here is to write a thin wrapper to implement the abstractions for the underlying infrastructure. Those wrappers are the components belonging to the team's code base that:

- Are generated from a behavior-first position (public interface definition first)

- Can be substituted with Test Doubles

We have found this to be great insight for understanding the technique. It restores the pre-eminence of design in the use of **Mock/Stub Objects**, which has often been overshadowed by its popularity for testing interactions with third-party libraries.

So, what if the external library changes? How can we test it? That's possible using an integration test, but we will go through that later.

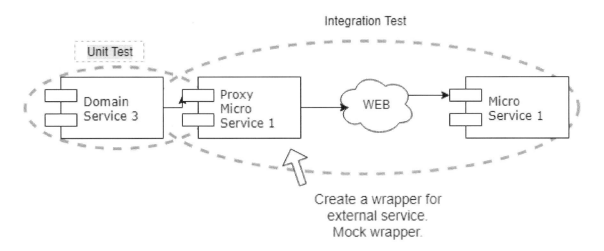

Figure 8.4: Only use Test Doubles for classes that you own

Verify as Little as Possible in a Test

When using Mock/Stub objects, it is important to find the balance between the specification of the **Subject Under Test** behavior and a flexible test that allows the easy evolution of the code base. One of the risks with TDD is tests becoming **fragile** – that is, failing due to unrelated changes to the application code. Usually, that happens when they have been over-specified to check the features that are implemented, not the expression of some requirement in the object.

A test suite that contains a lot of fragile tests will slow down development and compromise the ability to refactor. The solution is to review the fragile tests and see if either the specification should be weakened, or the object composition is not optimal and should be changed. "A *specification should be as precise as possible, but not more precise.*" Paraphrasing Einstein:

Everything should be made as simple as possible, but not simpler. Generally attributed to *Albert Einstein.*

Don't Use Test Doubles for Isolated Objects

If an object has no collaborations with other objects in the system, it does not need to be tested using **Mock/Stub Objects**. A test for such an object only needs to make assertions about its state through values returned from its methods. Typically, these objects store data, perform calculations, or represent atomic values. While this may seem an obvious thing to say, we have seen a lot of usage of Test Doubles where they weren't actually needed.

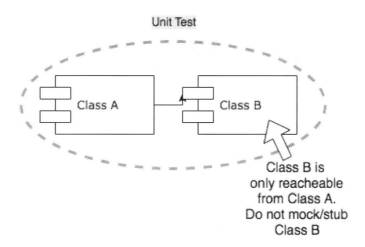

Figure 8.5: Don't use Test Doubles for isolated objects

Don't Add Behavior in Test Doubles

Mock objects might also be Stubs but should not add any additional complexity to the test environment. Their behavior should be obvious and self-explanatory. We have noticed that when real behavior has been added to Mock objects, it is usually a strong symptom of misplaced responsibilities.

A common example of this is when one Mock has to interpret its input to return a value, perhaps by parsing an event message. This has the consequence of testing the test infrastructure rather than the **Subject Under Test**, because a change in the original object would force a change in the stubbed object, making it a classic example of Shotgun Surgery code smell.

For example:

```csharp
// Too much logic in the test
var username = new Random().Next(1, 11) % 2 == 0
                ? "Pedro"
                : string.Empty;


var pedro = new User("Pedro");


userServiceMock
    .Setup(service => service.GetUser(username))
    .Callback((userName) => //Called before the service gets the user
    {
        //Change input parameters behavior
        if(userName = string.Empty)
        {
            userName = "Default";
        }
        Console.WriteLine($"args before returns {userName}");
    })
    .Returns(pedro)
    .Callback((user) => // Called after the service returned the user
    {
        //Change returned value behavior
        if(user == null)
        {
```

```
        user = new User("Default");
    }
    Console.WriteLine($"arg after returns {user.Name}");
});
```

Rather than this, write two independent, more focused tests.

Only Use Test Doubles for Your Immediate Neighbors

An object implemented in such a way that it has to navigate a tree of objects to complete its task is likely to be fragile because it has too many dependencies and crosses several abstraction layers. One evident symptom of this problem is the considerable complexity needed in the arrange phase, which often comports a dramatic degradation of readability. It is usually identifiable by the need to set up a network of nested **Mock/Stub Objects**.

In such a context, there is a high probability we can improve the design of the code base by looking for code smells like Feature Envy, Inappropriate Intimacy, and Message Chain and act accordingly. Usually, the leaked abstraction is caused by the violation of the **Law of Demeter**. (The Law of Demeter is the same concept as the Message Chain code smell.)

Unit tests work best when they focus on testing *only one behavior at a time*, *one Subject Under Test at a time*, and setting expectations *only on objects that are the nearest neighbors*.

The solution starts by assessing the behavior under test. Once that is identified, if we still have the problem, it might be time to act on the collaborators' design of the **Subject Under Test**. It might be solved by:

Introducing a public method on the neighbor, encapsulating the call to its own dependencies

Or

Creating a new class to hide the complexity between the object and its neighbors

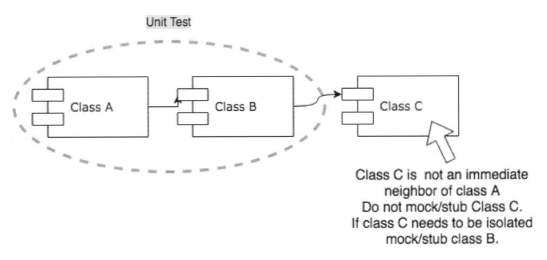

Figure 8.6: Only use Test Doubles for your immediate neighbors

Too Many Test Doubles

A similar problem arises when a test has to pass too many **Mock/Stub Objects** to the **Subject Under Test**, even if they are all immediate neighbors. Even if it doesn't break the *Law of Demeter*, this situation is, more often than not, the manifestation of Long Parameter List, Large Class, or Long Method code smells. Again, the test is likely to have a long *arrange* phase with consequent bad readability. And again, the solution might be to act on misaligned responsibilities, to introduce an intermediate class, or to break the object up into smaller entities, depending on which code smell has been identified.

CQS Principle Trade-OffS

Another flavor of this problem arises when we have a complicated procedure to set up and assert on **Objects** that are, at the same time, both **Stubs** and **Mocks**. Sometimes it's fine to not follow the **CQS Principle** in particular contexts; however, having such an **Object** in your test is a clear indication that you should consider acting on your design and split responsibilities.

Generally, there are two kinds of possible violations of the CQS principle:

- Returning a result for a command (*weak violation*)
- Changing state for a query (*strong violation*)

We understand that, in particular environments, it is not always possible to handle the unsuccessful commands that are throwing exceptions (think of highly transactional environments at large scale or very exceptional situations). In this scenario, returning a self-contained data structure holding the minimum significant information about the result is an acceptable trade-off. (Think about the HTTP protocol request/response returning HTTP status codes.)

What should be avoided, instead, is what we call *strong violation* occurrences, when a query has the side effect of changing any state of the system. This is a clear violation of the **Principle of Least Astonishment**.

See the section on *PoLA* in *Section 3* of *DESIGN VI – SOLID PRINCIPLES++*.

Katas

Character Copier by Urs Enzler

We found these katas on Urs Enzler's website: https://www.planetgeek.ch.

The character copier is a simple class that reads characters from a source and copies them to a destination one character at a time.

When the `Copy` method is called on the copier, then it should read characters from the source and copy them to the destination until the source returns a newline (**\n**).

The exercise is to implement the character copier using Test Doubles for the source and the destination (try using Spies – manually written Mocks – and Mocks written with a mocking framework). Start from these definitions:

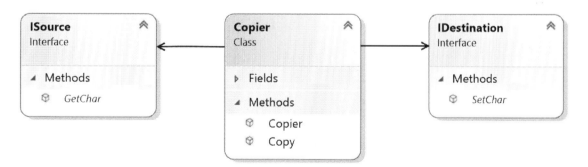

Figure 8.7: Character copier

```
public class Copier
{
  public Copier(ISource source, IDestination destination) {...}
  public void Copy() {}
}


public interface ISource
{
  char GetChar();
}


public interface IDestination
{
  void SetChar(char character);
}
```

Instrument Processor by Urs Enzler

In the **Instrument Processor** kata, we are going to implement a class that gets tasks from a **TaskDispatcher** and executes them on an **Instrument**.

The **InstrumentProcessor** must implement the following interface:

```
public interface IInstrumentProcessor
{
  void Process();
}
```

The task dispatcher must have the following interface:

```
public interface ITaskDispatcher
{
  string GetTask();
  void FinishedTask(string task);
}
```

The **GetTask** method returns the next task to execute on the instrument.

After the task has been successfully executed on the instrument, the **FinishedTask** method must be called by the **InstrumentProcessor**, passing the task that was completed as the method argument.

The **InstrumentProcessor** has the following interface:

```
public interface IInstrument
{
    void Execute(string task);
    event EventHandler Finished;
    event EventHandler Error;
}
```

The **Execute** method starts the instrument, which will begin to execute the task passed to it. The method will return immediately (we assume that the instrument implementation is asynchronous).

The **Execute** method will throw **ArgumentNullException** if the task passed in is null.

When the instrument finishes executing, then the **Finished** event is fired.

When the instrument detects an error situation during execution (note that the **Execute** method will already have returned the control flow to the caller due to its asynchronous implementation), it fires the **Error** event.

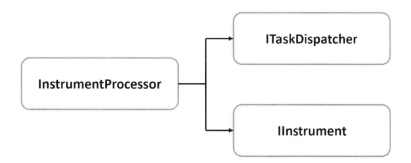

Figure 8.8: Instrument processor

The exercise is to implement the `InstrumentProcessor` in a way that:

- When the method `Process` is called, the `InstrumentProcessor` gets the next task from the task dispatcher and executes it on the instrument

- When the `Execute` method of the instrument throws an exception, that exception is passed on to the caller of the `Process` method

- When the instrument fires the finished event, the `InstrumentProcessor` calls the task dispatcher's `FinishedTask` method with the correct task

- When the instrument fires the Error event, then the `InstrumentProcessor` writes the `Error occurred` string to the console

Great Habits

In this lesson, we introduced new habits. Check it out in the following list.

Considerations When Writing a New Test

- Tests should test one thing only

- Create more specific tests to drive a more generic solution (triangulate)

- Give your tests meaningful names (behavior/goal-oriented) that reflect your business domain

- See tests fail for the right reason

- Ensure you have meaningful feedback from failing tests

- Keep your tests and production code separate

- Organize your unit tests to reflect your production code (similar project structure)

- Organize your tests in arrange, act, and assert blocks

- Write the assertion first and work backward

- Write fast, isolated, repeatable, and self-validating tests

- Consider using Test Doubles to isolate side effects on your tests (**New habit**)

Considerations When Making a Failing Test Pass

- Write the simplest code to pass the test
- Write any code that makes you get to the refactor phase more quickly
- Use the transformation priority premise
- Consider using object calisthenics to drive design decisions

Considerations after the Test Passes

- Use the Rule of Three to tackle duplication
- Refactor design constantly
- Apply object calisthenics to improve your design
- Stay in the green while refactoring
- Use the IDE to refactor quickly and safely
- Refactor code readability/understandability first
- Look out for code smells and refactor your code accordingly

When Should I Move on to the Next Lesson?

- When you understand the different *Test Doubles* (**Stub**, **Mock**, **Fake**, and **Spy**)
- When you understand the difference between a query and a command method
- When you can use Mocks and Stubs to test your production code
- When you can write your own **Fakes** and **Spies**

Resources

Web

- The Little Mocker, Robert C. Martin: http://blog.cleancoder.com/uncle-bob/2014/05/14/TheLittleMocker.html.

- Mocking katas, PlanetGeek.ch: https://www.planetgeek.ch/?s=mocking+kata.

- Mocks aren't Stubs, Martin Fowler: https://martinfowler.com/articles/mocksArentStubs.html.

- Mocks, Fakes, Stubs and Dummies, Gerard Meszaros: http://xunitpatterns.com/Mocks,%20Fakes,%20Stubs%20and%20Dummies.html.

- Mocks for Commands, Stubs for Queries by Mark Seemann: http://blog.ploeh.dk/2013/10/23/mocks-for-commands-stubs-for-queries/.

- Really Simple CQRS, Vaughn Vernon, Kalele blog: https://kalele.io/blog-posts/really-simple-cqrs/.

- Test Double, Gerard Meszaros: http://xunitpatterns.com/Test%20Double.html.

Books

- **Growing Object-Oriented Software, Guided by Tests**, Steve Freeman and Nat Pryce: https://www.goodreads.com/book/show/4268826-growing-object-oriented-software-guided-by-tests.

- **xUnit Test Patterns: Refactoring Test Code**, Gerard Meszaros: https://www.goodreads.com/book/show/337302.xUnit_Test_Patterns.

9
Testing Legacy Code

Code without tests is bad code. It doesn't matter how well written it is; it doesn't matter how pretty or object-oriented or well-encapsulated it is. With tests, we can change the behavior of our code quickly and verifiably. Without them, we really don't know if our code is getting better or worse. To me, legacy code is simply code without tests.

– Michael C. Feathers, Working Effectively with Legacy Code

Once upon a time, a friend who was very skilled in the subjects of this book went to a job interview for a consultancy in a large company. They gave him an exercise about refactoring some legacy code. He created a *seam* and used it to solve the exercise in a way they had never seen before.

At first, they wanted to reject the application. It was only when someone pointed out that this was a legitimate refactoring technique that they changed their mind and started the consultancy work. After six months working there, they appreciated his work so much that they tried to hire him permanently (without success, by the way).

Breaking Dependencies Using a Seam

Sometimes it is not possible to write tests due to excessive **coupling**. If your code is dealing with external dependencies, we can break the dependency to allow the *Subject Under Test* to be exercised independently.

If the dependency is injected through the constructor or setters, replacing the dependency with a test double should be enough. Unfortunately, that's not always the case. Sometimes you have to deal with static dependencies or locally generated ones. In those cases, you will have to segregate the dependency, introducing a *seam* in your code (as specified in *Working Effectively with Legacy Code* by Michael C. Feathers).

In clothing, a seam joins parts together to form a piece of clothing. In code, we can use this concept to find soft points where we can separate coupled parts. If your language supports passing functions as parameters, you can use the *Peel-and-Slice technique* by Llewellyn Falco.

We should be extremely careful when breaking dependencies, especially when we have low test coverage. This is a very delicate operation, so we want to minimize changes that are not covered by tests. Ideally, we want most of the changes on test code and not on production code.

Using Inheritance to Decouple Production Code

```
public class Game

{

  public void Play()

  {

    var diceResult = new Random().Next(1, 6);

    ...

  }

}
```

In this case, the `Game` class is coupled with the random number generator library. We need to control the dice rolling in order to test the `Game` class.

1. Add a **protected virtual** method to the `Game` class to encapsulate the behavior that has the coupling issue. We use a protected method to avoid extending the public interface of the `Game` class:

    ```
    public class Game
    {
      public void Play()
      {
    ```

```
        var diceResult = roll();
        ...
    }

    protected virtual int Roll()
    {
      return new Random().Next(1, 6);
    }
  }
```

2. In your *test code*, inherit from the **Game** class and change the behavior of the **protected** virtual method **Roll** to something you have control over:

```
public class TestableGame : Game
{
  private int roll;

  public TestableGame(int desiredRoll)
  {
    roll = desiredRoll;
  }

  protected override int Roll()
  {
    return roll;
  }
}
```

3. Write a test using the **TestableGame** class:

```
public class GameShould
{
  [Test]
  public void Do_Something_When_A_Six_Is_Rolled()
  {
    var game = new TestableGame(6);

    game.Play();

    //ASSERT
  }
}
```

This technique can also be applied when production code is calling static methods. The advantage of using this method is that it minimizes changes to production code and can be done using automated refactoring, thus minimizing the risk of introducing breaking changes to production code. Once you have good test coverage, you can refactor the Game class and remove the need for the seam by injecting the dependency in the Game class, for example.

Characterization Tests

Michael C. Feathers, who coined the term *characterization test*, defines it as a test that describes (characterizes) the actual behavior of a piece of code. These tests protect the existing behavior of legacy code against unintended changes via automated testing.

In other words, they don't check what the code is supposed to do like specification tests do, but what the code actually and currently does. Having a set of characterization tests helps developers working with legacy code because they can run these tests after modifying their code, ensuring that their modification did not cause any unintended or unwanted changes in functionality somewhere else.

1. Use a piece of code in a test harness.

2. Write an assertion that you know will fail.

3. Run the test and let the failure tell you what the actual behavior is.

4. Change the test so that it expects the behavior that the code actually produces.

5. Repeat until you are reasonably sure all the *degrees of freedom* are identified and tested.

6. Name the test according to the business behavior you are characterizing.

Kata

Characterization Tests on Gilded Rose Kata by Emily Bache

Add characterization tests to the GildedRose class. Try to name tests from a business perspective, in a way that describes what the code is doing. As with our first approach to testing, remember the degrees of freedom; before moving to the next exercises, stay in a behavior until you have characterized it fully.

You can find the repository for your language of choice on Emily's public repository here: https://github.com/emilybache/GildedRose-Refactoring-Kata.

Golden Master

The **Golden Master** technique is very useful when a clear input and output is easy to obtain on the system level. There are some cases where the Golden Master technique can be applied only with difficulty or where it cannot be applied at all. For all the given situations, we need to consider whether the system tests generated with the Golden Master are enough, or whether we need to add other types of tests such as unit tests, component tests, integration tests, and so on.

In the following subsections, we provide guidelines to create a Golden Master for a system.

Feasibility

1. Does the system have clear inputs and outputs? Examples may include the console, filesystem, network, and so on.

2. Does the system generate the same output for the same input? If not, can we use a test double to make it so? Isolate the side effects.

3. Can we capture the effect of the system on our tests without changing the behavior of the system? The options are to either redirect the output to a file or replace the data layer with an in-memory data layer.

4. Can we inject the input of the system on our tests without changing the behavior of the system? Same options as point 3.

Generate Input/Output (Golden Master)

1. Gradually create a fake input for the system and persist it on a file. **Hint**: look out for patterns in input and output.

2. Create a test that loads the fake input, injects it into the system, and captures and persists the output.

3. Measure the test coverage. Repeat until coverage is close to or at 100%.

Assert

1. Expand the previous test to assert that given the input (Golden Master input), we get the expected output (Golden Master) saved from the previous step.

2. Commit. Don't forget to include the Golden Master input and output files.

3. Experiment with small mutations on the production code to check that the test fails. Revert when done. If you're not pleased with the results, go back to the previous section and generate better input/output combinations, or write new tests with new input/output combinations.

If we follow the steps in the previous sections, we should now have a Golden Master test for our system. If we make any changes in the production code that break the behavior of the system, our Golden Master test(s) should fail.

Kata

Golden Master on Gilded Rose Kata by Emily Bache

Create a Golden Master for the Gilded Rose kata. You can find the repository here: https://github.com/emilybache/GildedRose-Refactoring-Kata.

> **Hints:**
>
> Read input from a file.
>
> Redirect output to a file. In this case, the output of the system is the console. To capture the system output, we can redirect the console to an in-memory stream and then save the stream to a file.

C#

```
var streamwriter = new StreamWriter(new FileStream("/location/out.txt",
FileMode.Create));

streamwriter.AutoFlush = true;

Console.SetOut(streamwriter);
```

Java

```
System.setOut(new PrintStream(new BufferedOutputStream(new
FileOutputStream("/location/out.txt")), true));
```

Python

```python
import sys

sys.stdout = open('/location/out.txt', 'w')
```

Ruby

```ruby
$stdout = File.new('/location/out.txt', 'w')

$stdout.sync = true
```

Approval Tests by Llewellyn Falco

Approval Tests is a testing framework conceived by Llewellyn Falco based on the idea of a Golden Master. It has a fluent API that allows for the definition of scenarios and verification of outputs. Typically, it will serialize the output of an execution that the human will mark as accepted. If anything in the code changes the output, the test will fail.

Llewellyn Falco: http://approvaltests.com/.

A less-known usage for **Approval Tests** is the *locking of code* for refactoring. By locking of code, we mean the activity of adding tests around a piece of code to make refactoring possible. Using a code coverage tool in conjunction with this technique provides feedback on how much code has actually been exercised by our new tests. When we reach a satisfactory level of coverage, we can then move to the refactoring phase. Once our code is in better shape and the components are extracted and isolated, they should be easier to understand. We can then add tests for each one of them so we can remove the locking tests.

Combination Tests

Combination Tests is a feature of *Approval Tests* that allows for parameters to be passed to the **System Under Test** in a combinatorial fashion. Given a known set of inputs, they will be combined in all possible ways to exercise as many execution paths as possible.

Beware of a combinatorial explosion! *With great power comes great responsibility*, so be careful when adding more values to your input sets. The resulting collection of parameters could increase so quickly that your test execution won't proceed, and the captured Golden Master will occupy a lot of space on your disk.

Revisiting the Refactoring Guidelines

Stay in the Green while Refactoring

In *Lesson 6, Refactoring*, we said, "Don't change production code that is not covered by tests. If we need to refactor some code that has no tests, then start by adding behavior tests." Now that we know how to test legacy code, we can expand our guidelines to include:

- Approval-based tests
- Characterization tests
- Golden Master tests
- Model-based tests
- Property-based tests

Kata

Gilded Rose Refactoring Kata by Emily Bache

If you have performed the previous exercises, there should now be a complete set of tests proving the behavior of the code for any degree of freedom.

Trusting your tests and staying in the green, you can finally go ahead and refactor the *Gilded Rose kata* by *Emily Bache*.

Conclusions

It takes time to become proficient in writing tests for legacy code and we understand that sometimes it is a daunting task. In this lesson, we distilled what in our opinion are the most important concepts on legacy code testing. Spending some time practicing the techniques we have outlined is an extremely useful exercise and we hope that it might give you some ideas helping to make that work a bit less daunting.

Guideline Questions

Is it important to understand the legacy code in detail?

If the answer is yes, **characterization tests** are probably the best solution. This is a slow process but gives us the best insight on how legacy code works.

Can we get by with a superficial understanding of the legacy code?

If the answer is yes and the system under test has clear inputs and outputs, we can probably use the **Golden Master technique** or **Approval Tests**.

We added a few web resources and books that go much deeper into this subject.

Great Habits

In this lesson, we introduced a new habit. Check it out on the following list.

Considerations when Writing a New Test

- Tests should test one thing only.

- Create more specific tests to drive a more generic solution (triangulate).

- Give your tests meaningful names (behavior-oriented/goal-oriented names) that reflect your business domain.

- See that the test fails for the right reason.

- Ensure you have meaningful feedback from failing tests.

- Keep your tests and production code separate.

- Organize your unit tests to reflect your production code (similar project structure).

- Organize your test in arrange, act, and assert blocks.

    - Arrange (also known as **Given**) all necessary preconditions.

    - Act (also known as **When**) on the subject under test.

    - Assert (also known as **Then**) that the expected results have occurred.

- Write the assertion first and work backward.

    - Write your test by first writing the assertion; don't even worry about naming the test properly.

    - Write the act section of your test.

    - Write the arrange block if required.

    - Finally, name the test.

- Write fast, isolated, repeatable, and self-validating tests.

- Consider using object calisthenics to drive design decisions.

- Consider adding tests to legacy code (**new habit**).

    - Approval tests, characterization tests, Golden Master tests.

Considerations when Making a Failing Test Pass

- Write the simplest code to pass the test.
- Write any code that makes you get to the refactor phase quicker.
- Use the transformation priority premise.
- Consider using object calisthenics to drive design decisions.

Considerations after the Test Passes

- Use the *Rule of Three* to tackle duplication.
- Refactor design constantly.
- Apply object calisthenics to improve your design.
- Stay on the green while refactoring.
- Use the IDE to refactor quickly and safely.
- Refactor code for readability/understandability first.
- Look out for code smells and refactor your code accordingly.

When Should I Move to the Next Lesson?

- When you are able to break dependencies to allow testing.
- When you are able to add tests to previously untested code.
- When you are able to refactor production legacy code.
- When you cannot tolerate bad names anymore.

Resources

Web

- Approval Tests by Llewellyn Falco: http://approvaltests.com/.

- Emily Bache's public GitHub repositories: https://github.com/emilybache.

- Peel and Slice technique, Llewellyn Falco: https://www.youtube.com/playlist?list=PLb4ON7iRsxZNNqZuA2dlQOW3MOQwQ6AjM.

- Using ApprovalTests in .NET by Llewellyn Falco: https://www.youtube.com/playlist?list=PL0C32F89E8BBB5368.

Books

Working Effectively with Legacy Code by Michael C. Feathers: https://www.goodreads.com/book/show/44919.Working_Effectively_with_Legacy_Code.

10

Design IV – Design Patterns

The basic laws of the universe are simple, but because our senses are limited, we can't grasp them. There is a pattern in creation.

– Albert Einstein

The first time I heard about Design Patterns I was still in Italy, in one of my first jobs. A colleague was talking about a previous interview, "When they started asking me about design patterns, I knew I was doomed! Ciaone!"

After the general laugh (my colleague, Matteo is a great developer and an amazing storyteller!), I had this exotic term blinking in my mind: *Design Patterns*. I didn't even know what these patterns were. I would have been doomed as well in such an interview. I had to know more.

I Googled it quickly and read a few random pages here and there, and I realized this wasn't a subject you can pick up easily. And when memorization is not among one's best qualities, it may appear to be a daunting task. A few months later, I found *Head First Design Patterns* on the shelves in the office of my next job.

This was the book that allowed me to finally connect the dots. *Common solutions to common problems*. Abstractions. I couldn't grasp it in the beginning because I was approaching it from the implementation side (typical bias of the young developer). Now, when I think of design patterns, I don't even remember the solution—I only remember the problems they are meant to solve. For anything else, we have Google (or DuckDuckGo).

The subject of Design Patterns is controversial. We debated whether or not to include it in this journey. We included it because we recognize the immense validity of the solutions that they lead to when applied correctly, and the value they bring in certain technical discussions about how to solve a coding task.

> **Note**
>
> Not everybody knows that at OOPSLA 1999, the Gang of Four were (with their full cooperation) subjected to a mock trial (the Chief Prosecutor was apparently Kent Beck). At the end, they were charged with numerous crimes against computer science, including misleading the world on what patterns were all about, and deluding others into thinking they could write code like the experts just because they could mention a few of them.

The problem is that, in our experience, we have seen many examples of software overengineering driven by applying Design Patterns extensively *by the book*. We usually call this *Design Pattern Golden Hammer* or *Design Patterns Obsession*.

The subject of Design Pattern subject fits perfectly into the *Rules, Principles, and Values* considerations. Memorizing them is like learning the rules: they give you a shortcut for solving particular problems. But the real value is in mastering the principles they are based on. You can blend them into particular scenarios, enhancing the expressivity and reusability of the final code. Ultimately, when you follow correct design principles and solve your problem in your very own way, your design might include pieces of patterns naturally, without even having to look them up.

Design Pattern Advantages

- They give you a range of scenarios of recurring problems that have been already solved in which to look for inspiration.

- They give you a vocabulary for talking about possible implementations of a solution, so that there is no need to go into detail.

- They give you a quick reference for a possible implementation of a solution if the problem fits.

- The implementations used are based on fundamental software design principles that have been widely accepted.

Design Pattern Pitfalls

- They almost never apply out of the box, but need to be shaped and customized to match a particular scenario.

- They fail miserably when it comes to expressing business concepts and domain vocabulary, focusing on implementation details instead of behavior.

> **Caution**
>
> Avoid leaking the name of the pattern in your code if possible. Naming should always focus on behavior related to the business functionality you are implementing. Showing off that you have implemented a *visitor pattern* with an *abstract factory* and a *command* doesn't express the functional goal of your code. And it doesn't make you look smarter, either.

A Quick Reference Catalogue

Creational Design Patterns

Creational patterns are all about creating instances of objects, since the basic process of object creation could result in design problems or added complexity:

Problem	Solution	Design Pattern
Are we instantiating families (or sets) of objects?	Provide an interface for instantiating families of related or dependent objects without having to specify their concrete classes.	Abstract Factory
Do derived classes need to create instances following some logic?	Define the interface for object creation, but delegate the decisions about instantiation to subclasses.	Factory Method
Do we need to follow several steps to instantiate our objects?	Separate construction of an object from its representation so that the same construction process can create different representations.	Builder

Figure 10.1: The creational design patterns

Behavioral Design Patterns

Behavioral patterns are those patterns that are concerned with communication between objects. They identify common communication patterns between objects, increasing behavior flexibility:

Problem	Solution	Design Pattern
Do we apply some rules or algorithms that are replaceable or can change?	Define families of algorithms, encapsulate each one behind an interface, and make them interchangeable.	Strategy
Do we have an algorithm that needs to change certain behavior in subclasses?	Define the abstract steps of a superclass, deferring some steps to subclasses.	Template Method
Do we need call back functionality or to keep track of history? Do requests need to be handled at different times or in different orders? Should we decouple the invoker from the object handling the invocation?	Encapsulate the method call in a first class object. This allows the request to be handled with traditional constructs such as lists, queues, and call backs.	Command

Figure 10.2: The behavioral design patterns (part 1)

Problem	Solution	Design Pattern
Do several different entities need to know about events that have occurred?	Define a one-to-many dependency between objects so that when one object changes state, all its dependents are notified. Create an event-based communication initiated by the dependent object going opposite the dependency flow.	Observer
Do we have a system with lots of states where the logic for the different states is complicated?	Allow an object to alter its behavior when its internal state changes. The object will appear as if it changes its class.	State

Figure 10.3: The behavioral design patterns (part 2)

Problem	Solution	Design Pattern
Do we have different objects that might do the job, but we don't want the client object knowing which is actually going to do it?	Avoid coupling the sender of a request to its receiver by giving more than one object a chance to handle the request. Chain the receiving objects and pass the request along the chain until an object handles it.	**Chain of Responsibility**
Do we have new tasks to be applied to our existing classes?	Represent an operation to be performed on the elements of a structure.	**Visitor**
Do we want to separate a collection from the client that uses it so we don't have to worry about the collection's implementation details?	Provide a way to access the elements of the collection sequentially without exposing its underlying representation.	**Iterator**
Do we have a lot of Coupling in a many-to-many relationship of object interactions?	Define an object that encapsulates how a set of objects interact, promoting loose Coupling by keeping objects from referring to each other explicitly, letting their interaction vary independently.	**Mediator**
Do we have an internal state of an object that must be saved and restored at a later time and cannot be exposed by interfaces without exposing implementation? Must encapsulation boundaries be preserved?	Without violating encapsulation, capture and externalize an object's internal state.	**Memento**

Figure 10.4: The behavioral design patterns (part 2)

Structural Design Patterns

These patterns are about class and object composition. Their purpose is to simplify the design by identifying a clean way to realize relationships between entities:

Problem	Solution	Design Pattern
Do we need to add some optional new functionality to something that already exists?	Provide an abstraction or placeholder for another object to control access to it.	Proxy
Do we have the right logic exposed with the wrong interface?	Convert the interface of a class into another, correct interface.	Adapter
Do we have multiple additional functions to apply, but order and cardinality is variable?	Add dynamic additional responsibilities to an object.	Decorator
Do we want to simplify, beautify and clean existing systems or subsystems?	Provide a unified interface to a set of interfaces in a system.	Facade
Do we have several different objects that need be logically aggregated in a whole?	Compose objects into tree structures to represent part-whole hierarchies.	Composite

Figure 10.5: Structural design patterns

Revisiting the Refactoring Guidelines

Refactoring Design

In *Lesson 6*, *Refactoring*, we mentioned simple design refactors. We can now expand these with design patterns. Once we know how to use patterns correctly, we will be able to refactor code toward them when it makes sense to do so:

- Extract private methods from deep conditionals.
- Extract smaller private methods from long methods, and encapsulate cryptic code in private methods.
- Return from methods as soon as possible.

- Encapsulate where we find missing encapsulation.

- Remove duplication.

- Refactor to patterns (**New**).

Kata

Refactoring Game of Life Kata to Patterns

In the lesson, **Object Calisthenics**, we introduced **Game of Life** as an exercise to practice the rules. If you have done this exercise, you should have it saved somewhere and that will be the starting point for this exercise. If you have not done it, we suggest you give it a go. Once you have done your implementation, you will be ready to carry on.

This exercise consists of refactoring your current Game of Life and solving it with different design patterns. Interesting implementations in this scenario could be:

- Command patterns

- State patterns

- Strategy patterns

Chose one pattern and refactor to it using the refactoring suggestions of previous lessons. Once done, choose another pattern and refactor to it. Rinse and repeat.

> **Caution**
>
> This exercise is meant to help internalize the implementation of a few patterns and prove that there are many ways to use patterns to solve a problem. Realistically, you should derive the pattern choice by the functional context and by how your code is meant to interact with other parts of the system.

Great Habits

In this lesson, we introduced a new habit. Check it out in the following lists.

Considerations When Writing a New Test

- Tests should test one thing only.

- Create more specific tests to drive a more generic solution (triangulate).

- Give your tests meaningful names (behavior/goal-oriented) that reflect your business domain.

- See that the test fails for the right reason.

- Ensure you have meaningful feedback from failing tests.

- Keep your tests and production code separate.

- Organize your unit tests to reflect your production code (similar to the project structure).

- Organize your test into arrange, act, and assert blocks.

- Write the assertion first and work backward.

- Write fast, isolated, repeatable, and self-validating tests.

- Consider using object calisthenics to drive design decisions.

- Consider adding tests to legacy code.

Considerations When Making a Failing Test Pass

- Write the simplest code to pass the test.

- Write any code that makes you get to the refactor phase quicker.

- Use the transformation priority premise.

Considerations After the Test Passes

- Use the *Rule of Three* to tackle duplication.

- Refactor the design constantly.

- Apply object calisthenics to improve your design.

- Stay on the green while refactoring.

- Use the IDE to refactor quickly and safely.

- Refactor code for readability/understandability first.
- Look out for code smells and refactor your code accordingly.
- Refactor to patterns when the context is appropriate (**New habit**).

When Should I Move to the Next Lesson?

- Can you refactor to some of the patterns without using the pattern name in your code?
- Can you resist the urge to apply design patterns everywhere?

When you answer yes to all of the previous questions, you are ready to move on.

Resources

Web

Here are some web resources that you can refer to for more information:

- Design Patterns, Refactoring Guru: https://refactoring.guru/design-patterns.
- Design Patterns, SourceMaking.com: https://sourcemaking.com/design_patterns.

Books

Here are some book resources that you can refer to for more information:

- Design Patterns: Elements of Reusable Object-Oriented Software, Erich Gamma, et al.: https://www.goodreads.com/book/show/85009.Design_Patterns?from_search=true.
- Head First Design Patterns: A Brain Friendly Guide, Eric Freeman, et al.: https://www.goodreads.com/book/show/85009.Design_Patterns?from_search=true.
- Patterns of Enterprise Application Architecture, Martin Fowler, et al.: https://www.goodreads.com/book/show/70156.Patterns_of_Enterprise_Application_Architecture.
- Refactoring to Patterns, Joshua Kerievsky: https://www.goodreads.com/book/show/85041.Refactoring_to_Patterns?from_search=true.

Running

11

Design V – Cohesion and Coupling

Coupling between A and B is defined as:

'if I change element A I also have to change element B [...]

Cohesion of an element A is defined as:

'if I change sub-element A.1, do I have to change all the other sub-elements A.2–n?'

So, cohesion is coupling within an element.

–Kent Beck

Coupling

Coupling measures the degree of interdependence between software components. In object-oriented design, we want coupling to be as low as possible, but not lower, or we end up with software that does very little. This allows us to make changes in a component without impacting other components.

Coupling is an indication of the independence among the components. Some indicators of possible high coupling are the following code smells:

- Divergent Change
- Feature Envy
- Inappropriate Intimacy
- Message Chains
- Middleman
- Shotgun Surgery

When we talk about *components* in object-oriented design, we are referring to libraries, programs, packages/namespaces/modules, classes, methods, and so on.

The types of coupling categorize how we connect components and how much one component knows about other component(s).

Types of Coupling

There are two main categories of coupling that create interdependence for very different reasons:

- **Interaction Coupling**: When the dependency is based on a component calling the methods of another
- **Inheritance Coupling**: When the dependency is based on a component inheriting from another

Interaction Coupling

This is by far the most common type of coupling. Based on the nature of the method call, its locality, and the parameters exchanged, we can further identify several different types of **interaction coupling**:

- Message coupling
- Data coupling
- Stamp coupling
- Control coupling

- External coupling
- Common coupling
- Content coupling

Message Coupling

Components communicate by using messages. This is the best coupling type, as different components only share a message.

Data Coupling

Components share data through parameters; it's a very common practice to call a method on another component. Compared with message passing, a component needs to know a bit more detail about the other component in order to perform a method call. We can refactor to message passing to lower the coupling.

Stamp Coupling

Components share a common data structure. We should avoid passing data structures amongst components. Remember the first class collections rule in *Object Calisthenics*? It helps to reduce this type of coupling to **data coupling**.

Control Coupling

One component is responsible for controlling the flow of another component. Refactoring to design patterns such as state or strategy can help fix this type of coupling.

External Coupling

Components share an external data format or protocol. Abstracting the knowledge of external data allows us to remove this type of coupling.

Common Coupling

Components share global data; any change in this global data format has a ripple effect, breaking multiple components (Shotgun Surgery code smell). We can abstract common data to minimize this coupling or remove global data and move to *Data Coupling* or message passing.

Content Coupling

Components depend on other components' internal elements' data. This is the worst form of coupling since one component can mutate another component's data. This makes the system very brittle and very difficult to change. Using encapsulation and abstractions is an effective strategy to minimize this type of coupling.

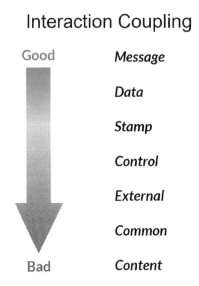

Figure 11.1: Relative ranking of interaction coupling types

Law of Demeter

The *Law of Demeter* helps avoid coupling components. It's a very simple but effective law. It says that *Method M* on *Object O* can only invoke methods of the following objects:

1. On O itself

2. On objects contained in attributes of itself (O) or a superclass (of O)

3. On an object that is passed as a parameter to method M

4. On an object that is created by the method M

5. On an object that is stored in a global variable (outdated)

Communication is the main reason for coupling. The Law of Demeter can be seen as the law of the neighborhood: "talk only to components close to you." The goal of this is to keep the communication of an object limited in scope, avoiding the exposure of internal complexity and collaborators. This encourages correct encapsulation because to achieve it, classes must hold and use logic cohesive with the data they own, hiding it behind a public method.

Method Coupling Premises

Another important aspect of *interaction coupling* is the number and kind of parameters passed into the methods, which we can think of as the impact of that method on the overall coupling. Something to always keep in mind is that there is an optimal way to design our methods for minimal impact. To help in these choices, we identified high-level *Method Coupling Premises*.

Method Coupling Premises

	Method's parameters	Relative coupling impact
-		
Less	– `void Method()`	➤ 0
	– `void Method(int x)`	➤ 1
COUPLING	– `int Method()`	➤ 1
	– `void Method(ClassA a)`	➤ 1 + FanIN
	– `ClassA Method()`	➤ 1 + FanOUT
	– `void Method(int x, int y)`	➤ 2
More	– `int Method(int x)`	➤ 2
+	– `void Method(ClassA a, ClassB b)`	➤ 2 + 2FanIN
	– `ClassA Method(ClassB b)`	➤ 2 + FanIN + FanOUT
	`etc...`	

Figure 11.2: Method coupling premises with relative impact

It is important to notice the relevance of the Law of Demeter for the *FanIN* and *FanOUT* impact on coupling for message passing. While they potentially could add a big coupling component to the system, respecting the Law of Demeter has the effect of limiting that impact, keeping it low, hence making *message coupling* very effective.

Inheritance Coupling

Inheritance coupling is the strongest type of coupling and happens every time a class inherits from another one. When that happens, the subclass binds itself completely to the superclass. If the superclass definition is modified, all the subclasses are affected.

Have you ever felt lost when trying to understand a very long hierarchy chain of inheritance? A high degree of inheritance coupling may not be a good idea.

Ideally, we should be careful and *use inheritance only for generalization/specialization semantics* (A-Kind-Of relationship). As we will see, this is exactly the goal of the *Liskow Substitution Principle* in the next lesson.

For any other case, we should really *use composition over inheritance.*

Cohesion

Cohesion (noun): When the members of a group or society are united.

Cohesive (adjective): United and working together effectively.

> **Note**
>
> Cambridge Dictionary: https://dictionary.cambridge.org/us/dictionary/english/cohesion#dataset-cald4.

Cohesion is a measure of how strongly related and focused the various responsibilities of a software module are, and it "refers to the degree to which the elements of a module belong together."

> **Note**
>
> Wikipedia: https://en.wikipedia.org/wiki/Cohesion(computerscience).

Cohesion is everywhere, not just in code. For example, companies try to create highly cohesive teams, with cross-functional roles (developers, business analysts, designers, and so forth) that work closely together to achieve a specific goal, such as a software product update.

A component should implement a single behavior or responsibility, and all the parts of the component should contribute to the implementation of it. Components should only be created if all parts they group are collaborating together to implement a behavior or responsibility. Cohesion indicates a component's functional strength and how much it focuses on a single point.

Low cohesion results in behavior being scattered instead of existing in a single component. Some indicators of possible low cohesion are the following code smells:

- Data class
- Lazy class
- Middleman
- Primitive obsession
- Shotgun Surgery

Other Indicators of Possible Low Cohesion in Design

- `Static` methods in a class

- `Helper` classes

- Criteria for grouping things (for example, in *folders* with names such as `helper`, `core`, and `utilities`)

- Namespaces, packages, and modules that are the equivalent of a junk drawer

We are not saying that we should never have `static` methods, but we should be aware that they are low-cohesion features. The same applies to `helper` classes or modules. Design is about choice, but that choice should be a deliberate one, and we should be aware of the consequences of our choices. Have a look at `Java.util`: https://docs.oracle.com/javase/8/docs/api/java/util/package-summary.html. What is the cohesion of this package?

Cohesion should be as high as possible, but not higher. We should strive for highly cohesive components; however, overdoing cohesion has bad consequences. A great example is a **God** class that concentrates all the behavior. Some potential indicators of too much cohesion are the following code smells:

- Data clumps

- Divergent change

- Duplication

- Large class

- Long method

- Long parameter list

Types of Cohesion

The types of cohesion categorize how we group elements into classes and components. There are different reasons why we group elements in software design; some are better, some are worse. The worst cases of cohesion are like leaving windows broken on a building—they invite others to break the remaining windows because no one seems to care.

Also, for cohesion, there are two main, distinct categories:

- **Class cohesion**: As the holistic cohesion at class level deducted from fields, methods, and their interactions

- **Method cohesion**: As the cohesion of the individual methods, focusing on how single-minded they are

Class Cohesion

- **Ideal**: A class has an ideal cohesion when it doesn't show any other types of *mixed cohesion.*

- **Mixed-role**: The class has one or more fields that relate objects of the class to other objects on the same abstraction layer, but the fields have nothing to do with the underlying semantics of the class.

- **Mixed-domain**: The class has one or more fields that relate objects of the class to other objects on a different abstraction layer. Hence, the fields are completely unrelated with the underlying semantics of the class.

- **Mixed-instance**: The class represents two different types of objects and should be split in two separate modules. Typically, different instances use only subsets of fields and methods of the class.

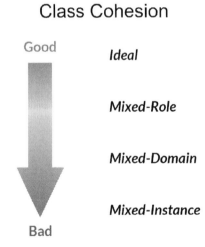

Figure 11.3: Relative ranking of class cohesion types

Method Cohesion

Cohesion is not only a matter of data and interaction with data, but should also take into consideration the semantics of methods in connection with the behavior they are expected to exhibit. Let's look at the different kinds, starting with the best one and moving to the worse ones.

- **Functional Cohesion**: Functional cohesion is the ideal scenario, when a method performs a particular function interacting with elements belonging to the component because they are all needed to perform that same function and responsibility, and/or share the same concern.

- **Sequential Cohesion**: In sequential cohesion, elements are grouped in the same method because it combines two functions where the output of an element is used as the input of another. The fact that one element uses as input the output of another component is not by itself a reason to group them together.

  An example would be the grouping of a JSON deserializer and some service that uses the result of the deserializer.

- **Communicational/Informational Cohesion**: This is when a method combines two functions just because they access the same data fields to execute.

  A component groups elements because they use the same input type or generate the same output type. This is a weak reason to group elements in the same component as they may perform very different functions in the system.

  An example would be the grouping of a JSON serializer used by a web controller and a JSON serializer used by a repository.

- **Procedural Cohesion**: This is when a method supports multiple, weakly related functions. Elements belong in a component because they execute in a certain sequence. Functionality-wise, these elements probably belong in other components.

  For example, there may be an element that formats the output and an element that prints to the console can be executed in a sequence, but this does not mean they are cohesive with each other. They shouldn't belong to the same component just because they need to be executed sequentially inside the same method.

- **Temporal Cohesion**: This is when a method performs multiple functions related only by the moment in time they execute. A component is created just for exposing a method to execute all elements in the same timespan.

  Examples would be initialization and finalization.

- **Logical Cohesion**: This is when a method supports multiple functions, but the choice of the specific execution is determined by a control parameter passed in as input. Often, elements are bundled into a component because they perform the same logic operation, but the functions they perform in the system are significantly different.

  An example would be creating an IO operations component that bundles disk IO, network IO, and so on. All perform IO, but functionality-wise may belong in other places.

- **Coincidental Cohesion**: This is when there is no clearly defined purpose for the method, or it performs multiple unrelated functions.

  Unrelated elements will be bundled into a component for no specific reason. Readability and understandability are difficult, and reusability is very low. This is the worst case of cohesion.

  Examples would be `util`, `core`, and `helper` (whether they be modules, packages, namespaces, or folders).

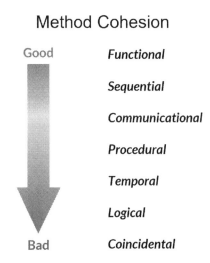

Figure 11.4: Method cohesion relative ranking

Katas

Connecting Code Smells with Cohesion/Coupling

In the following table, we have grouped code smells in relation to coupling or cohesion excesses. Because cohesion and coupling are more abstract concepts, we can make use of code smells to help us detect imbalances.

For each row in the **Degree** column and in the **Cohesion/Coupling** column, *highlight* the correct concept and then add a reason in the reason column. After the table, we have listed several sample reasons to use. In some cases, both coupling and cohesion apply.

Code smells	Degree	Cohesion/Coupling	Reason
Alternative classes with different interfaces	Too high / Too low	Cohesion/Coupling	
Comments	Too high / Too low	Cohesion/Coupling	
Data Class	Too high / Too low	Cohesion/Coupling	
Data Clumps	Too high / Too low	Cohesion/Coupling	
Dead Code	Too high / Too low	Cohesion/Coupling	
Divergent Change	Too high / Too low	Cohesion/Coupling	
Duplicated Code	Too high / Too low	Cohesion/Coupling	
Feature Envy	Too high / Too low	Cohesion/Coupling	
Inappropriate Intimacy	Too high / Too low	Cohesion/Coupling	
Large Class	Too high / Too low	Cohesion/Coupling	
Lazy Class	Too high / Too low	Cohesion/Coupling	
Long Method	Too high / Too low	Cohesion/Coupling	
Long Parameter List	Too high / Too low	Cohesion/Coupling	
Message Chains	Too high / Too low	Cohesion/Coupling	
Middle Man	Too high / Too low	Cohesion/Coupling	
Parallel Inheritance Hierarchies	Too high / Too low	Cohesion/Coupling	
Primitive Obsession	Too high / Too low	Cohesion/Coupling	
Refused Bequest	Too high / Too low	Cohesion/Coupling	
Shotgun Surgery	Too high / Too low	Cohesion/Coupling	
Speculative Generality	Too high / Too low	Cohesion/Coupling	
Switch Statements	Too high / Too low	Cohesion/Coupling	
Temporary Field	Too high / Too low	Cohesion/Coupling	

Figure 11.5: Connecting code smells with cohesion/coupling

Note

For answers, see the Appendices section on the page 388.

Some ideas for the Reason column

- The method is probably doing too much.
- The class is probably doing too much.
- A class knows too much about non-immediate neighbors.
- The class just delegates behavior and has no behavior or state.
- The class hierarchy is probably wrong.
- The class misses state or behavior.
- Behavior that should be in a type is scattered.
- Data and behavior in separate places.
- Duplication instead of encapsulation.
- `If` statements are duplicated.
- The field is not really part of the state of a class.

Connecting Object Calisthenics with Code Smells and Cohesion/Coupling

As shown in the previous table, we can refer to object calisthenics and other heuristics to avoid creating code smells when writing the code in the first place. This has an effect also on coupling and cohesion.

For each row in the **Cohesion/Coupling** column, *highlight* the correct concept... either cohesion or coupling.

Object calisthenics	Code smell	Cohesion/Coupling
Only one level of indentation per method.	Long Method	Cohesion/Coupling
Don't use the ELSE keyword.	Long Method / Duplicated Code	Cohesion/Coupling
Wrap all primitives and strings.	Primitive Obsession	Cohesion/Coupling
First class collections.	Divergent Change	Cohesion/Coupling
One dot per line.	Message Chains	Cohesion/Coupling
Don't abbreviate.	NA	Cohesion/Coupling
Keep all entities small.	Large Class / Long Method /Long Parameter List	Cohesion/Coupling
No classes with more than two instance variables.	Large Class	Cohesion/Coupling
No geers / seers / properties.	NA	Cohesion/Coupling
All classes must have state	Lazy Class / Middle Man	Cohesion/Coupling

Figure 11.6: Connecting object calisthenics with code smells and cohesion/coupling

Note

For answers, see the Appendices section on the page 389.

When to Refactor (Extended for Cohesion/Coupling)

Refactor in the following circumstances:

- When we find duplication in our code; that is, DRY violation. (Don't forget the Rule of Three.)
- When we break any object calisthenics rules.
- When code exhibits code smells.
- When code has low cohesion or high coupling.

Classic TDD Flow

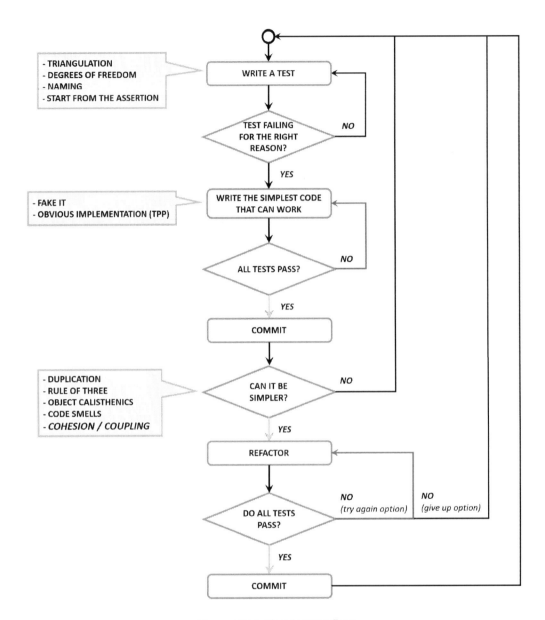

Figure 11.7: Classic TDD flow

The Big Picture

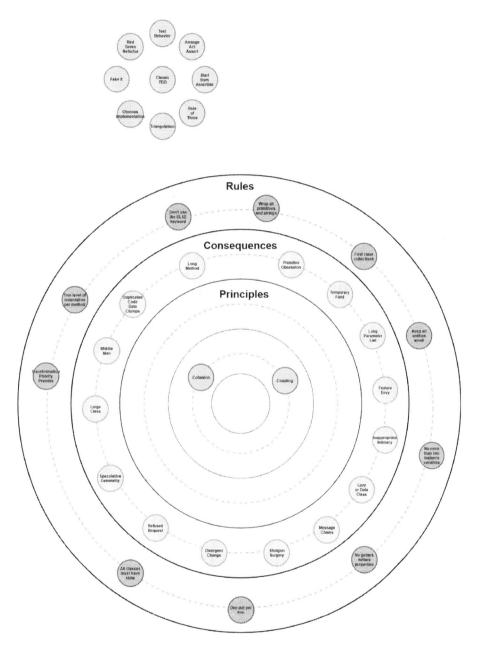

Has fewer Elements

Figure 11.8: Object-oriented design

When Should I Move to the Next Lesson?

- When you understand the connection between cohesion, coupling, and code smells.

- When you can design code using cohesion and coupling in a balanced way.

Resources

Web

- Cohesion – The cornerstone of Software Design, Sandro Mancuso, Codurance: https://codurance.com/software-creation/2016/03/03/cohesion-cornerstone-software-design/.

- Cohesion (computer science), Wikipedia: https://en.wikipedia.org/wiki/Cohesion_(computer_science).

- Coupling And Cohesion, C2 wiki: http://wiki.c2.com/?CouplingAndCohesion.

- Law of Demeter, Wikipedia: https://en.wikipedia.org/wiki/Law_of_Demeter.

- Software Complexity: Toward a Unified Theory of Coupling and Cohesion, David P. Darcy and Chris F. Kemerer: http://misrc.umn.edu/workshops/2002/spring/Darcy_020802.pdf.

Books

- Practical Guide to Structured Systems Design, Meilir Page-Jones: https://www.goodreads.com/book/show/1441004.Practical_Guide_to_Structured_Systems_Design.

12

Design VI – Solid Principles ++

"Everything should be made as simple as possible, but no simpler."

– Generally attributed to *Albert Einstein*

Single Responsibility Principle

In object-oriented programming, the **Single Responsibility Principle** (**SRP**) states that every object should have a single responsibility, and that responsibility should be entirely encapsulated by the class. All its services should be narrowly aligned with that responsibility.

The term was introduced by Robert C. Martin. Martin described it as being based on the principle of cohesion as described by Tom DeMarco in his book *Structured Analysis and Systems Specification*. Cohesion is a measure of the strength of association of the elements inside a module. A highly cohesive module is a collection of statements and data items that should be treated as a whole because they are so closely related. Any attempt to divide them up would only result in increased coupling and decreased readability.

Glenn Vanderburg said:

"This is also why we refer to a sound line of reasoning, for example, as coherent. The thoughts fit, they go together, they relate to each other. This is exactly the characteristic of a class that makes it coherent: the pieces all seem to be related, they seem to belong together, and it would feel somewhat unnatural [...] to pull them apart. Such a class exhibits cohesion."

Gather together those things that change for the same reason, and separate those things that change for different reasons. This is another aspect of the **SRP**. In short, it says that a subsystem, module, class, or even a function should not have more than one reason to change. Peter H. Salus, summarizing a portion of the UNIX philosophy, wrote, *"Write programs that do one thing and do it well. Write programs to work together."*

> **Note**
>
> Salus, in his book A Quarter-Century of Unix (1994), was summarizing from the Unix philosophy documented by Doug McIllroy in the Bell System Technical Journal (1978).

Let's look at a simple example and consider this code:

```
public class Car{
    public int CurrentMileage(){...}
    public void TravelTo(Location location){...}
    public void Save(){...}
}
```

Do you find anything strange in this **Car** class?

We can clearly see that the **CurrentMileage** and the **TravelTo** methods are related and change together.

What about the **Save** method? This method is obviously unrelated to the other two, acting on a different level of abstraction. The save action leaks the intent of collaborating with a persistence layer—a completely different responsibility than traveling and showing the current mileage. Here, without even having to see the implementations of those three methods, we can anticipate that the class has at least two responsibilities; hence, it violates SRP.

A great heuristic for the SRP is that we are able to describe what a class does without using *and* or *or*.

Open/Closed Principle

"The principle stated that a good module structure should be either open and closed. Closed, because clients need the module's services to proceed with their own development, and once they have settled on a version of the module should not be affected by the introduction of new services they do not need. Open, because there is no guarantee that we will include right from the start every service potentially useful to some client."

– Bertrand Meyer, Object-Oriented Software Construction

Closed with respect to X means that clients are not affected if X changes. Martin Fowler states that:

> **Note**
>
> Published Interface is a term I used [...] to refer to a class interface that's used outside the code base that it's defined in. The distinction between **published** and **public** is actually more important than that between **public** and **private**. The reason is that with a non-published interface you can change it and update the calling code since it is all within a single code base. [...] But anything published so you can't reach the calling code needs more complicated treatment.
>
> http://martinfowler.com/bliki/PublishedInterface.html.

Ideally, we should identify points of predicted variation and create a stable interface around them. The problem is that if we predict more variation than what is actually warranted, we waste effort on over-engineering a wrong abstraction. But if we fail to identify the variation over a common pattern of behavior, we usually end up with lots of breaking changes and a high probability of introducing code smells such as Shotgun Surgery or Divergent Change.

Also here, the rule of wrong abstraction is valid, so we find it's a good idea to use the *Rule of Three* before refactoring to open/closed principle. This is especially the case if we are building a brand-new system and we are not sure about predicting variations. When there are three components showing a pattern of behavior, it is usually easier to build the correct abstraction.

One of the great advantages of a correct implementation of the **open/closed principle** is that future developments of new functionality become much faster to achieve than before. This is usually achieved by identifying and modeling the common behavior into a higher layer of abstraction. To introduce new behavior, it will then be just a matter of implementing a new concrete component to be plugged in.

The responsibility of the common behavior is pushed onto its own component (an interface or an abstract class), leaving to the concrete singularities the only responsibility of executing their specific task. If we look closely at the open/closed principle in this way, we can think of it as a special case of applied *single responsibility principle* on a higher abstraction level. The end solution usually shows less code and fewer repetitions with an optimal level of code reuse.

Plugin-ability creates a system that is flexible enough to allow you to extend it without being too generic. There should be a balance between the concept of **You Aren't Going to Need It (YAGNI)** and plugin-ability; they are opposing forces. YAGNI tells you to have just enough code to express the desired behavior; plugin-ability tells you that you need to have extension points to allow new features without too much code change.

The balance between these forces is the *inflection point*. The inflection point defines the maximum amount of investment we are comfortable making in a desired type of flexibility at a given moment in time. Beyond this point, the investment is not worth it.

'I'll tell you what the problem is, mate,' said Majikthise, 'demarcation, that's the problem!

[...]

'That's right' shouted Vroomfondel, 'we demand rigidly defined areas of doubt and uncertainty!

– Douglas Adams, The Hitchhiker's Guide to the Galaxy

Let's see a simple example using our beloved **Car** domain:

```
public class CarEngineStatusReportController{
  public View DisplayEngineStatusReport(){
    var webView = new CarEngineWebView();
    webView.FillWith(carEngineViewModel);
    return webView;
  }


  public View PrintEngineStatusReport(){
    var printView = new CarEnginePrintView();
    printView.FillWith(carEngineViewModel);
    return printView;
  }
}
```

What happens if we have to, for example, add another way to visualize the *engine status* report on an alternative display for enhanced access? The obvious way would be to add a method like this:

```
public View AlternativeDisplayEngineStatusReport(){
    var webView = new EnhancedAccessCarEngineWebView();
    webView.FillWith(carEngineViewModel);
    return printView;
}
```

Every time we add a new view, we have to modify the controller, adding more code. Hence, *this controller is not closed for modification.* Furthermore, since the controller is created and destroyed for every request, it never uses more than one of these methods each time. We can definitely do better than that.

Let's see what happens if we identify and extract the point of variation, leaving in the controller just the common abstract behavior:

```
public class CarEngineStatusReportController{
    IDisplayEngineStatusReport _carEngineView;

    public CarEngineStatusReport(IDisplayEngineStatusReport carEngineView){
        _carEngineView = carEngineView;
    }

    public View EngineStatusReport(){
        _carEngineView.FillWith(carEngineViewModel);
        return _carEngineView;
    }
}
```

Here, **IDsiplayEngineStatusReport** is something like:

```
public interface IDisplayEngineStatusReport {
    void FillWith(CarEngineViewModel viewModel);
}
```

And we would now need three concrete implementations:

```
public class CarEngineWebView : IDisplayEngineStatusReport{

  void FillWith(CarEngineViewModel viewModel) {

 ...

    }

}


public class CarEnginePrintView : IDisplayEngineStatusReport{

  void FillWith(CarEngineViewModel viewModel) {

 ...

    }

}


public class EnhancedAccessCarEngineWebView : IDisplayEngineStatusReport{

  void FillWith(CarEngineViewModel viewModel) {

 ...

    }

}
```

The trick here is made by passing the correct instantiation of the view when the controller is created.

We now could go on forever adding more views; it would just be a matter of creating more concrete implementations of **IDisplayEngineStatusReport**, making sure they get plugged in correctly in their use cases. That's why this solution is *open for extension*. Furthermore, we can see that we will not have to modify **CarEngineStatusReportController** anymore for adding new views. That's why we can say that it is *closed for modification*.

Liskov Substitution Principle

"A *type hierarchy is composed of subtypes and super types. The intuitive idea of a subtype is one whose objects provide all the behavior of objects of another type (the super type) plus something extra. What is wanted here is something like the following substitution property: If for each object o1 of type S there is an object o2 of type T such that for all programs P defined in terms of T, the behavior of P is unchanged when o1 is substituted for o2, then S is a subtype of T."*

– *Barbara Liskov, Data Abstraction and Hierarchy*

If you don't understand this, don't worry. Neither do we! Instead, let's look at it from a less academic, mere mortal point of view.

In simple terms, the **Liskov Substitution Principle** (**LSP**) says that derived classes should keep promises made by base classes. This also applies to interfaces, and it means that classes that implement some interface should keep the promises made by that interface.

What does it mean for a class that it should keep the promises by the base class? Everything regarding the LSP is about the *behavior* of a class. So, the **is-a** relationship in Object-Oriented Programming (OOP) has to be seen from the perspective of exposed behavior, not the internal structure or the abstract meaning.

Imagine describing classes through their invariants, preconditions, and postconditions as explained in the design by contract of Bertrand Meyer. Following the LSP in terms of design by contract, it means:

- Preconditions cannot be more restrictive.

- Postconditions cannot be less restrictive.

- Invariants must be preserved.

> **Note**
>
> Wikipedia, Design by contract: https://en.wikipedia.org/wiki/Design_by_contract.
>
>
> Another way to state this principle is to say that subclasses should be contravariant of overridden method input types and covariant of overridden method output types, or, that a derived class should be less or equally restrictive on inputs and more or equally restrictive on outputs for overridden methods. (Mike James, Covariance And Contravariance – A Simple Guide) https://www.i-programmer.info/programming/ theory/1632-covariance-and-contravariance-a-simple-guide.html.

Remember that exceptions can be hidden return values; the same conformance rules still apply. Do not throw exceptions from derived classes that are not the same type or subtypes as exceptions thrown by the base class. Remember the *Refused Bequest* code smell? Inheritance is a *one-of-a-kind* relationship where subclasses are specializations of the base classes; they don't change the behavior–they make it more specific.

A good example is the famous **Rectangle** and **Square**. In this case, when we inherit **Square** from **Rectangle**, we are creating a more restrictive precondition; changing one size sets the other size to the same value, but this did not happen on the base class, **Rectangle**.

A simple test to verify whether your class is following the LSP is to replace its base type with the subclass; if the program doesn't change in meaning, then you are following the LSP.

A common mistake is to inherit from a type to get access to its state or expose some of its behavior. It seems a reasonable idea at first because it's a way of reusing code. The problem with this approach is that it tends to ignore the implications of the **is-a** relationship implied by the inheritance in OOP.

Let's think for a second about a *Person* class that is required to expose some behavior related to *Money*, and for that reason inherits from the *Wallet* type. If we allow *Person* to inherit from *Wallet*, *Person* gains access to the behavior exposed by *Wallet*.

The problem with this is that semantically we are stating that a *Person* is a *Wallet* and everywhere in our program we can use one in place of the other without changing the meaning of our software. This is the reason why this approach is often said to *favor composition over inheritance*.

Composition expresses the concept of *has a* and fits better in this example. Saying that a *Person has a Wallet* definitely makes more sense than a *Person is a Wallet*. So, when thinking about inheritance in OOP, remember that inheritance represents the *is-a* relationships, and subtypes refine the base types behavior, but maintain the meaning.

In the following example, we are breaking the **LSP** in the **Cook** method of the **Chef** class because you cannot replace *Oven* with any of its children without changing the meaning of what *Oven* achieves for *Chef*.

```
public class Oven {
   void Cook()
}


public class Microwave : Oven{
   void CookMicorwaving(){...}
```

```
    // If you replace Oven with Microwave and call Cook
    // it will change the meaning because this method
    // is throwing an exception, as a Microwave in this context
    // IS NOT an Oven
    void Cook(){throw ...}
}


class GrillOven : Oven{
  void CookGrilling(){...}
}


class FanOven : Oven{
  void CookHeating(){...}
}


public class Chef {
  public void Cook(Oven oven){
    switch(oven)
      case Microwave m:
        m.CookMicorwaving();
      case GrilOven g:
        g.CookGrilling();
      case FanOven f:
        f.CookHeating();
      default o:
        o.Cook();
  }
}
```

Interface Segregation Principle

The **Interface Segregation Principle (ISP)** states that *clients should not be forced to depend upon interfaces that they do not use*. The goal of the ISP is to reduce the side effects and the amount of changes needed in a system by splitting the software into multiple, smaller, independent parts grouped by functionality.

> **Note**
>
> Robert C. Martin, The Interface Segregation Principle, Engineering Notebook, C++ Report, Nov-Dec, 1996.

The dependency should be on the interface, the whole interface, and nothing but the interface. We refer to a sound line of reasoning, for example, as coherent. The thoughts fit, they go together, they relate to each other. This is exactly the characteristic of an interface that makes it coherent; the pieces all seem to be related, they seem to belong together, and it would feel somewhat unnatural to pull them apart. Such an interface exhibits cohesion.

Let's look at an example:

```
public class Car : IAmACar{

...

}


public interface IAmACar{
    void GoTo(Location location);
    void RefillGasoline(int gallons);
    int CurrentMileage();
}
```

This looks perfectly fine.

Now, let's suppose a new kind of car is coming out. This car doesn't run on gasoline; it's an electric car. What happens if we just add it to the current interface, like this:

```
public interface IAmACar{
    void GoTo(Location location);
    void RefillGasoline(int gallons);
    void RefillElectricity(decimal kiloWatts);
```

```
    int CurrentMileage();
}
```

In this way, we have just broken the ISP, which is the reason why we now have a *refused bequest* code smell. Since the two refill methods are mutually exclusive in their usage, we now have an interface that is always unfit to represent a real category of car. One of the two would always have to be implemented by **throw new NotImplementedException();**. Not nice at all.

How should we approach this problem instead? Well, by segregating the interfaces!

```
public interface IAmACar{

  void GoTo(Location location);

  int CurrentMileage();

}


public interface IUseGasoline : IAmACar{

  void RefillGasoline(int gallons);

}


public interface IUseElectricity : IAmACar{

  void RefillElectricity(decimal kiloWatts);

}
```

Now we can have cars correctly accepting either gasoline or electricity, without unimplemented methods. The interfaces correctly map the real functionality and correctly inherit the common behavior from the base interface.

Dependency Inversion Principle

In object-oriented programming, the **Dependency Inversion Principle** refers to a specific form of decoupling where conventional dependency relationships established from high-level, policy-setting modules to low-level, dependency modules are inverted for the purpose of rendering high-level modules independent of the low-level module implementation details.

To achieve that, you need to introduce an abstraction that decouples the high-level and low-level modules from each other. So:

- High-level modules should not depend on low-level modules. Both should depend on abstractions.

- Abstractions should not depend on details. Details should depend on abstractions.

Hence, both high-level and low-level modules depend on the abstraction. The design principle does not just change the direction of the dependency, as you might have expected from its name. It splits the dependency between the high-level and low-level modules by introducing an abstraction between them. So, in the end, you get two dependencies:

- The high-level module depends on the abstraction.

- The low-level depends on the same abstraction.

Let's see a simple example:

```
public class Kitchen{
    private Microwave _oven;

    public Kitchen(){
        _oven = new MicrowaveOven();
    }
    ...
}


public class MicrowaveOven{
    private MicrowaveGenerator _heater;

    public Microwave(){
        _heater = new MicrowaveGenerator();
    }
    ...
}
```

```
public class MicrowaveGenerator{

...

}
```

This is how a normal dependency hierarchy could look:

- The `Kitchen` class holds a dependency to the `MicrowaveOven` class.

- The `MicrowaveOven` class has a dependency to the `MicrowaveGenerator` heater component.

In the diagram that follows, we have a dependency arrow from `Kitchen` to `MicrowaveOven` and from `MicrowaveOven` to `MicrowaveGenerator`.

Let's see what happens when we apply the principle:

```
public interface IOvenCook{ ... }


public interface IGenerateMicrowaves{ ... }


public class Kitchen{
  private IOvenCook _oven;


  public Kitchen(IOvenCook oven){
    _oven = oven;
  }
...
}


public class MicrowaveOven : IOvenCook{
  private IGenerateMicrowaves _heater;


  public Microwave(IGenerateMicrowaves heater){
    _heater = heater;
  }
...
}
```

```
public class MicrowaveGenerator : IGenerateMicrowaves{

    ...

}
```

To apply the principle, we introduced abstraction layers in the form of interfaces. They act as catalysts for the dependencies, attracting the direction of the arrows of the dependency diagram.

The following diagram shows how the dependency flow has changed with this simple adjustment.

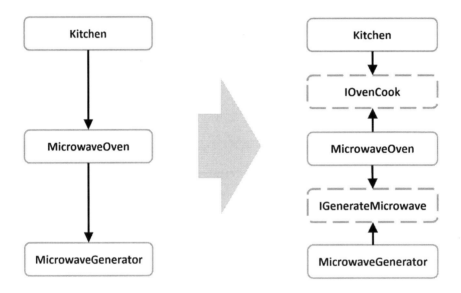

Figure 12.1: Depending on interfaces inverts the direction of dependencies

Balanced Abstraction Principle

Sandro Mancuso, in his blog, defines the **Balanced Abstraction Principle** as follows:

The Balanced Abstraction Principle defines that all code constructs grouped by a higher-level construct should be at the same level of abstraction. That means:

- All instructions inside a method should be at the same level of abstraction.
- All public methods inside a class should be at the same level of abstraction.
- All classes should be inside a package/namespace.
- All sibling packages/namespace should be inside a parent package/namespace.

Sandro Mancuso, Balanced Abstraction Principle, https://codurance.com/2015/01/27/balanced-abstraction-principle/.

Let's see how it relates to a little previous example. In the following snippet, the **Save** method is not at the same level of abstraction:

```
public class Car{

    public int CurrentMileage(){...}

    public void TravelTo(Location location){...}

    public void Save(){...}

}
```

The **Save** method implies that there will be some collaboration with an external persistency mechanism, while other methods imply work on business logic pertaining to the **Car** class. These are clearly two different layers of abstractions. This is an example where the violation of the Balanced Abstraction Principle is also a violation of the **SRP**.

Let's see an example of the principle applied to methods that conform to the SRP, but not to the Balanced Abstraction Principle:

```
public class LeapYear{

    public bool IsLeapYear(int year){

      if((year % 4 == 0) && !year.IsMultipleOf(100))

      {


  ...

      }


  ...

    }

}
```

In the **IsLeapYear** method, **year % 4 == 0** is not at the same level of abstraction as **year.IsMultipleOf(100)**. A better implementation, solving the issue while maintaining a balance level of abstractions and improving clarity, could be the following:

```
public class LeapYear{

  public bool IsLeapYear(int year){

    if(year.IsMultipleOf(4) && !year.IsMultipleOf(100))

    {


  ...

    }



  ...

  }

}
```

Principle of Least Astonishment

The **Principle of Least Astonishment** (also known as the **WTF principle**) states that "*People are part of the system. The design should match the user's experience, expectations, and mental models.*"

> **Note**
>
> Wikipedia, Principle of least astonishment: https://en.wikipedia.org/wiki/Principle_ of_least_astonishment.

The choice of *least surprising* behavior depends on the expected audience and, hence, on the context.

We are software developers, so the principle says that we shouldn't mislead the developers who will work on the code in the future with names that are not coherent with the behavior inside the constructs.

For example:

```
int Multiply(int a, int b)

{

  return a + b;

}
```

```
int SaveFile(string filename, string text)
{
  Console.WriteLine(text);
}
public class SomethingFactory {
  //returning void???? for a factory????
  public void DoSomething()
  {
    //write on Database
  }
}
```

Kata

Connecting Cohesion/Coupling and SOLID principles

For each row in the **Cohesion/Coupling** column, **highlight** the correct concept and then add a reason in the **Reason** column. We created a few sample reasons you can use. In some cases, both coupling and cohesion apply:

Solid Principle	Cohesion/Coupling	Reason
Single Responsibility Principle	Cohesion/Coupling	
Open/Closed Principle	Cohesion/Coupling	
Liskov Substitution Principle	Cohesion/Coupling	
Interface Segregation Principle	Cohesion/Coupling	
Dependency Inversion Principle	Cohesion/Coupling	

Figure 12.2: Connecting cohesion/coupling and SOLID principles

> **Note**
>
> For answers, see the Appendices section on page 389.

Some ideas for the **Reason** column are as follows:

- Consistency/usage
- Change
- Inheritance tree level

When to Refactor (Extended for SOLID Principles)

Refactor in these circumstances:

- When we find duplication in our code; that is, DRY violation. (Don't forget the Rule of Three.)

- When we break any object calisthenics rules.

- When our code exhibits code smells.

- When code has low cohesion or high coupling.

- When our code does not follow SOLID principles.

Classic TDD Flow

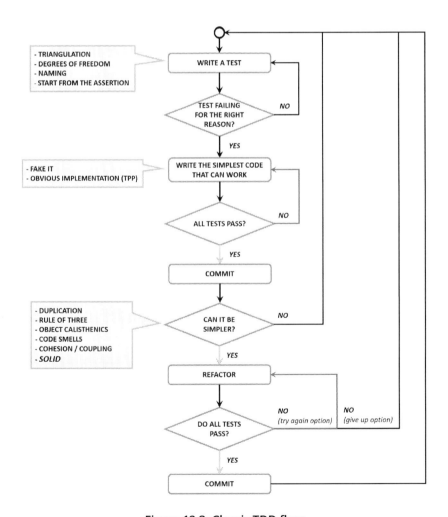

Figure 12.3: Classic TDD flow

The Big Picture

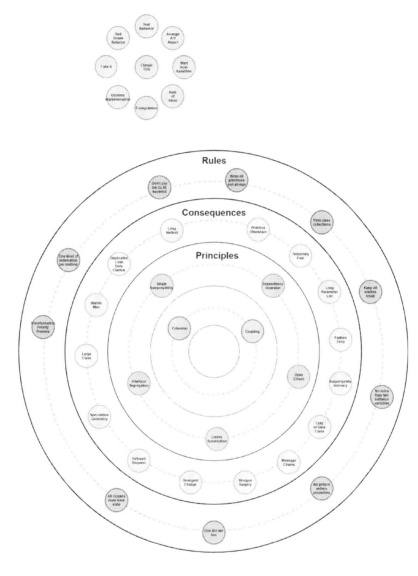

Has fewer Elements

Figure 12.4: The big picture

When Should I Move to the Next Lesson?

- When you understand the meaning of SOLID principles

- When you understand the connection between cohesion, coupling, code smells, and the SOLID principles

Resources

Web

- A Behavioral Notion of Subtyping, Barbara H. Liskov and Jeannette M. Wing: https://www.cs.cmu.edu/~wing/publications/LiskovWing94.pdf.

- Cohesion, Glenn Vanderburg: https://vanderburg.org/blog/2011/01/31/cohesion.html.

- Covariance And Contravariance – A Simple Guide, Mike James: https://www.i-programmer.info/programming/theory/1632-covariance-and-contravariance-a-simple-guide.html.

- Data Abstraction and Hierarchy, Barbara Liskov: https://dl.acm.org/citation.cfm?doid=62138.62141.

- Design by Contract, Wikipedia: https://en.wikipedia.org/wiki/Design_by_contract.

- Inflection point, Sandro Mancuso: https://codurance.com/2015/06/17/inflection-point/.

- SOLID deconstruction slides: http://yowconference.com.au/slides/yow2013/Henney-SOLIDDeconstruction.pdf.

- SOLID Design Principles Explained – Dependency Inversion Principle with Code Examples, Thorben Janssen: https://stackify.com/dependency-inversion-principle/.

Books

- Clean Code: A Handbook of Agile Software Craftsmanship, Robert C. Martin: https://www.goodreads.com/book/show/3735293-clean-code.

- Object-Oriented Software Construction, Bertrand Meyer: https://www.goodreads.com/book/show/946106.Object_Oriented_Software_Construction.

- Structured Analysis and Systems Specification, Tom DeMarco: https://www.goodreads.com/book/show/123719.Structured_Analysis_and_System_Specification.

13
Design VII – Connascence

Great things are done by a series of small things brought together.

– Vincent Van Gogh

Definition

The term **connascence** derives from Latin: co + nascence.

"co" means together and "nascence" derives from nascentem, which means arising young, immature. It's the present participle of nasci, to be born, hence the definition:

> **Note**
>
> The birth and growth of two or more things at the same time.

In software development, we can say that two or more elements (fields, methods, classes, parameters, variables, but also build steps, procedures of any kind, and so on) are *connascent* if a change in one element would also require a change in the others in order for the system to keep working correctly.

Connascence generalizes the ideas of cohesion and coupling, combining them in a more exhaustive classification using a proper taxonomy. In 2009, Jim Weirich, in a great talk at a conference, defined connascence as *The Grand Unified Theory of Software Development* because of its wide applicability in the analysis and improvement of information systems.

> **Note**
>
> James Nolan Weirich (November 18, 1956 – February 19, 2014) was well known in the software industry as a developer, speaker, teacher and contributor to the Ruby Programming Language community. His talks have been the main inspiration for this lesson. Thanks, James!

Connascence makes the argument for several levels of encapsulation in a system, often called information hiding.

- **Level 1 encapsulation** refers to the encapsulation attained by combining lines of code into a method, and it is addressed by **Method Cohesion** and **Interaction Coupling**.

- **Level 2 encapsulation** refers to the encapsulation achieved by creating classes, combining both methods and fields, and it is addressed by **class cohesion** and **inheritance coupling**.

Connascence, as a generalization of both cohesion and coupling, addresses either Level 1 or Level 2 encapsulation.

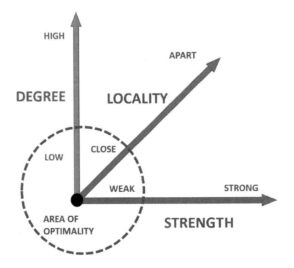

Figure 13.1: The three dimensions of connascence

Dimensions

Every case of connascence can be measured over three dimensions: *degree*, *locality*, and *strength*.

Degree

Degree is the size of the impact as estimated by the number of occurrences and the number of entities it affects. The acceptability of connascence is strongly related to its degree: the higher the degree, the higher the pain when a modification is needed. *We should aim to have the minimal possible degree.*

Locality

Locality is the closeness of the affected entities with respect to each other in terms of abstraction. The closer the better and the more acceptable (leading to cohesion). On the other end, connascence of entities that are very far apart from each other is often an indication of design or architectural pitfalls. *We should try to keep the connascent elements as close as possible.* If you remember the *Law of Demeter*, it is meant to limit the distance of method calls, hence acting on the locality.

Strength

Strength is the likelihood that connascence requires compensating changes in connascent elements and how hard it would be to make those changes. The stronger the form of connascence, the more difficult and costly it would be to refactor the elements in the relationship. *We should try to use only the weakest forms:*

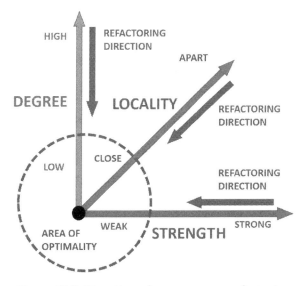

Figure 13.2: Direction of connascence refactoring

As you may have already noticed, these definitions imply that there are different kinds of connascence, so let's see them in more detail with clarifying examples.

Connascence of Name and Type (CoN and CoT)

The concept of connascence pervades anything we do when we work on software development. Every line of code displays some element of it as the logical building blocks of programs.

To understand how the concept of connascence influences so much of what we do in our code, let's look at an example:

```
public class Time {

    int _hour;

    int _minute;

    int _second;


    public Time(int hour, int minute, int second){

        _hour = hour;

        _minute = minute;

        _second = second;

    }


    public string Display(){

        return _hour + ":" + _minute + ":" + _second + ":";

    }

}
```

We can see that every line of our code has things repeated two or more times. How many instances of connascence can you spot by looking at the name of the variables and their types?

1. **Connascence of Name** for the **_hour**, **_minute**, and **_second** fields (three appearance each).

2. **Connascence of Name** for the **hour**, **minute**, and **second** parameters (two appearance each).

3. **Connascence of Type** for the **hour**, **minute**, and **second** parameters and the respective fields, **_hour**, **_minute**, and **_second** (two appearance each).

These are are the good types of connascence and should be the only ones we find in the system. We will see that other types of static connascence can always be reduced to this form.

The elements in that code snippet would be useless if they appeared only once: *the repetitions of their appearance in the code is what allows the data to be part of some logical construct* for transforming information and making it flow. This concept represents the building blocks of software development and optimizing it would lead to better design, simpler code, and minimum waste.

Can we find other kinds of connascence in that example? There are two others—not of a very good kind:

1. **Connascence of Position** for the `hour`, `minute`, and `second` parameters.

2. **Connascence of Value** for the `hour`, `minute`, and `second` parameters.

As you can see in the following graphic, these last two kinds of connascence score at the top of our weak-to-strong list. In the sections that follow, we'll explain why.

Figure 13.3: Types of connascence

Connascence of Position

Connascence of Position (CoP) occurs when *multiple components must be adjacent or must appear in a particular order, often when passed within a positional structure such as an array or a tuple.* It is the strongest form of static connascence and must be carefully avoided, especially for higher degrees.

Let's see an example:

```
public class NotificationSystem {

    public void SendEmail(string recipient, string sender, string message) {

        Email email = new Email();

        email.To(recipient);

        email.From(sender);

        email.Body(message);

        _smtpService.SendEmail(email);

    }

}


_notificationSystem.SendEmail("recipient@email.com", "sender@email.com",
"text");
```

Here, the connascence of position is about the order of the arguments of the **SendEmail** method because we have to make sure that we pass those arguments in that exact order, otherwise our message isn't going to get where it's supposed to go, which could be disastrous.

This example is easy to solve for languages such as Ruby or C# because when we call the method, we can use the named parameter construct to decouple from the order of the parameters.

In other languages, we find that using custom types representing the meaning of the parameter is a valid way to solve it:

```
public class NotificationSystem {

    public void SendEmail(Recipient recipient, Sender sender, Message
message) {

        Email email = new Email();

        email.To(recipient.Address);

        email.From(sender.Address);

        email.Body(message.Body);
```

```
            _smtpService.SendEmail(email);
        }
    }
    public class Recipient {
        public Address => _address;
        private string _address;


        public Recipient(string address){
            _address = address;
        }
    }
    public class Sender {
        public Address => _address;
        private string _address;


        public Sender(string address){
            _address = address;
        }
    }
    public class Message {
        public Body => _body;
        private string _body;


        public Message(string body){
            _body = body;
        }
    }
    _notificationSystem.SendEmail(
        new Recipient("recipient@email.com"),
        new Sender("sender@email.com"),
        new Message("notification text"));
```

There we go—CoP has been removed and replaced with the weaker CoT.

Did you notice something else in this example related to *code smells*? CoP is often related to the *Primitive Obsession* code smell. That's exactly what we clean up here; instead of using strings to express the concepts of *recipient*, *sender*, and *message*, we have now more expressive constructs to represent them.

Another way to solve a similar case is by using a custom type to encapsulate the information passing into this method. This solution has the advantage of reducing the overall method of coupling as well as conforming to the *Method Coupling Premises* mentioned in *Lesson 11, Cohesion and Coupling*:

```
public class NotificationSystem {

    public void SendEmail(Notification notification) {

        Email email = new Email();

        email.To(notification.Recipient);

        email.From(notification.Sender);

        email.Body(notification.Message);

        _smtpService.SendEmail(email);

    }

}
```

We have solved the *Connascence of Position* on the **NotificationSystem** class, but what about the new **Notification** class? Essentially, we have now just pushed the problem to the collaborator. How can we build the notification without the same type of connascence? In such a case, a simplified version of the builder pattern can be helpful:

```
public class Notification {

    public string Recipient => _recipient;

    public string Sender => _sender;

    public string Message => _message;


    private string _recipient;

    private string _sender;

    private string _message;


    public Notification To(string recipient){

        _recipient = recipient;

        return this;

    }
```

```
    public Notification From(string sender){

        _sender = sender;

        return this;

    }


    public Notification WithMessage(string message){

        _message = message;

        return this;

    }

}


_notificationSystem.SendEmail(

    new Notification()

        .To("recipient@email.com")

        .From("sender@email.com")

        .WithMessage("notification text"));
```

Another common example of Connascence of Position (which is easier to recognize given the immediate drop in code expressivity) occurs when positional structures are used in message passing.

Let's look at this example:

```
public class OrderProcessor {

  public void ProcessOrder(Tuple<Order, bool> orderInfo)

  {

    ProcessOrder(order.Item1);


    if (order.Item2)

      SendInvoice(order.Item1);

  }


  public void ProcessOrder(Tuple<Order, bool, int, datetime, string, bool>
  orderInfo)

  {
```

```
        ProcessOrder(order.Item1);


        if (order.Item2)
          SendInvoice(order.Item1);


        NotifyEmployee(orderInfo.Item1,orderInfo.Item3,orderInfo.Item4,orderInfo.
   Item5);
      }

   }
```

The **tuple** structure here apparently allows for *flexibility* when the methods are defined. But what happens when another class has to call this method? Let's see:

```
   _orderProcessor.ProcessOrder(new Tuple(order, true));


   _orderProcessor.ProcessOrder(new Tuple(order, true, 12345, DateTime.UtcNow,
   "Jack", false));
```

If we look at this from a point of view internal to the **Order Processor** class, using a tuple might not appear to be a bad idea. However, when we step out of the class and try to use the method, the problems become evident.

The first call shows *CoP of Degree* 2, while the second is of Degree 6. It's easy to see the progressive fading of expressivity for these two calls. In the Degree 2 call, we have completely lost the meaning of the second Boolean, even if with a little effort we can work it out (but it's not nice, anyway).

What about the second call? With a Degree 6 CoP we are left with a sequence of apparently arbitrary information to pass in, making it an absolute nightmare to guess the correct usage!

The good news is that it's easy to get back on track with a quick refactoring; we can introduce a class for message passing and rewrite the calling method as follows:

```
   public class InvoiceableOrder{
       Order Order;
       bool IsInvoiceable;
   }
```

```
public void ProcessOrders(InvoiceableOrder invoiceableOrder){

    ProcessOrder(invoiceableOrder.order);


    if(invoiceableOrder.IsInvoiceable)

        SendInvoice(invoiceableOrder.order);

}
```

Connascence of Value (CoV)

Connascence of Value (**CoV**) occurs when *two or more components' values are related or have an intrinsic range of validity in their input not expressed by their primitive types.*

Let's consider the initial example:

```
public class Time {

    int _hour;

    int _minute;

    int _second;


    public Time(int hour, int minute, int second){

        _hour = hour;

        _minute = minute;

        _second = second;

    }


    public string Display(){

        return _hour + ":" + _minute + ":" + _second + ":";

    }

}
```

What happens if we instantiate it like this:

```
var myTime = new Time (27, 76, 82);
```

That's obviously not a valid time. Is it wise to rely on the user's knowledge about the concept of **time**? The best thing we can do to improve our design is to try to eliminate it by making *invalid states unrepresentable.*

What if we do something like this:

```
public enum Hour {
    Midnight = 0,
    OneAm = 1,
    TwoAm = 2,
    ThreeAm = 3,
    FourAm = 4,
    FiveAm = 5,

    ...
    TenPm = 22,
    ElevenPm = 23
}


public class Time {
    Hour _hour;
    int _minute;
    int _second;

    public Time(Hour hour, int minute, int second){
        _hour = hour;
        _minute = minute;
        _second = second;
    }

    public string Display(){
        return _hour + ":" + _minute + ":" + _second + ":";
    }
}
```

We can see that now our parameter takes an enumeration called **Hour**, and it is basically impossible to pass something incorrectly. However, the resulting enumeration becomes quite long and feels like overkill in this situation. What about minutes and seconds? Those would be even longer.

Preceding on that road clearly depends on how the class will be used in its context. If there will be a lot of manual instantiations it might be worth doing it. (Remember, typing is not the bottleneck!) Otherwise, there is a minimum viable solution for this form of connascence.

The real issue with CoV is that it is discoverable only at runtime, so we should try to minimize the response time of the negative feedback and validate the input as soon as possible. In this way, we make sure that *this class participates in the information flow if – and only if – its state is valid.*

```
public class Time {
    int _hour;
    int _minute;
    int _second;


    public Time(int hour, int minute, int second){
        _hour = hour;
        _minute = minute;
        _second = second;
        Validate()
    }


    public string Display(){
        return _hour + ":" + _minute + ":" + _second + ":";
    }


    private void Validate(){
        if(_hour < 0 || _hour > 23)
            throw new InvalidHourException();
        if(_minute < 0 || _minute > 59)
            throw new InvalidMinuteException();
        if(_second < 0 || _second > 59)
            throw new InvalidSecondException();
    }
}
```

Let's see another example of CoV where the need of validation is not so intuitive:

```
ublic class Triangle {

    int SideA;

    int SideB;

    int SideC;


    public Triangle(int sideA, int sideB, int sideC){

        SideA = sideA;

        SideB = sideB;

        SideC = sideC;

    }

}
```

The values of the sides need to satisfy a particular relation for it to be a triangle, as shown in the diagram. So, here we have the same validation problem, and validation must occur in the constructor as well:

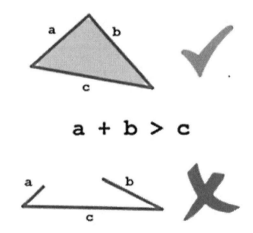

Figure 13.4: Sides relation for being a triangle

What about making invalid states unrepresentable? Can we do it?

Studying the properties of triangles a little allows us to create an alternative design for our class. Let's look at the angles in this example. Can we use this to make our constructor less fragile?

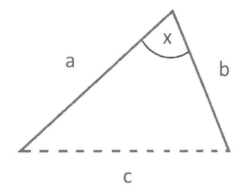

Figure 13.5: Triangle defined by a, b, and x

Well, it's actually interesting to see that if we have the data of just two sides and their connecting angle, we can work out the third side!

So an alternative class could be as follows:

```
public Triangle(int sideA, int sideB, Angle x){
    SideA = sideA;
    SideB = sideB;
    SideC = CalculateSide(sideA, sideB, x);
}
```

We still have to validate the angle in order to be valid in our situation, but we removed the relation between data.

Given that the angle is valid, we are always in a position to calculate the third side.

Connascence of Meaning

We have **Connascence of Meaning (CoM)**, or **convention**, when *two or more components must agree on the meaning of specific values, hence using a convention*. This kind of connascence is not considered strong, but it is particularly annoying because it's quite common, easy to fix, and can become really tedious in debugging mode.

Let's suppose we are writing a simple web page for a survey about how people come to work. We might need a checkbox that looks similar to this:

```
<input type='checkbox' name='transport' value='1' />
I travel by bike <br />


<input type='checkbox' name='transport' value='2' />
```

```
I travel by car <br />


<input type='checkbox' name='transport' value='3' />
I travel by train <br />


<input type='checkbox' name='transport' value='4' />
I travel by bus <br />
```

And in our controller, we might need something like this:

```
private SetTransport(string transport){
    switch(transport){
        case "1":
            AddBike();
        case "2":
            AddCar();
        case "3":
            AddTrain();
        case "4":
            AddBus();
        break;
    }
}
```

Let's suppose we have deployed our website, but we notice that the stats don't add up. We debug our controller, and we see that **transport** is **3**. That's not helpful. We'll always need one more step (or to memorize the mapping) in order to identify the correct meaning of **3**.

In this case, just using the text values **bike**, **car**, **train**, and **bus** would have prevented this kind of problem. But what if we really need to keep the integers because we have to feed a legacy system that really, really, really loves integers? Are we doomed?

Nope. As we said, it's easy to fix! We can just introduce some *constants*:

```
const string BIKE = "1";
const string CAR = "2";
const string TRAIN = "3";
const string BUS = "4";
```

```
<input type="checkbox" name="transport" value="<%= BIKE %>" />
I travel by bike <br />
<input type="checkbox" name="transport" value="<%= CAR %>" />
I travel by car <br />
<input type="checkbox" name="transport" value="<%= TRAIN %>" />
I travel by train <br />
<input type="checkbox" name="transport" value="<%= BUS %>" />
I travel by bus <br />
private SetTransport(string transport){
    switch(transport){
        case BIKE:
            AddBike();
            AddCar();
        case CAR:
        case TRAIN:
            AddTrain();
        case BUS:
            AddBus();
        break;
    }
}
```

There we go. As always, we replaced **CoM** with more expressive **Connascence of Name and Type**.

Connascence of Algorithm

Connascence of Algorithm (**CoA**) occurs when *two or more components must agree on using a particular algorithm.*

Perhaps the most popular example of this kind of connascence is `checksum` for file verification; applying the algorithm remotely allows for a mathematical proof that the file has not been changed.

Unfortunately, if we have this kind of connascence in our code, the result is not useful. Let's see an example of a dumb **checksum** implementation that assumes we want to build it with a simple logic consisting of adding a character at the end of an integer so that the sum of the single numbers could be divided by 10:

```
AddChecksum("32143")    =>    "321437"

Check("321437")         =>    true

Check("321432")         =>    false
```

Let's see this snippet implementing it:

```
public string AddChecksum(string inputData){
    var sum = SumCharsOf(inputData);
    var difference = sum % 10;
    return inputData + difference;
}


public bool Check(string inputData){
    var sum = SumCharsOf(inputData);
    return sum % 10 == 0;
}
```

Do you see anything wrong with it? What if at some point we have to change the algorithm? What would happen? Well, in that case we would be forced to modify the code inside both methods; a *by the book* example of the **divergent change** code smell.

The problem here comes from the fact that our algorithm has not been encapsulated into its abstraction layer; hence, it cannot be reused. Look at **sum % 10**, for instance. It might be simple, but in this case, that's our algorithm. It appears twice in two different methods. Does it respect DRY? No, it doesn't. This is a classic example of CoA.

Once this kind of connascence is identified, it's usually not difficult to solve. The trick is just pushing the logic into another reusable construct. This is usually a class if the algorithm is complicated enough. In our example, a method would be enough (assuming this would be the only usage):

```
public string AddChecksum(string inputData){
    return inputData + Checksum(inputData);
}


public bool Check(string inputData){
```

```
        return Checksum(inputData) == 0;
}


  private int Checksum(string inputData){
        var sum = SumCharsOf(inputData);
        return sum % 10;
}
```

As always, we transform it back to connascence of Name so we will be in a better position when it's maintenance time. Do you notice how something so simple helps the expressivity of this little code so much? Imagine if the algorithm was much more sophisticated. It's always a good idea to encapsulate reused, complicated logic behind its own level of abstraction!

Connascence of Execution Order

Connascence of Execution Order (CoEO) happens when *the caller of a component must have some unexpressed knowledge about the correct order of the methods to be called.* It is quite common in imperative languages and in the weakest of the dynamic forms of connascence. Nevertheless, it can become a source of deep pain in the maintenance phase because often it's quite difficult and time consuming to figure it out by just reading the code.

Let's see a short example of a class that is supposed to send and archive receipts:

```
  public void SendReceipts(){
        var receiptSender = new ReceiptSender();
        var receiptId = NextUnsentReceiptId();


        while(receiptId != null){
            receiptSender.SendToCustomer(receiptId);
            receiptSender.Archive(receiptId);


            receiptId = NextUnsentReceiptID();
        }
}
```

What happens if in our calls to the **ReceiptSender** we invert the order and call the **Archive** method before the **SendToCustomer** with the same **receiptId**? If that would result in a failure on the second call, we have CoEO.

If this is the only usage of the **ReceiptSender** class, we clearly have a leaking abstraction in its behavior. The **Archive** method is meant to always be called *after* **SendToCustomer**. So why are both methods public, leaving incorrect usage to chance? Here, one method should be enough, and the correct execution order hidden and enforced inside.

However, sometimes this form of connascence is meant to exist because of the nature of our context. Think of the **Builder** pattern, for instance. The builder pattern is essentially an elegant way to use CoEO by expressing the correct usage by convention; we first have to somehow set up the builder and, *after* that's done, call the **Build()** method.

Let's look at this little car builder example:

```
public class CarBuilder : IBuildCars {

    public IBuildCars WithBrand(Brand brand){

        _brand = brand;

        return this;

    }


    public IBuildCars WithEngine(Engine engine){

        _engine = engine;

        return this;

    }


    public IBuildCars OfColor(Color color){

        _color = color;

        return this;

    }


    public Car Build(){

        return new Car(_brand, _engine, _color)

    }

}
```

The interface is as follows:

```
public interface IBuildCars {

    IBuildCars WithBrand(Brand brand);

    IBuildCars WithEngine(Engine brand);

    IBuildCars WithColor(Color brand);

    Car Build();

}
```

What if we now need to enforce an execution order and, for whatever reason, must have the **Brand**, **Engine**, and **Color** specified in exactly that particular sequence? Is it even possible without Connascence of Execution Order?

A very elegant way, in our opinion, is leveraging **interface segregation**.

Let's see how we could break down our interface:

```
public interface IBuildCarsWithBrand{

    IBuildCarsWithEngine WithBrand(Brand brand);

}


public interface IBuildCarsWithEngine{

    IBuildCarsWithColor WithEngine(Engine engine);

}


public interface IBuildCarsWithColor{

    IBuildCars WithColor(Color color);

}


public interface IBuildCars{

    Car Build();

}
```

Now, just a little modification to our concrete class will do the trick:

```
public class CarBuilder : IBuildCarsWithBrand, IBuildCarsWithEngine,
IBuildCarsWithColor, IBuildCars {
    private CarBuilder(){}

    public static IBuildCarsWithBrand New(){
        return new CarBuilder();
    }

    public IBuildCarsWithEngine WithBrand(Brand brand){
        _brand = brand;
        return this;
    }

    public IBuildCarsWithColor WithEngine(Engine engine){
        _engine = engine;
        return this;
    }

    public IBuildCars WithColor(Color color){
        _color = color;
        return this;
    }

    public Car Build(){
        return new Car(_brand, _engine, _color)
    }
}
```

We made the constructor private so we can force the call of the *Factory Method* for instantiating the concrete as `IBuildCarsWithBrand`. This interface now just has the `WithBrand` method, so it enforces the beginning of the sequence correctly. Furthermore, it returns the concrete as `IBuildCarsWithEngine` this time, which returns `IBuildCarsWithColor`.

Chaining interfaces in this way will lead exactly to the sequence we wanted. Only the last one will return `IBuildCars`, where the `Build()` method can finally be called and the concrete car returned. We have essentially used chained interfaces to enforce a call sequence over methods of a concrete class.

Note that Connascence of Execution Order is still there, because it is part of our requirements. However, we achieved something very interesting; we have pushed its locality completely inside the code! When we leave the programmer to figure out the correct execution order, we have a dangerous loss of information. One of the connascent elements becomes undocumented (until we have an eventual runtime failure).

Using *interface segregation* in this way allows us to instead express the correct execution sequence, making the expected usage very easy to understand. Remember Murphy's Law? *Anything that can go wrong will go wrong.*

So many attributions and recollections exist as to the origination of Murphy's Law that is impossible to pinpoint with any certainty.

Connascence of Timing

Connascence of Timing (CoTm) happens when *the success of two or more calls depends on the timing of when they occur.* The concept is not very different from CoEO, but here we have an explicit relation with *the point in time* the call gets executed, not just *before* or *after.*

One of the most classic occurrences of CoT is race conditions in multithreading. You'll find another example when you see in the code something like `Wait`, `Sleep`, or `Timeout` followed by an actual arbitrary explicit timespan.

The problem with CoTm is that we usually are not in control of the time, so it obviously has the potential to introduce great flakiness into the system. And intermittent problems are usually the hardest to identify and resolve. That's why we feel that it's always a good idea to try to avoid CoTm like the pox, when possible.

Sometimes, however, we can't really get rid of it. For example, think of some integration tests for a **Service Bus**. We always have CoTm in an asynchronous kind of test like that. We need to decide an arbitrary amount of time to wait for the message, right?

Let's see an example, assuming for simplicity our message handler queues the messages internally after receiving them:

```
[TestFixture]
public class ServiceBusMessageHandler_Should{
    var messageHandler = new MessageHandler();


    [Test]
    public void ReceiveMessages(){
        var expectedMessage = new TestMessage();
        SendMessageToIntegrationTestBus(expectedMessage);
        Thread.Sleep(1000);


        var receivedMessage = messageHandler.ReadLastMessage();


        Assert.That(receivedMessage, Is.Equal(expectedMessage))
    }
}
```

Between sending the message and reading it, we need to wait some arbitrary amount of time. If we don't wait, we will check for the message before it gets received, and our test cannot pass. Timing here is crucial. We can't escape this. But can we do something better?

Well, if we remember that *time is money*, we can.

We can optimize it so that we do not always depend on an *arbitrary* amount of it. Let's see an alternative snippet:

```
[TestFixture]
public class ServiceBusMessageHandler_Should{
    var awaiter = new AutoResetEvent(false);
    var messageHandler = new MessageHandler();
    messageHandler.OnNewMessage += ()=>awaiter.Set();


    [Test]
    public void ReceiveMessages(){
```

```
        var expectedMessage = new TestMessage();

        SendMessageToIntegrationTestBus(expectedMessage);

        awaiter.WaitOne(1000);


        var receivedMessage = messageHandler.Read();


        Assert.That(receivedMessage, Is.Equal(message))
    }
  }
```

What's the difference in this implementation? We used an event in the message handler to notify the external world that a new message has been queued up. Assuming no one listens to the event in production, there is no impact on the behavior.

How does this influence our tests? It gives us the option of hooking up an awaiter directly on that event, so that when the message arrives at destination, we know we can dequeue it! The behavior would be exactly the same only if the message doesn't get delivered in one second since `awaiter.WaitOne(1000)` will trigger the timeout and the test would fail. Here, we have effectively removed CoTm for our tests' happy path!

We're aware that some readers will argue that we actually modified our production code for the sake of testing. Obviously, this is a trade-off, and we always appreciate this kind of critical thinking. However, consider that the event would be fired *if and only if* there is a handler attached to the event—so production behavior doesn't change at all.

Ultimately, what makes it worthwhile is related to the time we save when we run our tests! If there are many integration tests or the latency could vary (and hopefully you run them often), the advantages of removing this CoTm become evident very soon.

Connascence of Identity

We have **Connascence of Identity** (**CoI**) when *one or more components must reference exactly one particular instance of another entity* to work correctly.

This is the strongest form of connascence in code and it is usually not easy to spot. The code apparently looks fine, but gives errors under certain conditions. The dependency in this case is within the creational context of a particular entity. Given the distributed nature of modern systems, it is almost never a good idea to rely on a particular instance of any object.

Let's see a simple example (and let's forget about thread safety):

```
public class GlobalCounter{
    int count = 0;

    public void Increment(){
        count++;
    }

    public int CurrentCount(){
        return count;
    }
}


public class Controller{
    GlobalCounter _counter;

    public Controller(GlobalCounter counter){
        _counter = counter;
    }

    public ActionResult Home(){
        _counter.Increment();
    }
}
```

Such an implementation works correctly if and only if the controllers share the same instance of **GlobalCounter**. In this case, a better solution would be using some external persistence mechanism so that the counter would just send a command for the increment without relying on a shared state.

Connascence of Manual Task

The power of the concept of connascence resides in the fact that it is not just limited to code! Let's see this real life story to understand better the worst type of connascence of all.

I was once in a team that was building a new service for consuming messages from a new queue. The "classic" way they used was to configure a list of messages in the configuration, and for each message, configure a handler. So, for every new message, they had to add not just the handler, but also an entry in the configuration; hence, the two were connascent.

While sometimes this is unavoidable, I always try to minimize connascence, and I tried to remove it. So I decided to make the new service slightly different, smart enough to self-configure at startup and removing the connascent step of the configuration line. The result was great when testing it locally, but when the code was promoted to the integration environment, I discovered that it didn't work there for some reason I couldn't grasp. I was relatively new to the team, so after a quick investigation, I asked for help from a more seasoned team member.

He couldn't see anything evidently wrong either. We decided to investigate further, opening the deployment scripts, and there we found the culprit: more connascence at the deployment level! For every new message handled, they had to add a step in the deployment process, instructing the script to create a new subscription for it, with a dependency on the message type.

Do you see the big problem there? The *locality* of this connascence was so far away that even the older member of the team couldn't remember it. We had to open the build scripts to realize there was another manual extra step to do before it could work! "Add enough hidden steps like these and teams will spend more time trying to make things work, fidgeting with scripts and configuration, than actually focusing on writing clean, well-designed code."

This kind of connascence is far worse than any other, because it goes against the very first reason we want CI and DevOps. Ultimately, we write software to automate an information flow so our mindset should be focused on achieving full smooth automation for the deployment process on our physical (or cloud) infrastructure. Any manual task is a drag in reaching that goal. We call this type of connascence the *Connascence of Manual Task*.

The way we solved it was straightforward. In the same way the service was able to self-configure at startup, we added the ability to check if the subscription was set up in the environment, setting it up when missing. Easy to do, once you think about it!

Classic TDD Flow

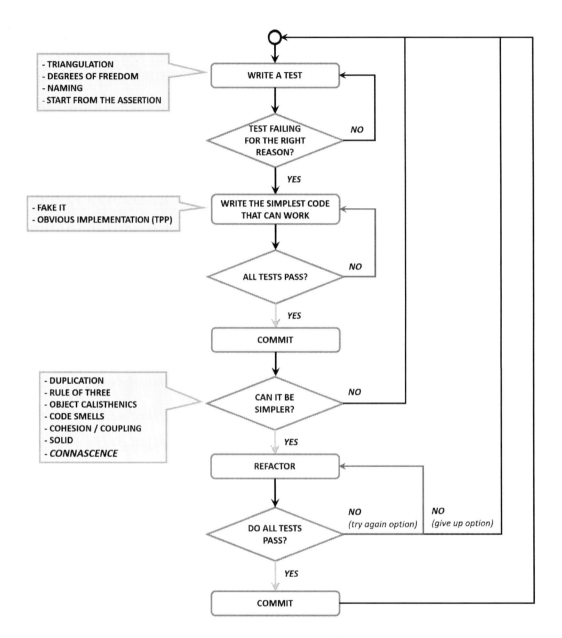

Figure 13.6: Classic TDD flow

The Big Picture

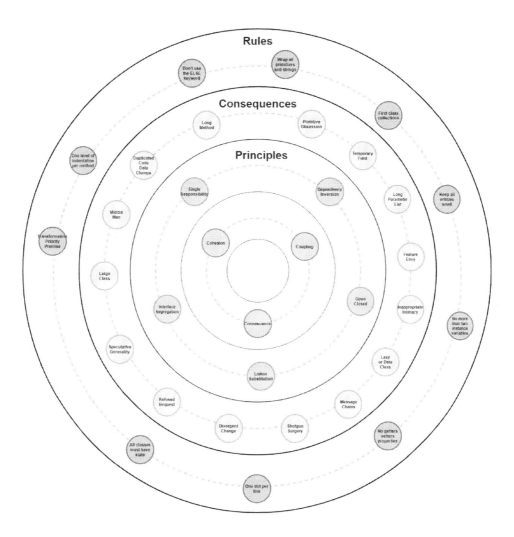

Figure 13.7: The big picture

When Should I Move to the Next Lesson?

- When you understand the concept of connascence and can identify it.

- When you understand the connection between connascence, cohesion, coupling, code smells, and the solid principles.

Resources

Web

- About Connascence, Codesai: https://www.codesai.com/2017/01/about-connascence.

- The Building Blocks of Modularity, Jim Weirich: https://www.youtube.com/watch?v=l780SYuz9DI.

- Comparing Techniques by Means of Encapsulation and Connascence, Meilir Page-Jones: http://wiki.cfcl.com/pub/Projects/Connascence/Resources/p147-page-jones.pdf.

- Connascence Examined, Jim Weirich: https://www.youtube.com/watch?v=HQXVKHoUQxY.

- The Grand Unified Theory, Jim Weirich: https://www.youtube.com/watch?time_continue=2890&v=NLT7Qcn_PmI.

- The Page-Jones refactoring algorithm, Kevin Rutherford: https://silkandspinach.net/2016/06/09/the-page-jones-refactoring-algorithm/.

- Understanding Coupling and Cohesion, Corey Haines, et al.: https://www.youtube.com/watch?v=hd0v72pD1MI.

Books

- Fundamentals of Object-Oriented Design in UML, Meilir Page-Jones: https://www.goodreads.com/book/show/179210.Fundamentals_of_Object_Oriented_Design_in_UML.

- Practical Guide to Structured Systems Design, Meilir Page-Jones: https://www.goodreads.com/book/show/1441004.Practical_Guide_to_Structured_Systems_Design.

- Structured Design: Fundamentals of a Discipline of Computer Program and Systems Design, Edward Yourdon and Larry L. Constantine: https://www.goodreads.com/book/show/946145.Structured_Design.

- What Every Programmer Should Know About Object-Oriented Design, Meilir Page-Jones: https://www.goodreads.com/book/show/1694645.What_Every_Programmer_Should_Know_about_Object_Oriented_Design.

14

Design VIII – The Four Elements of Simple Design

Simplicity is the ultimate sophistication.

– Generally attributed to Leonardo Da Vinci

I personally love the four elements of simple design. It is the highest-level set of principles, more like a set of goals to pursue with a defined priority than rigid rules to apply or break. This meshes well with my personality, but it also works really well when you have to make trade-off decisions while refactoring the design.

In my opinion, the key element of the set is the focus on *expressivity*, considered one of the fundamental properties of good design. While the other three elements are very important, and we have seen many practices and principles that support them, I feel that there is generally not enough consideration about code expressing its intentions.

Working on a very clean and expressive code base is the most satisfying technical experience for me as a developer. Knowing that I can easily find out where a particular thing occurs or where we should add a class in order to expand the behavior is priceless. And usually that also means getting stories flying over the kanban board, making the stakeholders happy. I have experienced this only on teams writing expressive code.

What Are the Four Elements of Simple Design?

- Passes its tests.

- Minimizes duplication.

- Maximizes clarity.

- Has less elements.

> **Note**
>
> JB Rainsberger, The Four Elements of Simple Design: http://www.jbrains.ca/permalink/the-four-elements-of-simple-design.

It makes sense to follow rules in the order they are enunciated. Applying these rules, we can create correct, compact, expressive, and succinct code. The four rules of simple design define what good design looks like.

What Does Each Element Mean?

Passes Its Tests

TDD is a very effective way to limit the amount of code we write, as we are only writing enough code to make the failing test pass. Tests help prove that the system is implementing the expected behaviors. There is no point in having a beautifully designed system if it does not implement the expected behaviors; this is why *Passes its tests* is the first rule.

Tests also allow us to refactor the design with caution, allowing us to tackle design issues safely and effectively. Finally, tests serve as documentation to improve the clarity of the system.

Minimizes Duplication

Duplication is the first code smell we examined in this book. It is an important indicator we can use to detect problems in our code. Removing duplication often leads us to create new abstractions that more clearly express the intent of the code, thus increasing clarity.

Code duplication leads to many problems in design. This is the reason why this is the second rule. After each test, we should look for duplication and refactor it out of our system.

Maximizes Clarity

We should always favor the reader when writing code. Clarity can be achieved by naming, but also by creating meaningful abstractions that encapsulate details. Often the need for new abstractions emerges from duplication issues that must be solved.

"...usually names tend to go through four stages: nonsense, accurate-but-vague, precise, and then meaningful or intention-revealing, as Kent Beck described it. I focus my efforts on gradually moving names to the right of this spectrum. Instead of agonizing over the choice of a name, I simply pick a name, confident that I always look for opportunities to move names towards becoming meaningful."

> **Note**
>
> JB Rainsberger, The Four Elements of Simple Design: http://www.jbrains.ca/permalink/the-four-elements-of-simple-design.

"Many people try to come up with a great name all at once. This is hard and rarely works well. The problem is that naming is design: it is picking the correct place for each thing and creating the right abstraction. Doing that perfectly the first time is unlikely."

– Arlo Belshee

Very often you hear that you have to write readable code to make it more maintainable. Making it readable is not enough; try to write obvious code. If you reach the point where you think, *Do I really need to be this explicit?*, then you have achieved the goal.

Clarity is achieved not just from good names but also from good abstractions that express intent in design. Code smells, solid violations, low cohesion, high coupling, and high connascence reduce clarity.

Has Fewer Elements

If we can have a system that passes its tests, minimizes duplication, and maximizes clarity, we have already achieved an exquisite design. The next step is to check if we can maintain the mentioned design characteristics by employing fewer elements. This last rule is the icing on the cake.

Alternative Definitions of Simple Design

Since the four elements of simple design express high-level goals instead of low-level rules, they allow for a great degree of personalization in how they are expressed. That's because everyone uses their own favorite set of principles and values to express what is key to achieving these goals. Hence, we have found several different versions of the elements, each one different, yet all expressing the same goals. Here are a few of them:

Definition #1

- Passes the tests

- Reveals intention

- No duplication

- Fewest elements

> Martin Fowler, BeckDesignRules: https://martinfowler.com/bliki/BeckDesignRules.html.

Definition #2

- Passes all the tests

- Expresses every idea that we need to express

- Says everything once and only once

- Has no superfluous parts

Definition #3

- Unit tests tell you when you are done

- Self-documenting code

- Once and only once, don't repeat yourself, redundancy is inertia

- You aren't going to need it, minimum number of classes and methods

Definition #4

- Runs all the tests

- Maximizes cohesion

- Minimizes coupling

- Says everything once and only once

Definition #5

- Runs all the tests

- Contains no duplication (once and only once)

- Expresses all the ideas you want to express:

  – Do not put the implementation of unrelated ideas in the same method

  – Classes should organize ideas in a readily understandable way

  – Use appropriate names so you don't have to explain method, member, or class names with additional documentation

  – Methods and classes should be implemented so they can be understood totally from their public interfaces. This not only allows for up-front testing, but decreases coupling.

- Minimizes classes and methods. This is actually redundant, but it's a reminder that we are trying to make this simple and concise.

Definition #6

- Pass all tests

- Clear, expressive, and consistent

- Duplicates no behavior or configuration

- Minimal methods, classes, and modules

> **Note**
>
> Definitions #2 - #6: Xp, Simplicity Rules: http://wiki.c2.com/?XpSimplicityRules.

Our Personal Definitions of Simple Design

Let's also look at our own personal definitions of simple design:

Pedro

- Correct and provable behavior
- Favors the reader
- Balanced cohesion and coupling
- Minimal elements

Marco

- Proves business correctness with tests
- Expresses functional behavior
- Minimizes entropy

Alessandro

- Correct and provable behavior
- Obvious code
- Behavior attractors
- Minimal moving parts

Kata

Elevator Kata by Marco Consolaro

Implement a controller for an elevator system considering the following requirements.

For evaluation purposes, assume that it takes one second to move the elevator from one floor to another and the doors stay open for three seconds at every stop.

Part I

The building has a total of five floors, including the basement and the ground floor. The elevator can be called at any floor only when it is not in use via one call button.

Given the elevator is positioned on the ground floor:

> When there is a call from floor 3 to go to the basement
>
> And there is a call from the ground floor to go to the basement
>
> And there is a call from floor 2 to go to the basement
>
> And there is a call from floor 1 to go to floor 3
>
> Then the doors should open at floor 3, basement, ground, basement, floor 2, basement, floor 1, and floor 3 in this order

Part II

The elevator is not fast enough, so as an experiment to speed it up, the idea is to allow the elevator to queue the requests and optimize the trips.

The elevator can now queue the stop requests from the floors and collect people along the way, but cannot change direction once it's started until all calls in the same direction have been fulfilled.

Given the elevator is positioned on the ground floor:

> When there is a call from floor 3 to go to the basement
>
> And there is a call from the ground floor to go to the basement
>
> And there is a call from floor 2 to go to the basement
>
> And there is a call from floor 1 to go to floor 3
>
> Then the doors should open at floor 3, floor 2, the ground floor, the basement, floor 1, and floor 3, in this order.

Nonfunctional requirement: The total time spent in the process of Part II should be less than the time spent with the algorithm of Part I.

Classic TDD Flow

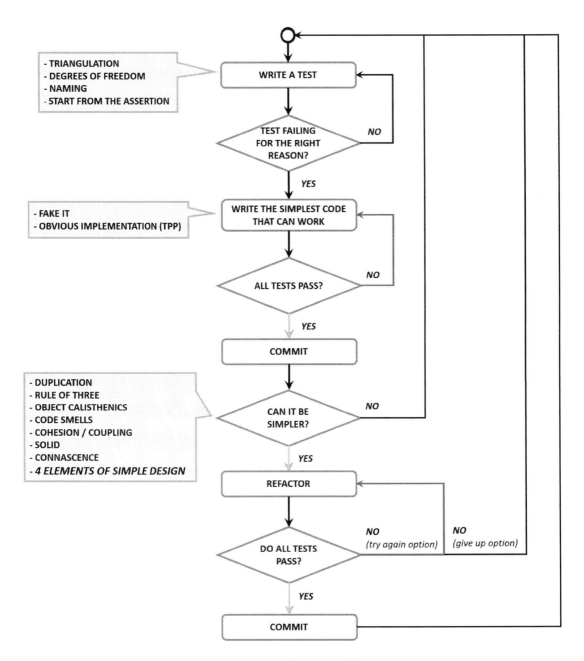

Figure 14.1: Classic TDD flow

The Big Picture

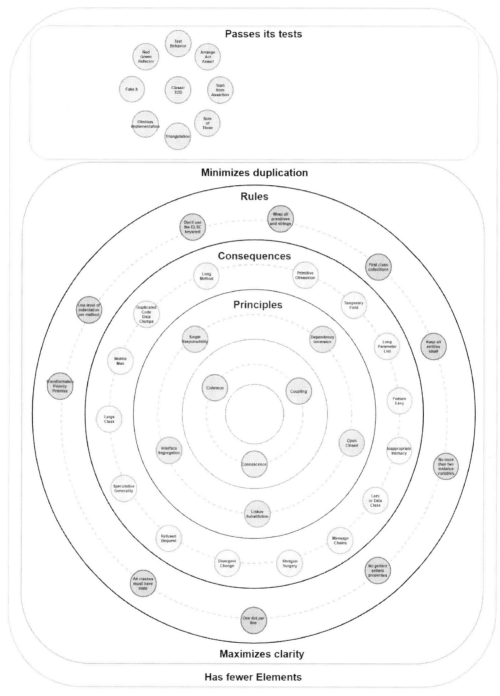

Figure 14.2: The big picture

When Should I Move to the Next Lesson?

When you have connected the dots on calisthenics, code smells, refactoring, solid, cohesion, and coupling.

Resources

Web

- Beck Design Rules, Martin Fowler: https://martinfowler.com/bliki/BeckDesignRules.html.

- The Four Elements of Simple Design, JB Rainsberger: http://www.jbrains.ca/permalink/the-four-elements-of-simple-design.

- Good naming is a process, not a single step, Arlo Belshee: http://arlobelshee.com/good-naming-is-a-process-not-a-single-step.

- Putting an Age-Old Battle to Rest, JB Rainsberger: http://blog.thecodewhisperer.com/2013/12/07/putting-an-age-old-battle-to-rest.

- Simple Made Easy, Rich Hickey: https://www.infoq.com/presentations/Simple-Made-Easy.

- XP simplicity rules: http://c2.com/cgi/wiki?XpSimplicityRules.

Books

- Understanding the Four Rules of Simple Design, Corey Haines: https://leanpub.com/4rulesofsimpledesign.

15
Conclusion

"We know the past but cannot control it. We control the future but cannot know it."

–Claude Shannon

This Claude Shannon quote is controversial and usually generates interesting conversations. The main observation is this: we don't really have full control of the future. That's actually a meaningful observation if we consider the latter portion of the quote about the future at a higher philosophical level (our inability to change the past being much less debatable).

What if we apply the latter portion of the quote to software development? Theoretically, in software development, we fully control the future, in that it's the way we are going to write the next piece of code. And the amount of control we have is proportional to how much we understand and how effectively we can act on the code base. In your code, the control you can have over your future is deeply connected to how you have been building in the past.

You could also argue (also controversially) that it's not absolutely correct to say we cannot control the past. What is refactoring, if not improving the code written in the past? That's another reason for refactoring as soon as possible, without delaying to a future moment – to keep the current state of the code in its best shape. Even refactoring itself will be much easier by enabling a positive feedback loop in your development effectiveness.

Eric Evans, in his epic *Domain-Driven Design* book, writes:

The returns for refactoring are not linear. Usually there is a marginal return for a small return and the small improvements add up. They fight entropy and they are the frontline protection against a fossilized legacy. But some of the most important insights come abruptly and send a shock through the project. [...]

Often, though, continuous refactoring prepares the way for something less orderly. Each refinement of code and model gives developers a clearer view. This clarity creates the potential for a breakthrough insights. [...] This sort of breakthrough is not a technique; it is an event.

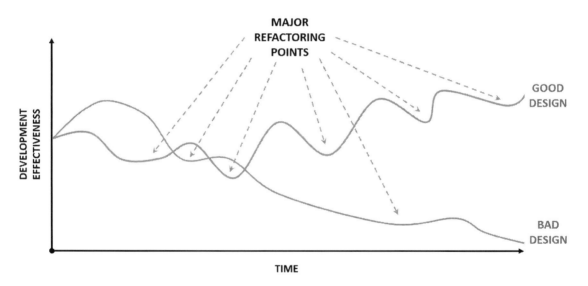

Figure 15.1: Good design and bad design, refactoring impact over time

So, in the long run, *development effectiveness* (understanding and acting quickly and effectively on a software system) depends on design. That is what really gives us the keys for controlling the future; the better the design, the more the control. That's why we focus so much on it.

Cohesion and Coupling as Forces

We can use the gravity force as an analogy for cohesion and coupling. Cohesion would be planet Earth's gravity, pulling everything inward. Coupling would be the Sun, pulling planet Earth and keeping it in its orbit.

Using this analogy, too much cohesion would create a black hole, and too little cohesion would create a barren planet, unable to support life as we know it. The same applies for coupling. Too much coupling and planets would collide with each other or would be swallowed by the Sun; too little coupling and we would not have the **Solar System** because each planet would wander by itself in the *Universe*.

Coupling and cohesion are in reality the same force. Cohesion is felt inwards and coupling outwards. We believe this to be the fundamental force in object-oriented design, just as gravity is the essential force in Newton's laws. The secret to great design is finding a good balance between cohesion and coupling.

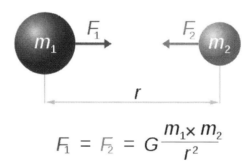

$$F_1 = F_2 = G\frac{m_1 \times m_2}{r^2}$$

Figure 15.2: Newton's law of universal gravitation

The 3 Cs of Design: From Cohesion and Coupling to Connascence

Just as the forces are deeply connected, so are the concepts of coupling, cohesion, and connascence. Let's look at this example to better understand this point:

```
public class OrderFlow
{
    public void Execute(int customerId, int categoryId, int[] itemIds)
    {
        var orderId = GenerateOrderId();
        orderProcessor.ProcessOrder(orderId, customerId, categoryId, itemIds);
```

```
            invoiceProcessor.ProcessInvoice(orderId, customerId, categoryId,
    itemIds);

        ...

    }

}
```

Look at this code from the point of view of coupling and cohesion. How does it look? Not really good, right? We have a long list of parameters that clearly make the method coupling score pretty high for the **Execute** method in the **OrderFlow** class, the **ProcessInvoice** method in the **InvoiceProcessor** class, and the **ProcessOrder** method in the **OrderProcessor** class. This is a classic example of data coupling.

The same **Execute** method also has cohesion problems because it generates order IDs internally. The main behavior of this method/class is to orchestrate the order flow (as its name suggests), not to generate order IDs. This is also a single-responsibility violation.

If we instead look from a point of view of **Code Smells**, we can call this a classic example of long parameter list code smell.

Finally, from the connascence perspective, it is an example of **Connascence of Position (CoP)**.

Let's see what happens if we refactor this code, trying to improve it:

```
public class OrderFlow

{

    public void Execute(Order order)

    {

        order.Process();

        invoiceProcessor.ProcessInvoiceFor(order);

        ...

    }

}
```

Is this version better? It looks definitely more readable, but how about coupling and cohesion?

From the point of view of coupling and cohesion, we removed the data coupling by introducing a more cohesive **Order** class, which drastically reduces the coupling score of this method. Moving the behavior closer to the data in the **Order** class also enhanced the cohesion of this code.

From the code smell aspect, we have removed the long parameter list smell.

Finally, we have also removed CoP for three classes: `OrderFlow`, `Order` and `Invoice`.

Fixing cohesion had an effect on coupling and connascence. Fixing coupling had an effect on cohesion and connascence. Fixing connascence had an effect on coupling and cohesion. It's as if *they are all the same force!*

Cohesion, coupling, connascence, the SOLID principles, and code smells are different manifestations of the same thing, and they are deeply connected. This is similar to electromagnetism, where there is always an interrelation between electric and magnetic fields.

Rules and principles help you before you write the code. Smells, cohesion, coupling, and connascence give you feedback on the design after the code is written.

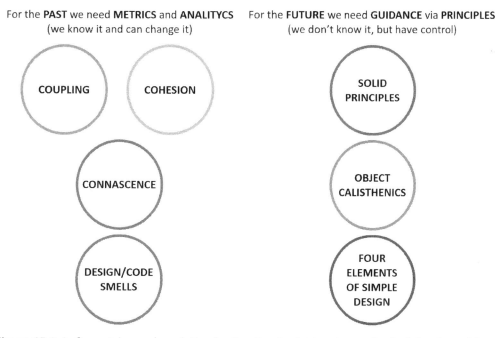

Figure 15.3: Left: metrics and analytics for feedback; right: rules and principles for guidance

From a higher perspective, cohesion/coupling/connascence are gauges for different aspects of the *entropy of the system*. They are actually a very powerful aspect from which to get feedback. From a systemic point of view, we can think of them as an index of contribution to the overall system entropy.

> **Note**
>
> Wikipedia, Entropy (information theory): https://en.wikipedia.org/wiki/Entropy_(information_theory).

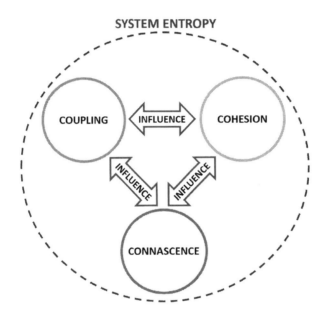

Figure 15.4: Coupling, cohesion, and connascence as gauges for entropy

Systems Entropy

Every single line of code we add to our system increases its overall entropy. If we allow it to grow without control, the maintainability and understandability of the system decreases very quickly. While we are developing a certain functionality, the concepts of cohesion, coupling, and connascence allow us to better understand the type and strength of the entropy we are adding. This is the reason that refactoring is such an important task. We use the feedback from our principles to refactor a system from high to low entropy.

The Relevance of Systems Entropy

In 1948, Claude Shannon published a paper, A *Mathematical Theory of Communication*, which is considered to be the beginning of an entirely new field of study called **Information Theory**. In this paper, he defines the concept of information entropy as a measure of the uncertainty in a message.

> **Note**
>
> Wikipedia, A Mathematical Theory of Communication: https://en.wikipedia.org/wiki/A_Mathematical_Theory_of_Communication.

We focus on the high-level concept of entropy, which can be seen in various aspects; all have mathematically proven equivalents. (We leave the math for the more curious readers – see the references at the end of this lesson).

> **Note**
>
> John J. Johnson IV, et al., A Theory of Emergence and Entropy in Systems of Systems: https://www.sciencedirect.com/science/article/pii/S1877050913010740.

In a very simplified but effective way, the concept of entropy in a system can be seen as:

- The energy dispersal rate of the system
- The degree of disorder in a system
- An increasing function of the number of possible states of a system

If entropy is the degree of disorder, it is evident that our goal is to minimize it.

> **Note**
>
> Erwin Schrodinger, in 1944, wrote a controversial book titled, What is Life?, where he said that if we look at living systems from the point of view of entropy, they do not maximize it. They appear instead to increase internal organization, hence minimizing entropy, using the external environment as a source of energy. We think minimization of entropy is key for success of any kind of system. https://en.wikipedia.org/wiki/What_Is_Life%3F, http://www.whatislife.ie/downloads/What-is-Life.pdf.

Software Development as System Building

Any program, as a means to move information from one place to another, or transform it from one form to another, is nothing more than a system. So, if we think of writing a program as equivalent to building a system, we can use a good deal of knowledge from information theory while developing software, and apply it for guidance.

The creativity involved in software development resides in the fact that any programming language exposes several tools that can be combined together in infinitely different ways. Among the tools provided by object-oriented design, perhaps the most relevant one is the concept of the **object**.

> **Note**
>
> From a purely probabilistic position, we can understand why writing good software it is so difficult!

So, from a systemic point of view, what is an object? Well, an object is... *a system*.

The outermost object represents the whole program (often called *Main... coincidence?*), which is the whole system. It is the interface with the external world, and it holds inside itself other objects that exchange information and work in collaboration to achieve a common goal. These objects are themselves systems. So the difference between a primitive and an object is that the former is seen as a mere part or component, while the latter is viewed as a proper system. Hence, from a general point of view, our programs are *systems of systems*.

Good Design as a Low-Entropy System

Seeing matters in this way allows us to think about *system entropy* in a much more pragmatic way. If the entropy is related to the *number of possible states of a system*, a simple object with only primitive fields is calculable as a combinatorial function of all possible values of its components.

That's not good news, because it means that there is a combinatorial entropy growth for every new field we add. It's not a surprise that the Single Responsibility Principle makes a lot of sense now.

What if instead of primitive fields, we had another object? That's the good news! In a system of independent systems (we can think here to independency related to testability; if I can test an object in isolation, it is independent from the state of other parts of the system), the overall entropy is given by the sum of the entropy of the single systems.

This means that we can transform a combinatorial growth into a linear one by embedding some parts in a new subsystem with its logic, and collaborate at the system level, instead of at the level of a basic part. In our development process, this means refactoring to a better abstraction that follows the principles expressed so far.

This basic idea is in agreement with all the practices and principles expressed in this book as far as we can think to good software design as a low-entropy system.

The Big Picture

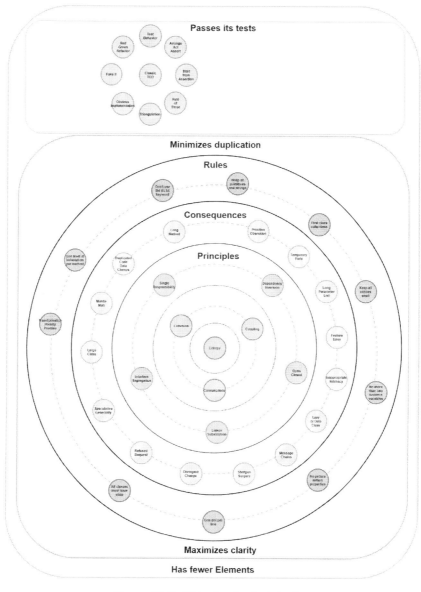

Figure 15.5: Object-oriented design

Resources

Web-based resources:

- Entropy (information theory), Wikipedia: https://en.wikipedia.org/wiki/Entropy_(information_theory).

- Entropy in thermodynamics and information theory, Wikipedia: https://en.wikipedia.org/wiki/Entropy_in_thermodynamics_and_information_theory.

- Information theory, Wikipedia: https://en.wikipedia.org/wiki/Information_theory.

- A Mathematical Theory of Communication, Clause Shannon: http://math.harvard.edu/~ctm/home/text/others/shannon/entropy/entropy.pdf.

- A Possible Ethical Imperative Based on the Entropy Law, Mehrdad Massoudi: https://www.mdpi.com/1099-4300/18/11/389.

- A Theory of Emergence and Entropy in Systems of Systems, John J. Johnson IV, et al.: https://www.sciencedirect.com/science/article/pii/S1877050913010740.

- Understanding Shannon's Entropy Metric for Information, Sriram Vajapeyam: https://arxiv.org/ftp/arxiv/papers/1405/1405.2061.pdf.

- What is life? Erwin Schrodinger: http://www.whatislife.ie/downloads/What-is-Life.pdf.

Books:

- Domain-Driven Design, Tackling Complexity in the Heart of Software, Eric Evans: https://www.goodreads.com/book/show/179133.Domain_Driven_Design.

- Structured Design: Fundamentals of a Discipline of Computer Program and Systems Design, Edward Yourdon: https://www.goodreads.com/book/show/946145.Structured_Design.

Flying

"He who would learn to fly one day, must first learn to stand and walk and run and climb and dance; one cannot fly into flying."

– Friedrich Nietzsche

16

Outside-In Development

"The key in making great and growable systems is much more to design how its modules communicate rather than what their internal properties and behaviors should be."

– Alan Kay

In this lesson, we start a journey where we move from building things right, to building the right things. Building things right is a more technical journey and revolves around the principles covered so far. Building the right things is a matter of business alignment and that involves several other abilities.

We will see in the following lessons that a business is made up of interactions between people, so while technical excellence is important, it is not enough, per se. We feel that real mastery encompasses this understanding. So let's begin this final part of the journey with one last technique which, in our experience, seamlessly enables a shift in perspective on development toward the business.

Outside-in is a development mindset, focused by default on the business view, bridging the gap between the two worlds naturally. This mindset derives from the **Outside-In TDD** approach, also called *London School* or *Mockist*. It is an alternative approach to **Test-Driven Design (TDD)**, leading us to first consider a point of view external of our class, starting with the design of the public interface. This, in turn, forces the developer to put himself in the shoes of the user, considering that person's needs first.

The beauty of this technique, in accordance with the Alan Kay quote at the beginning of the lesson, resides in the *servant approach* afforded by the focus on the functionality provided to the world outside the class, rather than its internals. This has many benefits:

- It naturally fits with a business-first view, using business functionality to drive the internal growth of the system.

- It naturally addresses **YAGNI (You Aren't Going to Need It)**, since nothing would be developed if not explicitly required by the business.

- It naturally minimizes entropy, because its focus on the public interface leads to the simplest way to communicate with the outside world, hiding the complexity of the internals.

- It naturally encourages expressivity, readability, clean code, and simple design, because the focus on public interfaces lends itself to immediate feedback on design and readability.

All of these points can also be achieved by using classic TDD, but it requires more effort from the software developer and does not come as naturally as in the outside-in approach.

The Classic TDD Approach

The classic TDD approach revolves around the idea of creating messy code and constantly refactoring it to clean it up. The mess in classic TDD is critical, since it provides feedback for refactoring the design.

The ideas of implementing the simplest thing that can work, and deferring important design decisions, are at the heart of classic TDD. The refactoring phase in classic TDD is vital; hence, good refactoring skills are key to its success. So having an understanding about code smells, the SOLID principles, and cohesion/coupling and connascence is a major advantage in changing the shape of the code before the mess turns into code that's too difficult to refactor.

The importance of the mess is highlighted by the **Rule of Three**, which stops us from premature refactors, maximizing the feedback to find the right pattern. The secret to this style of TDD lies in having the right amount of mess to provide feedback for design decisions, but not so much that refactoring becomes too painful.

There are some problems with classic TDD:

- It gravitates toward a more technical solution, and it's easier to lose the business focus.

- It can sometimes be a bit inefficient when exploration is not in heavy demand.

- It can lead to implementing behavior that is not required, especially if we start from the inside of the system toward the outside. There is a constant temptation to implement features that we *think* we will need on the outside of the system, thus not addressing the risk of YAGNI very well.

All of this being said, classic TDD, when in the hands of experienced software engineers who are aware of the pitfalls described here, is an amazing way to develop software. In the following diagram, we try to capture the high-level flow of software growth using classic TDD:

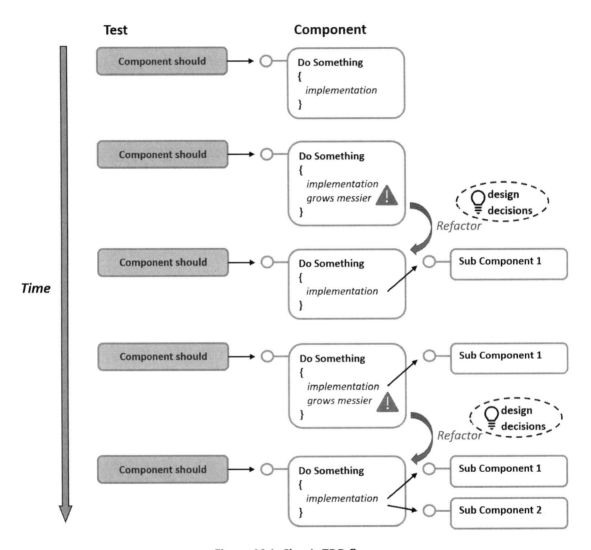

Figure 16.1: Classic TDD flow

Acceptance Tests

We borrow this concept from other engineering fields such as mechanical, chemical or civil engineering. Wikipedia defines *acceptance tests* as follows:

In engineering and its various sub-disciplines, acceptance testing is a test conducted to determine if the requirements of a specification or contract are met. It may involve chemical tests, physical tests, or performance tests.

– Wikipedia

The **ISTQB** (**International Software Testing Qualifications Board**) defines acceptance tests in the context of software design as follows:

Formal testing with respect to user needs, requirements, and business processes conducted to determine whether or not a system satisfies the acceptance criteria and to enable the user, customers or other authorized entity to determine whether or not to accept the system.

– International Software Testing Qualifications Board

> **Note**
>
> International Software Testing Qualifications Board, ISTQB Glossary: http://glossary.istqb.org/search/.

Acceptance tests are the formalization of an acceptance criteria, defined by ISTQB as follows:

The criteria that a component or system must satisfy in order to be accepted by a user, customer, or other authorized entity.

– International Software Testing Qualifications Board

> **Note**
>
> International Software Testing Qualifications Board, ISTQB Glossary: http://glossary.istqb.org/search/.

Acceptance criteria defines *what needs to be done*, and acceptance tests define *how it should be done*.

Acceptance tests are organized similar to the arrange-act-assert sections of a unit test. However, in acceptance tests, these sections are usually known as give-when-then: *given* some context, *when* some action is carried out, *then* a set of consequences should happen.

We will go more in detail on this subject in the next lesson. Patience is the virtue of the strong.

Acceptance tests are also similar to unit tests since they can only have one of two states: pass or fail. Where they differ is with their goals; acceptance tests are related to a use case scenario, and consequently to a business scenario. Acceptance tests are used to verify that business requirements are met, so are closely tied to the business requirement that they are trying to prove.

Acceptance Test Styles

Unit test style

This is constructed using a unit test framework, as follows:

```
class CarShould
{
  [Test]
  void decrease_speed_when_brakes_are_applied()
  {
      var car = new Car();
      car.Accelerate(10);
      var beforeBreakingVelocity = car.Speed();


      car.Break(5);


      Assert.That(car.Speed(), Is.LessThan(beforeBreakingVelocity));
  }
}
```

Given, when, then (GWT) style

English language style, example: Gherkin language:

```
Given I have a car
And I accelerate for 10 seconds
And I break for 5 seconds
When I measure the velocity
Then the velocity should be lower than the one measured before breaking.
```

Tabular style

This involves Excel-like notation. An example is FitNesse.

> **Note**
>
> FitNesse: http://docs.fitnesse.org.

Test Boundaries

The introduction of acceptance tests forces a discussion on test boundaries. What are the boundaries of an acceptance test? What about the boundaries of unit tests, integration tests, and end-to-end tests? In the following diagram, we try to convey our views on different tests boundaries.

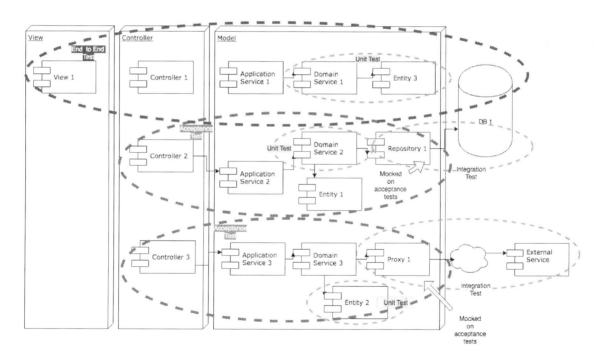

Figure 16.2: Test boundaries

The problem is that test terminology is not very standardized, and in our experience, we have seen some confusion about the different concepts of tests. Hopefully, the following definitions clarify the terminology:

- **End to end tests**: Focused on business requirements. Exercise the complete flow, including external systems. Usually, these tests are slow to execute.

- **Acceptance tests**: Focused on business requirements. Exercise all parts of the flow in our system. Compromise on feedback and speed of execution. Faster than end to end tests, but not as thorough.

- **Integration tests**: Focused on technical implementation. Exercise parts of our system that connect with external systems. Can be slow to execute, depending on external system and the integration with it.

- **Unit tests**: Focused on atomic behaviors. Exercise parts of the flow in our system. Very fast to execute.

Double Loop TDD

Double loop TDD introduces the concept of acceptance tests in the Red -> Green -> Refactor classic TDD loop. The idea is to have a high-level test that covers a business requirement. As the name implies, we add a second loop to our TDD loop. This is an outer loop and also has Red -> Green -> Refactor stages. In this acceptance test, with the outside loop, we are effectively creating an **executable definition of "done."**

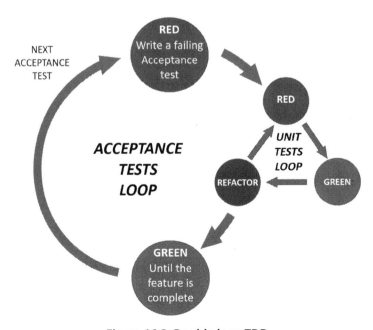

Figure 16.3: Double loop TDD

When starting a new feature, we begin by writing an acceptance test. This test will inevitably fail since we are lacking an implementation. Before we move on, we need to make sure our acceptance test is failing because it doesn't meet the acceptance criteria. This usually forces us to define the external API of our system.

Once we have a failing acceptance test, we move to the inner loop and stay on it until the acceptance test becomes green. The inner loop corresponds to the TDD unit test loop that we covered in the previous lessons. As our design evolves, we may have to revisit the initial high-level design decisions we made in the acceptance test. This is absolutely fine. We still want to make most design decisions in the inner or unit test loop.

Before going too deep into this subject, we recommend that you have a good grasp of the lesson about `Test Doubles`, because they are heavily used for Outside-in style. If you feel you need to refresh the topic of `Test Doubles`, please do so before moving forward.

The Outside-In Approach

Outside-in is not just a testing strategy; it is a development approach. There is a misunderstanding that considers outside-in as a *Mockist* testing approach. You can do outside-in development using a classic testing approach. You can even do outside-in development without tests. Outside-in, from a systemic point of view, means focusing first on one of the most important aspects, **the public interface**, which for a system represents the communication with the external world. Remember that we see software as a system of systems? This is the reason for the quote of Alan Kay at the beginning of this lesson.

Furthermore, using this way of development fits incredibly well with the most popular IDE frameworks. Sketching the outside-in methods allows us to use quick shortcuts for almost every operation involving interface creation, class creation and method creation. It makes development mainly a matter of naming things and using the autocomplete functionality of the IDE, leveraging its full potential, letting it do all the heavy work without typos. We highly suggest you try out this way of developing; we still haven't met anyone yet who, once they've learned it, went back to their previous way.

An Outside-In Mindset

Outside-In is a great way to align with the business, growing the code and sketching the collaboration between different subsystems. It is focused on delivering the value for the business first, moving to the implementation and unit testing strategy afterward.

The outside-in mindset works as follows:

- From the outside to the inside
- From high-level responsibilities to low-level details
- From the main goal, to the steps to reach it
- From strategic to tactical
- Following the dependency flow

Let's go over a quick example. Imagine we are building a microwave oven class. The outside-in flow starts with the sketching of the class we are going to build first, which in this case is the `MicrowaveOven` class. Let's leave tests aside for a moment and use instead the `Main` method to start, at the outermost boundary:

```
public void Main(){

    var oven = new MicrowaveOven();

}
```

At this point, we don't have the implementation of the class yet, so the IDE shows it highlighted in red. But if we prompt the suggestions, one of them says something like, create type `MicrowaveOven`. Let's select it and let it do the magic. Now we have something like this:

```
public void Main(){

    var oven = new MicrowaveOven();

}


public class MicrowaveOven(){

}
```

At this point, we can move the **MicrowaveOven** class to its own file, or carry on in the same file and delay this operation later. To move on, now we need to implement the **Cook** method. First, we sketch it:

```
public void Main(){


  var oven = new MicrowaveOven();

  oven.Cook(5);



}


public class MicrowaveOven(){


}
```

The IDE will show it in red again, because it is not implemented. Let's open its **Suggestions Helper**. We now see one of the options saying `create Method`. Let's select it and rename the parameter to **minutes**. We would have something like this:

```
public void Main(){


  var oven = new MicrowaveOven();

  oven.Cook(5);



}


public class MicrowaveOven(){


  public void Cook(int minutes){

    throw new System.NotImplementedException();

  }


}
```

We have now sketched the `MicrowaveOven` public interface. We put ourselves in the shoes of the user first and started the implementation from the outside. The main goal of this approach is making sure that the public interface is *intuitive to use*; that is, it is immediately understandable for whoever will use it in the future.

Next, we can step inside its own level of abstraction by implementing the `Cook` method.

Inside that method, we now realize that we need to do just one thing; switch the microwave generator on for the number of minutes stated in the method. So, we need a collaborator, and here we have two choices:

1. We can create a strong dependency and let the oven be responsible for it.

    OR

2. We can inject it so we could change it at runtime and test the generator in isolation.

Let's go with the first option for simplicity and see how the flow carries on using an `IGenerateMicrowaves` interface.

```
public class MicrowaveOven(){


    private IGenerateMicrowaves _microwaveGenerator = new MicrowaveGenerator();


    public void Cook(int minutes){
        throw new System.NotImplementedException();
    }
}
```

We now have two red items in the new line of code: the `IGenerateMicorwaves` interface and the concrete `MicrowavesGenerator`. Let's use the suggestions again, beginning from the interface. Here the *create interface* suggestion is straightforward, and we can afterward move on the concrete and use again the *create type*. The IDE is quite smart in this situation, already making the type inherit from the interface:

```
public class MicrowaveGenerator : IGenerateMicrowaves

{
}
```

```
public interface IGenerateMicrowaves

{

}
```

Let's leave these empty and keep focusing on our **MicrowaveOven** class; we still have an ugly **throw** there to remove. Now we can finally tell the generator to switch itself on, as we were planning! We start again by sketching its public interface:

```
public class MicrowaveOven(){


    private IGenerateMicrowaves _microwaveGenerator = new MicrowaveGenerator();


    public void Cook(int minutes){
        _microwaveGenerator.SwitchOnFor(minutes);
    }
}
```

The method, as usual, is highlighted red. Let's open the automatic suggestion and select the option to create the **IGenerateMicrowaves.SwitchOn** method and rename the parameter to **minutes**. Voilà! The interface now becomes:

```
public interface IGenerateMicrowaves

{
    void SwitchOnFor(int minutes);
}
```

We can see something else turning red now: the **MicrowaveGenerator** class marked with the problem of not implementing the **IGenerateMicrowaves** interface, because it is obviously missing that method. But we have the handy suggestion to *implement missing members*, which will add the method automatically:

```
public class MicrowaveGenerator : IGenerateMicrowaves

{
    public void SwitchOnFor(int minutes)
    {
        throw new System.NotImplementedException();
    }
}
```

Typically, at this point, we have two choices. We can use a breadth-first strategy and carry on with the implementation of the `Cook` method in case there are other things to do there, and keep the focus of the current level of abstraction, or implement the `SwitchOnFor` method in the `MicrowavesGenerator` class. The flow would again be the same: write the public interface first and delay the implementation. Rinse and repeat.

If, instead of starting from the `Main` method, we used a test to drive the code and inject the dependencies of the collaborators using mocks/stubs, this approach becomes even more powerful. That's the idea behind the *London School of TDD*.

Outside-In TDD: The London School

Outside-in TDD is also commonly know as the *London School of TDD*, **acceptance test driven development** (**ATDD**) or **Mockist TDD**. In Outside-In TDD, we use mocks to sketch the design of parts of the system we don't know much about yet.

Contrary to classic TDD, we don't wait to create a mess to extract sub-components; we use mocks to sketch them as soon as we write a test. Whereas in classic TDD, most design decisions happened in the refactoring phase, in Outside-In TDD, the design decisions about public interfaces happen in the red stage.

Here, the concept of responsibility becomes key. Identifying the different responsibilities gives us an idea of the kind of collaboration we might need. There is no need to implement the sub-module in this stage, however, because we can stub it and fake its behavior for our test.

This operation is a crucial design decision in itself, because what we are doing here is *designing the public interface of the collaborator*, deferring the context switch to its implementation. It's essentially a way to break down the problems into sub-tasks, solving it one abstraction layer at a time, instead of immediately going deep. This approach has an incredible advantage in keeping the mind focused on one sub-problem at a time, on one responsibility at time, and on one abstraction level at a time.

Another big difference between Outside-In TDD and classic TDD is the nature of assertions. In classic TDD, we usually write state-based assertions (`assert some-value-returned-by-function is equal to some-expected-value`). Outside-In favors the *Tell, don't ask* heuristic of commands over queries. So assertions are usually based on collaboration with some other components (**Mock**).

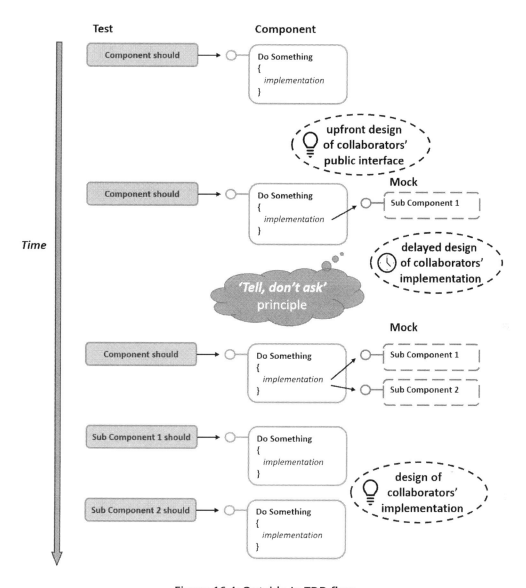

Figure 16.4: Outside-In TDD flow

In the previous diagram, we tried to capture the flow of software growth using Outside-In TDD. As with classic TDD, we start by writing a test, but now we immediately try to sketch a collaborator and write the assertion around that collaboration. Once we have a passing test, we can either move inside and use the same strategy with the collaborator (that now becomes the new test subject) and find its collaborator(s), or we find other collaborators for the current component and use the same strategy.

Restrain from mocking every abstraction layer in your module. Test it as black box through the public interface while being declarative and assertive about your interaction with other modules.

Example

In this example, we are implementing a scenario where we have to add a product to a customer's shopping cart on a website. In this case, the customer is a **Gold** customer and is entitled to a discount.

We start by writing an acceptance test for this scenario:

Given I have a product.

And I have a customer that is a gold customer.

When I add the product to the customer shopping cart with a quantity of 1.

Then the shopping cart should be saved with the gold customer discount applied.

In this case, we just specify the acceptance test without showing the implementation for the sake of space. In the following implementation, we use the acceptance test to guide us on what unit tests to write.

After the acceptance test, we move to the inner unit test loop. Starting from the outside, we first write a test for the shopping cart controller. We start by identifying the controller collaborator, in this case the shopping cart. Once we have an idea of the collaborator, we create a mock for it and decide how the controller should collaborate with the shopping cart. Using the mock for the shopping cart, we write an assertion on the collaboration.

```
class ShoppingCartControllerShould
{
  [Test]
  void add_product_to_shopping_cart()
  {
      var ABookId = 12345;
      var ACustomerId = 54321;
      var AQuantity = 1;
```

```
        var shoppingCart = new Mock<ShoppingCart>();

        var shoppingCartController = new ShoppingCartController(shoppingCart);


        shoppingCartController.Post(ACustomerID, ABookId, AQuantity);


        shoppingCart.Verify.Add(ACustomerId, ABookID, AQuantity).WasCalled();
    }
}
```

The next test uses the same strategy, but we are now testing the shopping cart and its collaboration with the discount calculator.

```
class ShoppingCartShould
{
  [Test]
  void add_product_to_shopping_cart_with_discount_for_gold_customers()
  {
      var ABookId = 12345;
      var ACustomerId = 54321;
      var AQuantity = 1;
      var discountCalculator = new Mock<DiscountCalculator>();
      var repository = new Mock<ShoppingCartRepository>();
      var shoppingCart = new ShoppingCart(discountCalculator, repository);


      shoppingCart.Add(ACustomerId, ABookID, AQuantity);


      discountCalculator.Verify.ApplyDiscount(shoppingCart).WasCalled();
  }
}
```

Finally, we test the shopping cart collaboration with a repository to persist its state.

```
class ShoppingCartShould
{
  [Test]
  void save_shopping_cart()
  {
      var ABookId = 12345;
      var ACustomerId = 54321;
      var AQuantity = 1;
      var discountCalculator = new Mock<DiscountCalculator>();
      var repository = new Mock<ShoppingCartRepository>();
      var shoppingCart = new ShoppingCart(discountCalculator, repository);


      shoppingCart.Add(ACustomerId, ABookID, AQuantity);


      repository.Verify.Save(shoppingCart).WasCalled();
  }
}
```

The Direction of Dependencies

Dependencies have a direction. So, what is the correct direction? Let's consider this with the following diagram:

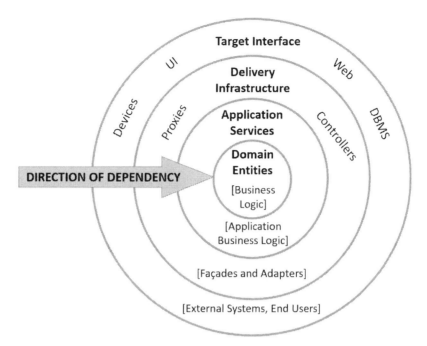

Figure 16.5: The direction of dependencies

The dependencies should follow a direction of movement from what is more likely to change, toward what is less likely to change; hence, abstraction should not depend on details. The domain should be the pure part of our code, ideally with no dependencies to anything else, since it's the least likely to change.

If you think about it, this makes sense; the business logic should be self-containing and should work correctly without caring if the information is saved on this or that database, displayed on the web, or in a CSV file. Changing a webpage to display information in an alternative way should be possible without changing the domain, and it happens way more often than modifications of the domain itself.

Outside-In naturally follows the same direction of dependencies.

Should I Use Classic TDD or Outside-In TDD?

Both. They are two different approaches, and different situations require different strategies. The question is not *"should I use classic TDD or Outside-In TDD?"*, but rather *"when should I use classic TDD and when should I use Outside-In TDD?"*

When our knowledge of the problem/domain is not very high, classic TDD is a great way to discover/explore solutions. If you are a beginner, classic TDD is a lot more accessible, since you don't have to take design decisions without feedback. Outside-In TDD requires a deeper knowledge of design since we don't get the feedback loop of the mess, but it can be a lot more efficient and focused on the business. In the end, *context is king*, and we should use the most appropriate technique required by the context.

Kata

Stock Portfolio

Implement the following user story using Outside-In TDD starting from an acceptance test.

Portfolio user story

```
As a customer of our stock exchange broker

I would like to see my current portfolio

So I can better plan my financial strategy
```

Portfolio scenario

We need to provide a class able to record the buy and sell operations of a customer and display the information as per the acceptance criteria. For simplicity, you can assume it should work for just one user at a time.

Portfolio criteria

```
Given I bought 1000 shares of "Old School Waterfall Software LTD" on
14/02/1990

    and I bought 400 shares of "Crafter Masters Limited" on 09/06/2016

    and I bought 700 shares of "XP Practitioners Incorporated" on 10/12/2018

    and I sold 500 shares of "Old School Waterfall Software LTD" on 11/12/2018

    and the current share value of "Old School Waterfall Software LTD" is
$5.75

    and the current share value of "Crafter Masters Limited" is $17.25

    and the current share value of "XP Practitioners Incorporated" is $25.55

When I print my current portfolio
```

Then the outcome displayed should be as follows:

```
company | shares | current price | current value | last operation
Old School Waterfall Software LTD | 500 | $5.75 | $2,875.00 | sold 500 on
11/12/2018
Crafter Masters Limited | 400 | $17.25 | $6,900.00 | bought 400 on 09/06/2016
XP Practitioners Incorporated | 700 | $25.55 | $17,885.00 | bought 700 on
10/12/2018
```

Sorted by first operation date ascending.

Katacombs of Shoreditch by Marco Consolaro

This kata is a little more structured and challenging, so you can try to put many concepts and principles into practice in a domain that can benefit from them. This is quite a large kata, so expect to spend some time with it.

Inspired by Colossal Cave Adventure, this is a kata for building a text-based adventure game that can be expanded *incrementally* and *indefinitely*, and is limited only by your imagination.

> **Note**
>
> https://en.wikipedia.org/wiki/Colossal_Cave_Adventure.

The game is based on a console application that describes a fictional underground world to be explored by the player via a set of commands. The world is a collection of locations linked to each other geographically (in terms of North, South, East or West) or via specific connection points (doors, passages, gates, stairs, and so on). The player can move among the locations using cardinal points for directions, or exploiting the connection points with actions or items.

Other important aspects:

- It is possible to simply look in every direction, but not all the directions are always available for being looked at, nor to move to.

- The world will have treasures hidden in several locations, which can be revealed if players enter the location or uses the correct item in the correct location.

- The game terminates when the player finds the exit of the katacombs, and the score is the sum of the value of the treasures collected.

- When looking somewhere without anything interesting, the system should reply, *Nothing interesting to look at there!*

- When a general action is not available, the system will reply, *I can't do that here!*

- When the system can't understand the command, it should prompt, *I don't understand that. English please!*

Part I

Starting the game

The game at startup shows the **title** and **main description** of the initial location. When the player moves to another location, the system always prompts **title** and **main description** for the new location.

```
LOST IN SHOREDITCH.

YOU ARE STANDING AT THE END OF A BRICK LANE BEFORE A SMALL BRICK BUILDING
CALLED THE OLD TRUMAN BREWERY.

AROUND YOU IS A FOREST OF RESTAURANTS AND BARS. A SMALL STREAM OF CRAFTED
BEER FLOWS OUT OF THE BUILDING AND DOWN A GULLY.
```

Exploring the world:

Moving

Movement is expressed with GO, followed by the letter of the cardinal point.

```
> GO N => move to the NORTH
> GO E => move to the EAST
> GO S => move to the SOUTH
> GO W => move to the WEST
```

Stairs

Movement on stairs is expressed with GO followed by UP or DOWN, depending on which direction the stairs are leading.

```
> GO UP => use stairs to go up
> GO DOWN => use stairs to go down
```

Looking

LOOK allows the player to look in every direction to get an idea of the surroundings or a better description of an item.

```
LOST IN SHOREDITCH.
YOU ARE STANDING AT THE END OF A BRICK LANE BEFORE A SMALL BRICK BUILDING
```

CALLED THE TRUMAN BREWERY. AROUND YOU IS A FOREST OF RESTAURANTS AND BARS. A SMALL STREAM OF CRAFTED BEER FLOWS OUT OF THE BUILDING AND DOWN A GULLY.

> LOOK N

I CAN SEE A BRICK BUILDING WITH A SIGN SAYING "TRUMAN BREWERY" AND A WOODEN WHITE DOOR.

World correctness

There are only two requirements for the world. The first is that there should not be two different locations with the same title. The second is that the locations must have mutually reversed references to each other. This means that if, from location A going South, the player ends up in location B, then from location B going North I must end up in location A. The same principle should be valid for all cardinal points, but also when going up and down stairs.

Game utilities:

Help

? lists all the available commands and their usage.

```
> ?
GO [direction], LOOK [direction/item], OPEN [item], TAKE [item], DROP
[item], BAG, USE [item]
```

Quit

QUIT terminates the game.

PART II

Interact with the environment

There are several commands for interacting with the environment. These commands are always composed of two parts: the action and the object. Usually, the object is specified in the main description or in the result of the LOOK command.

Opening

OPEN tries to open the object of the command. Usually, it's about doors or gates, but this should be a magic world...

I CAN SEE A BRICK BUILDING WITH A SIGN THAT READS "TRUMAN BREWERY" AND A WOODEN WHITE DOOR.

> OPEN DOOR

YOU ARE INSIDE THE MAIN ROOM OF THE TRUMAN BREWERY. THERE IS A STRONG SMELL OF HOPS AND A DOZEN EMPTY CASKS.

Taking and dropping items

TAKE collects an item from the environment and puts it in the bag. **DROP** allows the player to leave an item in the environment. Every item can be taken and dropped anywhere, and the game has to list the items in the environment just after the main description.

```
INSIDE THE BUILDING.

YOU ARE INSIDE THE BUILDING, A WELL HOUSE FOR LARGE SPRINGS.

THERE ARE SOME KEYS ON THE FLOOR.

> TAKE KEYS

KEYS: TAKEN.

> DROP KEYS

KEYS: DROPPED.
```

Checking BAG

BAG shows a list of items in the bag. The bag can contain only 10 items.

```
> BAG

THE BAG CONTAINS: SOME KEYS, A SWISS KNIFE, A CANDLE AND A COMPASS.
```

Using items

USE performs an action with the item if the environment is set up for it, and if the player has the item in the bag. The action can result in an extra sentence in the main description, such as unlocking a passage toward a hidden location or releasing a new item in the location.

```
> USE KEYS

THE RED DOOR HAS BEEN UNLOCKED!

> OPEN DOOR

YOU ARE INSIDE THE RED CHAMBER.
```

Collecting gold

The treasures we can find in the cave are in the form of gold coins. They are collected automatically the first time the player moves to a location with gold, or the first time the player opens an item containing gold. The total amount of gold retrieved can be seen in the bag.

The Big Picture

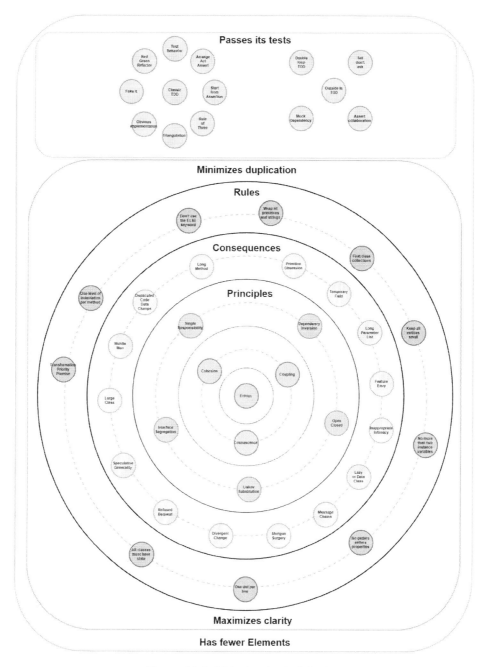

Figure 16.6: Object-oriented design

Great Habits

In this lesson, we introduced a new habit. Check it out in the following list.

Considerations When Writing a New Test

- Tests should test one thing only.
- Create more specific tests to drive a more generic solution (triangulate).
- Give your tests meaningful names (behavior/goal-oriented) that reflect your business domain.
- See the test fail for the right reason.
- Ensure you have meaningful feedback from failing tests.
- Keep your tests and production code separate.
- Organize your unit tests to reflect your production code (similar project structure).
- Organize your test in arrange, act, and assert blocks.
- Write the assertion first, and work backward.
- Write fast, isolated, repeatable, and self-validating tests.
- Consider using object calisthenics to drive design decisions.
- Consider adding tests to legacy code.
- Consider using classic TDD or Outside-In TDD (**New habit**).

  If using Outside-In TDD, start with an acceptance test and follow the double-loop TDD.

Considerations When Making a Failing Test Pass

- Write the simplest code to pass the test.
- Write any code that makes you get to the refactor phase quicker.
- Use the Transformation Priority Premise.

Considerations After the Test Has Passed

- Use the Rule of Three to tackle duplication.

- Refactor design constantly.

- Apply object calisthenics to improve your design.

- Stay on the green while refactoring.

- Use the IDE to refactor quickly and safely.

- Refactor code for readability/understandability first.

- Look out for code smells and refactor your code accordingly.

- Refactor to patterns when the context is appropriate.

Resources

Web-based resources:

- A Case for Outside-In Development, Sandro Manusco: https://codurance.com/2017/10/23/outside-in-design/.

- The London School of Test Driven Development, Emily Bache: http://coding-is-like-cooking.info/2013/04/the-london-school-of-test-driven-development/.

- Mocking as a Design Tool, Sandro Manusco: https://codurance.com/2018/10/18/mocking-as-a-design-tool/.

- Outside-In development with Double Loop TDD, Emily Bache: http://coding-is-like-cooking.info/2013/04/outside-in-development-with-double-loop-tdd/.

- Tell, Don't Ask, Alec Sharp](https://pragprog.com/articles/tell-dont-ask.

Books:

- Growing Object-Oriented Software, Guided by Tests, Steve Freeman and Nat Pryce: https://www.goodreads.com/book/show/4268826-growing-object-oriented-software-guided-by-tests.

17
Behavior-Driven Development

The causes of defects lie in worker errors, and defects are the results of neglecting those errors. It follows that mistakes will not turn into defects if worker errors are discovered and eliminated beforehand.

– Shiego Shingo

I was still in Italy the first time I was responsible for the development of a very important project for a successful startup. The company wanted to improve their systems in terms of scaling. They had an old system written in **Visual Basic (VB)**, which wasn't optimized for the always-increasing volume of items coming into the warehouse.

This was when.NET Framework had just come out, and the startup wanted to replace their old system. However, the most exciting aspect was that the scope wasn't limited to a simple code rewrite. The software was meant to generate data from a manual operation of cataloging real items. The company was aware that the process needed improving as well, so they hired José, a manager who specialized in optimizing supply chain operations, with the goal of creating a top-quality, cross-functional team in charge of the project.

We didn't have any written requirements, business analysts, architects, product owners or project managers. At that time, the word *agile* wasn't being hyped as it is today and was still limited to physical activities. But without being aware of the significance, the team was already valuing the individual and interactions over processes and tools, working software over documentation. In fact, José and I never wrote any official requirements, because *José was my requirements*. We continuously refined the product and tested it in the field until he was happy with the outcome; documented requirements would have been stale after days. Furthermore, I was the only one actually coding, so spending time on writing requirements wasn't an option.

After few weeks, we delivered an amazing system despite a restricted startup budget. José and I were very proud of the achievement, and in the process developed a strong professional relationship based on mutual respect that has lasted through the years.

The key to our success resided in the direct, continuously open communication flow between us, without intermediates, which created a super-fast feedback loop. Hence, we naturally converged on the optimal solution without wasting any time in the process.

Poka-Yoke

If we think about the very deep principles on which software developers base their work, it's amazing to realize that many concepts are not new at all. Using tests in our code is an effective way to reduce bugs, but the idea has been similarly applied in other contexts several decades ago.

Poka-yoke is a Japanese term that means *mistake-proofing* or *inadvertent error prevention*. The key word in the second translation, often omitted, is *inadvertent*. There is no poka-yoke solution that protects against an operator's sabotage, but sabotage is a rare behavior among people. A poka-yoke is any mechanism in any process that helps an equipment operator avoid (yokeru) mistakes (poka). Its purpose is to eliminate product defects by preventing, correcting, or drawing attention to human errors as they occur. The concept was formalized, and the term adopted, by Shigeo Shingo as part of the Toyota Production System.

The idea behind poka-yoke is that no defect found should be passed on downstream. **Downstream** applies not only to the consumer, but also to anybody in the organization. On a Toyota assembly line, the entire line is stopped, rather than passing a detected problem to the next person in line. This is very different in comparison to most Western car manufacturers, where a special group often exists at the end of the line to fix all the problems, and detected defects are simply handed down since they are somebody else's responsibility.

Shingo argued that errors are inevitable in any process involving human work, but that if appropriate poka-yokes are implemented, then mistakes can be caught quickly and prevented from resulting in defects. By eliminating defects at the source, the cost of mistakes within a company is reduced.

Mistakes versus Defects: Feedback Is the Cure (Again)

Shingo differentiates between *mistakes*, which are inevitable as part of the nature of human beings, and *defects*, which are mistakes that manage to get through the system and reach the customer. Poka-yoke seeks to prevent mistakes from becoming defects.

In the context of software development, we use the catchy word *bugs* to identify defects, and the test suites are our poka-yoke.

So the key enabling factor in preventing defects is having a mechanism to gather feedback in our processes for all the important aspects of development. The quicker the feedback, the more effective, because identifying mistakes early is what prevents the waste of working on an incorrect product and sending it downstream.

If you see things in this way, most of the activities we do, be they methodological or technical, derive from an agile mindset and are oriented to gathering quick feedback for the different aspects of our work.

Figure 17.1: Agile feedback loops

Bugs and Communication

From a product point of view, Philip Crosby, a widely acclaimed guru of Quality Management, defined quality as 'conformance to requirements'. As simple and blunt as that. Hence, if we think of defects as things that diverge from requirements, we can deliver the best possible value to the business when we strive to eliminate any kind of bugs from our code base.

> **Note**
> Bob Marshall, Dialogue: https://flowchainsensei.wordpress.com/2018/10/28/random-walks/.

Taiichi Ohno, one of the main personalities behind the Toyota Production System, believed that if it's not possible to reduce the number of defects, then there is a lack of ability, and if it's not possible to get close to zero defects, then there is a lack of perseverance.

So with this in mind, let's think more deeply about the nature of bugs in relation to requirements, and see if we can find something to help in acquiring ability. From this point of view, on a very high level, we could categorize software defects into three different groups:

- **Category 1**: The requirements were correct, but the code doesn't work as expected to fulfill them.

- **Category 2**: The requirements were incorrect (or incomplete), but the code works correctly (but is irrelevant, however).

- **Category 3**: The requirements were correct, but misunderstood by the developer, so the code does something else.

Introducing test automation as an integral part of our development process and improving the design of the system has many benefits, which are evident if we consider Category 1. However, Categories 2 and 3 are problems of a different nature because they are caused by issues related to *communication*.

Category 2 is a miscommunication occurring upstream in the organization, well before the requirements reach the development team. It's quite rare to experience them in small organizations, where the communication line is short and there is regular, direct interaction between stakeholders, product owners, and development teams. From a mere development point of view, there is not much we can do about it except leverage our agility and promptly fix them after clarification with the business client.

Category 3 problems instead are related to miscommunication between the business and the development team, so here we can actually take some actions.

Communication is one of the most important aspects of every organization, and it is crucial for the success of projects. As we have seen in the *Systems Entropy* section in the *Design Conclusions* lesson, Claude Shannon proved that communication is subject to entropy, and it naturally degrades the information at every step. So, handling information through too many lines raises the chance of misunderstanding. If you add in the lack of a standardized, rigorous and effective format to exchange information, we have the main ingredients for a recipe for misunderstanding. Did you ever play the **telephone game** when you were a kid? The same force is also in play for requirements.

> **Note**
>
> Wikipedia, Claude Shannon: https://en.wikipedia.org/wiki/Claude_Shannon.
>
> Wikipedia, A Mathematical Theory of Communication: https://en.wikipedia.org/wiki/A_Mathematical_Theory_of_Communication.
>
> And: https://en.wikipedia.org/wiki/Chinese_whispers.

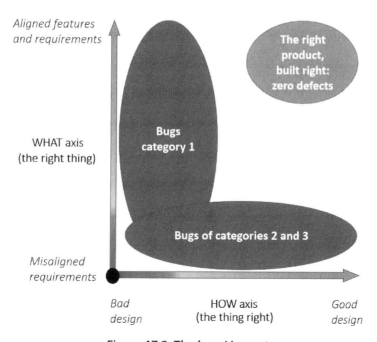

Figure 17.2: The bugs' impact

User Stories

If communication is so important, it is easy to grasp why the agile principles put so much focus on it. In particular, the 6th principle states, "*The most efficient and effective method of conveying information to and within a development team is face-to-face conversation.*"

> **Note**
>
> Kent Beck, et al., Principles behind the Agile Manifesto: http://agilemanifesto.org/principles.html.

In this context, it's interesting to remember our favorite definition of *user story* as a *placeholder for a conversation*, with the goal of achieving a *shared understanding*.

The user story is about the conversation that ideally happens between the people that want the product and those that are going to build the product. It is about the conversation, not just about how much detail we can put into a user story so that someone else can just read it, try to interpret it, and build it.

> **Note**
>
> Brian Sjoberg – Writing User Stories, It's About the Conversation: http://anagilemind.net/2017/10/21/lets-take-a-journey-on-writinguser-stories/.

So, having that conversation is key, but how can we make sure that it results in the correct features being developed?

This is where Dan North's Behavior-Driven Development reveals all its power, providing a structure for capturing the relevant aspects of that conversation. This has the consequence of enabling great things to happen, such as the automation of the proof for business correctness, the establishment of a shared business-related vocabulary (the *ubiquitous language*), and gathering data about the nature of bugs for a team to improve its performance.

Behavior-Driven Development

Behavior-driven development (**BDD**) takes the position that you can turn an idea for a requirement into implemented, tested, production-ready code simply and effectively, as long as the requirement is specific enough that everyone knows what's going on. To do this, we need a way to describe the requirement such that everyone – the business folks, the analyst, the developer and the tester – have a common understanding of the scope of the work. From this they can agree on a common definition of 'done,' and we escape the dual gumption traps of '*that's not what I asked for*' or '*I forgot to tell you about this other thing*'.

The Structure of a Story

The idea is that the *Title* and optionally the *Narrative* of a user story are what is visible on our Kanban board. It's the one-sight identification of a deployable unit of work and needs to be as short as possible; just enough to remember what it is about.

Before the user story is developed, the three amigos get together and have the conversation we talked about before. In our experience, the best results occur when this activity is done "Just In Time" because the concepts will stay fresh in the mind, and that usually minimizes the need for questions later on. However, the most important thing is that the conversation happens with the right people (https://dannorth.net/whats-in-a-story/):

- Who knows what the business wants (product owner or business analyst)

- Who knows how to make the system achieve it (developers)

- Eventually, a third party in charge to witness the discussion and agree on how to prove its correctness (testers)

> **Note**
>
> George Dinwiddie – The Three Amigos Strategy of Developing User Stories: https://www.agileconnection.com/article/three-amigosstrategy-developing-user-stories.

This activity has the final goal of producing the *Acceptance Criteria*, which should be added there and then, documenting the growth of the shared understanding of the work to be done. This task is the most important because it enables the chain of value that BDD builds into the system. It is the "glue" between the business and the information system and the first step for its complete automation. It's this automation that gives us one of the most important feedback points of all: the feedback about *functional correctness*.

This must be the ultimate proof that what we have developed is what the business wants. If it isn't there, the business didn't request it.

Title (one line describing the story)

Narrative:
As a [role]
I want [feature]
So that [benefit]

Acceptance Criteria: (presented as Scenarios)

Scenario 1: Title
Given [context or pre-conditions]
 And [some more context]...

When [event or Behavior under test]

Then [outcome or assertion]
 And [another outcome]...

Scenario 2: ...

Figure 17.3: The structure of a sample story

Acceptance Criteria: It's All about the Examples

"But if anyone has not yet got the concepts, I shall teach him to use the words by means of examples and by practice. – And when I do this I do not communicate less to him than I know myself."

– *Ludwig Wittgenstein, Philosophical Investigations*

The best way to fight misunderstanding is by being as clear as possible when discussing requirements. Having a shared vocabulary for identifying business concepts is fundamental, but that's not enough when functionality needs to be injected into an information system.

The best way to eliminate any doubt and double-check the understanding of a scenario is by using examples. Examples are ideal because they use data, transcending language and concepts deriving from it. They are a simple way to achieve a repeatable and predictable proof of correctness and can be easily inserted into an automation suite of tests that guarantee the software solution really does what the business wants. This kind of functional correctness is essential for eradicating Category 3 bugs (the requirements were correct, but misunderstood by the developer so the code does something else).

Successful application of specification by example is documented to significantly reduce feedback loops in software development, leading to less rework, higher product quality, faster turnaround time for software changes, and better alignment of activities of various roles involved in software development such as testers, analysts, and developers.

> **Note**
>
> Adzic Gojko – Specification by Example: https://www.goodreads.com/book/show/10288718-specification-by-example.

From Criteria to Acceptance Tests

Once the acceptance criteria are well-defined using examples, it becomes trivial to transpose them into a suite of Acceptance Tests. Furthermore, using an Outside-In approach, the team can drive the development of the scenarios, using the tests as a feedback for the work yet to be done in order to consider the story implemented.

Given that the acceptance criteria are expressed using business language, they also represent a great source for documenting the status of the project because they will never become stale and will always reflect faithfully what the system does in that moment in time.

Another great advantage of this approach is that when a bug is identified, it's possible to precisely analyze the reasons for it. In fact, the code responsible for the defect is always traceable to the user story that required it from a functional perspective; hence, it is possible to double-check it against its acceptance criteria. This allows the team to identify the root reasons for the occurrence.

Two situations are possible: either there's wrong/missing acceptance criteria or there's a code execution problem. Thus, it's always possible to identify the bug as being of Category 1, 2, or 3, which provides the necessary insight to make systemic improvements with surgical accuracy.

Acceptance Tests Done Right

An **Acceptance Test** suite must have well-defined properties in order to provide benefits. It is important to set goals early on so we can always have a clear idea of what we want to achieve and make trade-off decisions based on those goals.

Readable by Business Folks

In this context, the expressivity of the four elements of simple design have a key role. If it is not possible to sit with an analyst or a product owner in front of the acceptance criteria to have the discussion mentioned earlier, we have a clear red alarm signal. It means that the "glue" with the business is not working properly, and the risk is very high that we'll end up with acceptance tests that are ineffective and/or useless.

It is not necessary to use heavyweight frameworks to achieve this as long as we keep the scenario specifications well sorted and separate from the implementation. Businesspeople are not intimidated if we use an underscore instead of a blank space in a method name. It is the complexity of the implementation that scares them (rightly).

However, using design skills or specific properties of the languages matched with a little bit of creativity, it's not difficult to keep the specifications clean enough. For example, C# has the "partial class" construct, which is very effective for this purpose, in our experience. If you are unsure, ask a business analyst to sit with you and together read the acceptance criteria from code; this feedback is key.

Here is a brief example of how a simple acceptance test could look without dependencies, just pushing methods implementation at the bottom of the file – enough to have a base for the discussions:

```
//this is a "Refund" story
//we can use this to DRIVE THE CONVERSATION WITH THE BUSINESS
public partial class RefundSpecifications {
    //this is a scenario
    [Test]
    public void Refunded_items_should_be_returned_to_stock()
    {
        Given_customer_previously_bought_an_item();
        And_I_currently_have_four_items_in_stock();
        When_he_returns_the_item_for_a_return();
        Then_I_should_have_five_items_in_stock();
    }


    //we would have more scenarios here
    // ....
```

```
    //and implementations of methods afterward
    private void Given_customer_previously_bought_an_item()
    { ... }
    private void And_I_currently_have_four_items_in_stock()
    { ... }
    private void When_he_returns_the_item_for_a_return()
    { ... }
    private void Then_I_should_have_five_items_in_stock()
    { ... }
}
```

We could use a collaborator to keep the implementation in another file and make it even more readable:

```
public partial class RefundSpecifications {
    private readonly RefundContext _ = new RefundContext();


    [Test]
    public void Refunded_items_should_be_returned_to_stock()
    {
        _.Given_customer_previously_bought_an_item();
        _.And_I_currently_have_four_items_in_stock();
        _.When_he_returns_the_item_for_a_return();
        _.Then_I_should_have_five_items_in_stock();
    }
    //more scenarios ...
}


//and implementations of methods in a context class
public class RefundContext
{
    private void Given_customer_previously_bought_an_item()
    { ... }
    private void And_I_currently_have_four_items_in_stock()
```

```
    { ... }
    private void When_he_returns_the_item_for_a_return()
    { ... }
    private void Then_I_should_have_five_items_in_stock()
    { ... }
}
```

Here is another brief example without heavyweight dependencies, just using the EasyBdd microframework based on one abstract class. It would easily allows the previous example to reuse the methods inside the Given/When/Then/And structures:

```
public partial class RefundSpecifications {
    [Test]
    public void Refunded_items_should_be_returned_to_stock()
    {
        Given(Customer_previously_bought_an_item);
        And(I_currently_have_four_items_in_stock);
        When(He_returns_the_item_for_a_return);
        Then(I_should_have_five_items_in_stock);
    }
    //more scenario ...
}
//this partial class contains the implementation
//we hide this in a different file
[TestFixture]
public partial class RefundSpecifications : BddSpecification{
    private void Customer_previously_bought_an_item()
    { ... }
    private void I_currently_have_four_items_in_stock()
    { ... }
```

```
    private void He_returns_the_item_for_a_return()

    { ... }

    private void I_should_have_five_items_in_stock()

    { ... }

}
```

> **Note**
>
> Microframework for .NET in C# providing just Given, When, Then functionality, by Marco Consolaro https://github.com/conso/EasyBdd. This is very micro because it is made by just one abstract class. The following is the opinion of a friend about EasyBdd when asked about a popular BDD Framework (which we will call **X**): EasyBdd is like X without the chunkiness and fragility, but also without 100% natural language. The price you pay is `my_test_does_this` versus my test does this. The benefit is the IDE can refactor your tests properly, you can navigate your code base using standard Visual Studio and IDE navigation techniques, you don't need plug-ins, and it runs a lot quicker. I personally see X as a bit of a vanity project. Geeky types love its cleverness. But overall, the cost is too high for me. I don't yet know anyone who has tried both and gone back from EasyBdd to X. If you use .NET you can try it out if you want – it's free!

Feature Complete

An Acceptance Test suite needs to be functionally complete in order to be considered the very final contract between a business and development team. As developers, we cannot take for granted parts of a story or have only partial coverage. In our experience, we have noticed that most of the time, with enough mature team members, bugs of Categories 1 and 3 tend to disappear almost completely. At that point, we have still seen bugs of Category 2 coming out in the form of missing criteria for unconsidered situations. While sometimes it's hard to consider every aspect of scenarios, it's still important to keep this in consideration and help the business by asking the right questions.

Fast

While good acceptance tests maintain their main business value even if they don't run very fast (think about the classic test pyramid), we feel that the slower they execute, the less value they give for development purposes. In general, one of the properties of helpful system feedback is how quick it is, and business acceptance is one of the most important among developers when developing an information system. If we are building the wrong thing, then the sooner we know it, the faster we can correct the mistake (remember the poka-yoke?). If tests take all night to run (and we have seen it with our own eyes in some teams), we might waste an entire day of work before we know it! Not good at all.

Furthermore, very fast acceptance tests can be run every so often, which is priceless for those who write the code: **feedback on the progress of the development of the feature**. This is an amazingly helpful aspect because, to implement something, we have to break the task down in our mind in smaller problems and tackle them one at the time. We often have to focus on a high-level component first, and then move to a lower-level one (and/or vice versa) before the information pipeline is completely built. This is a particular case of context-switching that can easily drive us away from the higher-level feature. If we have a quick test we can run, we can delegate completely the higher-level aspects to automation and focus better on the internals. This allows us to write them beforehand and use that feedback to drive the growth of the functionalities of the system in a very effective way.

Boundaries

There are several opinions about the correct boundaries for acceptance tests that can have a big impact in how fast they execute. While it is true that a proof of a working system is achievable only by running tests on the real infrastructure, we find that the cost for the slower tests' execution is too high for the value provided. It isn't uncommon to see developers avoid running the tests when they are too slow, which would provide feedback too late and make them ineffective.

At the end of the day, in terms of acceptance, we are interested in proving the business behavior. And if we design our system well, that kind of abstraction lives in a very specific layer of our system, as we have seen in the previous lesson. Hence, it's a perfectly acceptable trade-off to run our acceptance suite, skipping infrastructural delivery components and hitting the application layer.

If we correctly separate UI concerns and business concerns, for example, by using the application layer for acceptance of business use cases, it is very effective, both in terms of speed and functional proof. We can then segregate UI tests into their own suite, providing better granularity. After all, having a problem with the UI displaying some data wrong is quite different than having the wrong data in the database because of a mistake in domain model functionality. Again, having a well-designed system gives us a lot of options to chose from for our test strategy.

The Walking Skeleton

A Walking Skeleton is a tiny implementation of the system that performs a small end-to-end function. It need not use the final architecture, but it should link together the main architectural components. The architecture and the functionality can then evolve in parallel.

– Alistair Cockburn

We highly suggest this approach when you are beginning development from scratch. Since we can't really get feedback before the pipeline is complete and, especially in distributed systems, integration points are one of the main sources of pain (including misconfigurations, access keys, availability of network), building the thinnest end-to-end slice of the system is very valuable, because it forces us to face the difficult infrastructural problem first while we still have time and the code base is almost empty.

The great advantage is that once the walking skeleton is working, it means that all the infrastructure we need for running our code and acceptance tests is set up, successfully connected, and ready to grow.

Kata

The Messy Delivery Office Requirements

Transform the following unstructured requirements into a BDD-style specification. Ideally, it should be done using acceptance criteria in a Given/When/Then structure and within an automation suite in order to be part of a continuous automation environment. If you feel like it, you can even carry on and implement them, using Outside-In TDD!

Estimated dispatch date service

Create a service with a **DispatchDate** method which, given the ID of a customer order collected via our website, returns its estimated dispatch date.

An order consists of an order date and a collection of products that a customer has added to their shopping basket. Each of these products is supplied to our company *Just In Time* through a number of third-party suppliers. As soon as an order is received by a supplier, the supplier will start processing the order.

The supplier has an agreed lead time in which to process the order before delivering it to the company's Delivery Office. Once the Delivery Office has received all products in an order, it is dispatched to the customer. Suppliers start processing an order on the same day that the order is received. For example, a supplier with a lead time of one day, receiving an order today before midnight, will send it to the Delivery Office tomorrow. Once all products for an order have arrived at the Delivery Office from the suppliers, they usually will be dispatched to the customer on the same day.

The exception is caused by the fact that the Delivery Office doesn't work over the weekend. Packages received from a supplier on a weekend will be dispatched the following Monday. Furthermore, none of the suppliers work during the weekend, so if an order is received on Friday with a lead time of 2 days, the Delivery Office would receive and dispatch on Tuesday.

Resources

Web-based resources

- An agile Mind blog: http://anagilemind.net.
- Bob Marshall's blog: https://flowchainsensei.wordpress.com.
- Dan North's blog: https://dannorth.net.
- Entropy (information theory), Wikipedia: https://en.wikipedia.org/wiki/Entropy_(information_theory).
- Sub-second acceptance tests, (repository): https://github.com/subsecondtdd/codebreaker-js.
- Sub-Second Acceptance Tests, Aslak Hellesoy (SCLConf 2018): https://www.youtube.com/watch?v=PE_1nh0DdbY.
- The Three Amigos Strategy of Developing User Stories, George Dinwiddie: https://www.agileconnection.com/article/three-amigos-strategy-developing-user-stories.

Books

- BDD in Action: Behavior-driven development for the whole software lifecycle, John Ferguson Smart: https://www.goodreads.com/book/show/20578311-bdd-in-action.

- Crystal Clear: A Human-Powered Methodology for Small Teams, Alistair Cockburn: https://www.goodreads.com/book/show/3353.Crystal_Clear.

- Quality Is Free, Philip B. Crosby: https://www.goodreads.com/book/show/1031937.Quality_Is_Free.

- Specification by Example, Gojko Adzic: https://www.goodreads.com/book/show/10288718-specification-by-example.

- Structured Analysis and System Specification, Tom DeMarco, P.J. Plauger: https://www.goodreads.com/book/show/123719.Structured_Analysis_and_System_Specification.

18

Understand the Business

"*The fact is that the system that people work in and the interaction with people may account for 90 or 95 percent of performance.*"

– *William Edwards Deming*

In general, one of the most common patterns observed in software developers is that they tend to see software development as a discipline apart–almost disconnected from any other fields of science or business. This view makes them think very passionately, deeply and seriously about it, but the same depth and passion fade out very quickly for other topics that are equally or even more important for the success of the business and the software development itself.

This quote of William Edwards (Bill) Deming reveals a great truth: software development is a team activity. Success and failure is team success or failure. According to him, if the working dynamics of teams aren't good, the relevance of the technical abilities of single developers account for just 5% of team's overall performance. That's the reason why David J. Anderson in his masterpiece *Kanban* book says that "a team with just a spread of talent can produce world-class results with the right process, good discipline, and leadership.

> **Note**
>
> David J. Anderson, Kanban: Successful Evolutionary Change for Your Technology Business, https://www.goodreads.com/book/show/8086552-kanban.

Knowledge versus Understanding

Russell Ackoff, one of the pioneers in the field of Systems Thinking, stated that "*you will never reach a complete explanation or understanding of everything, but your understanding increases the larger the system you comprehend. The knowledge increases the smaller the element you comprehend.*"

> **Note**
>
> Aleksis Tulonen: Ackoff and Systemic Thinking: http://aleksistulonen.com/2018/10/28/ackoff-and-systemic-thinking/.

This seems to imply that *to know* and *to understand* are not the same thing. So, what is the difference between the two? Let's see what the dictionary says:

To know: Be aware of through observation, inquiry, or information.

To understand: Perceive the significance, explanation, or cause of something.

Seeing solitary facts in relation to a general principle is the essence of understanding. What is an understanding then? An understanding is a generalized meaning or insight. An insight is a basic sense of, or feeling for, relationships; it is a meaning or discernment. A tested generalized insight is an understanding; it is a meaning or discernment that one may profitably apply to several or even many similar, but not necessarily identical, situations or processes. The most valuable insights are those confirmed by enough similar cases to be generalized into an understanding.

> **Note**
>
> Professor Y.K. Ip, National University of Singapore, Knowing is Not the Same as Understanding: What is Understanding: http://www.cdtl.nus.edu.sg/success/sl20.htm.

So we can say that *knowledge* answers the question *what* about something, while *understanding* answers the question *why*. We can know things we don't understand. We know facts, but understand ideas. So, understanding explains knowledge. It's on a higher level of abstraction (to use software-design terminology).

So, whatever your goal is, think about whether you're going to need intellect, intuition, or emotion in order to achieve it. Then design your *practice* to rewire this part of your brain, and get ready for the long journey from knowledge to understanding.

> **Note**
>
> The True Difference Between Knowledge and Understanding, Colin Robertson, Willpowered Evolution http://www.willpowered.co/learn/knowledge-understanding.

From Ackoff's point of view, to increase our understanding, we need to make an effort and push our intellectual boundaries well beyond our small development team and even the broader IT department. We should never forget that software development teams aren't working for their own goals; they work to be of service to the business. Their goal is to build an information system that supports and enables the achievement of business goals in a more effective way. So, the larger system that we should really comprehend is the whole business. That is what makes the real difference in terms of effectiveness, not only for software development but for anyone working for the organization.

Theory of Constraints

The **theory of constraints (TOC)** is an overall management philosophy introduced by Eliyahu M. Goldratt in his 1984 book titled *The Goal*, which is geared to help organizations continually achieve their goals. Goldratt adapted the concept to project management with his book *Critical Chain*, published in 1997.

> **Note**
>
> Wikipedia, Theory of constraints: https://en.wikipedia.org/wiki/Theory_of_constraints.

The basic idea of the TOC is very simple, yet very powerful when we focus on improvement because it is meant to help in identifying what we should work on in a System in order to achieve the quickest and the most effective benefit. Despite being first articulated in the context of manufacturing, the principles underlying it are very general and can be adapted to every systemic context.

The theory follows from the fact that every organization has room for improvements and the current performances are bounded by the most limiting constraint. Removing the constraint would have the effect of instantly improving the overall system, which would then be limited by a different constraint. The focus on the improvement efforts should always be on the most limiting constraint, and once it's removed should be focused on the following one.

To use a metaphor, you can think of a system as a chain of rings. If we put tension on the chain, the chain will break at the weakest ring. So, to improve the whole chain, we should strengthen the weakest ring.

To apply the TOC, you should consider the concept of *throughput* of a system as the rate at which it delivers value. In every value stream, there is always a constraining step limiting the overall throughput.

- **Identifying the constraint** is the first step, which involves understanding the system and looking for the bottleneck. In software development, it is often easily identifiable on a Kanban board with an overloaded column, but in manufacturing contexts, they were looking for "*a big pile of stuff and idle people standing around waiting.*"

- **Exploiting the constraint** pushes its limit and maximize current overall throughput without further investment. This might be the equivalent of optimizing a stored procedure, for example, when a particular database operation depending on it has been identified as the bottleneck.

- **Subordinate everything to the constraint** by finding ways to reduce the pressure, optimizing the systems interacting with it. In the previous stored-procedure example, this step would be optimizing the systems calling the stored procedure to use it less often, maybe caching some results.

- **Elevate the constraint** is about devoting more resources to it until it's not a constraint for the system anymore. In the previous example, this could mean scaling the database up or out, or rewriting the system responsible for the operation.

- At this point, you **repeat the process**, searching for the next constraint.

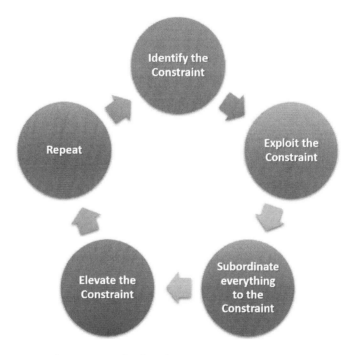

Figure 18.1: The five focusing steps of the TOC

Note

This example has been used with reference to the article of our friend, Matthew Butt, titled How Applying TOC Helped Us Optimize Our Code, on Matthew Butt's blog at https://blog.matthewbutt.com/2016/12/18/how-applying-theory-of-constraints-helpedus-optimise-our-code/.

This basic principle hides a few very important consequences, the main one being that in a system, if we don't improve the most limiting constraint, improving other aspects will not have any visible consequences for the system as a whole, essentially being wasted effort. Furthermore, if there is not an easy way to monitor the system in order to always identify the current constraint (the usual feedback), once our improvement efforts on the current constraint succeed in removing it, we should immediately stop working on it and switch our focus on identifying the next constraint. To keep working on the old one from that moment onward would become a waste.

In our experience, we have found this idea a great source of wisdom in many situations, not just involving effective teams and organizational improvement, but also in relation to self-development and the need to step out of our own comfort zone to *elevate* the relevant constraint. This is the ultimate reason for going beyond merely technical knowledge and learning subjects that involve organizational understanding. That's why, in our distillations, this lesson had to be included.

Domain-Driven Design: What Domain?

The main misconception about **Domain-Driven Design (DDD)** is "thinking that it is just a handful of implementation patterns as many articles and blogs focus on the modelling patterns. It is much easier for developers to see tactical patterns of DDD implemented in code rather than conversations between business users and teams on a domain that they do not care about or do not understand".

> **Note**
>
> Scott Millett and Nick Tune, Patterns, Principles, and Practices of Domain-Driven Design, https://www.goodreads.com/book/show/25531393-patterns-principles-and-practices-of-domain-driven-design.

So, the **Domain** of the first D is not the Domain Model. It is the **Business Domain**.

Furthermore, DDD is not advocating **Big Design Upfront**. "Driven" doesn't necessarily mean "build the full domain model first." What it means is, since the business domain is so important, the domain model is the heart of the system; thus, it must be the one we give more love to. Essentially, the closer we are to the domain model, the less we should be open to trade-offs that impact the design.

Software projects fail when you don't understand the business domain you are working within well enough. Typing is not the bottleneck for delivering a product; coding is the easy part of development. [...] Creating and keeping a useful software model of the domain that can fulfill business-use cases is the difficult part.

However, the more you invest in understanding your business domain the better equipped you will be when you are trying to model it in software to solve its inherent business problems.

> **Note**
>
> Scott Millett and Nick Tune, Patterns, Principles, and Practices of Domain-Driven Design, https://www.goodreads.com/book/show/25531393-patterns-principles-and-practices-of-domain-driven-design.

So, from this point of view, understanding the business as a whole is a huge advantage. It's not just because understanding what comes from upstream and what goes downstream helps us to model the software for delivering the best functionality and interacting with other parts of the organization. If that understanding could provide useful insights at a business level, improving its functionality and optimizing the whole system, we would also improve the performances of all the departments of the business, including our very own team, as Deming said.

This is the great power of DDD as a development philosophy, defined by Eric Evans in his epic work, *Domain-Driven Design: Tackling Complexity in the Heart of Software*. Its goal is enabling teams to effectively manage the construction of software for complex problem domains via collaboration with domain experts in order to build a shared understanding of the business context that the software should support, automate and, ultimately, improve. We should always remember that any automation has the philosophical reason to save time on the execution of a task, so that people can use that time for activities of higher purpose or intellectual requirements.

Beyond Requirements: Knowledge Crunching

Collaboration with domain experts is at the core of DDD, which coined the term "knowledge crunching" to express it. "*Knowledge crunching is the art of distilling relevant information from the problem domain in order to build a useful model that can fulfill the needs of business use cases.*"

> **Note**
>
> Scott Millett and Nick Tune, Patterns, Principles, and Practices of Domain-Driven Design, https://www.goodreads.com/book/show/25531393-patterns-principles-and-practices-of-domain-driven-design.

The goal of knowledge crunching is to go toward the path of understanding collectively, so that the requirements are focused on the features that give the most value to the business; features that in turn maximize the value that the software implementing them can provide.

What enables effective collaboration is communication, again in agreement with the agile principles, as we saw in the previous lesson. In agreement with this aspect of DDD, we strongly feel that excelling only in pure technical aspects is often not enough to achieve real effectiveness. Sometimes, it is important to be able to step out of the comfort zone of sitting behind the screen and take actions that enable communication to happen.

The frustration of discovering that you have been building right the wrong thing is proportional to the time and effort you have spent building it. So it's better to make sure as early as possible that's not the case, right?

Luckily, there are several techniques that can help prevent this from happening. They focus more on soft skills, facilitation and collective learning, with the goal of understanding and probing the wider system. In many situations, your technical skills might not be enough.

5 Whys

In our experience, we have found that the best way to achieve understanding is by asking questions. In Italy, there is a proverb: "*Chiedere e' lecito, rispondere e' cortesia.*" *Never be afraid to ask questions.* However, to maximize the value we get from the answers, it is important to ask the right questions.

One of the most powerful questions to ask for reaching understanding is very simple: *Why?* It's not a coincidence that kids, in their path to make sense of the world pass through the "Why?" phase, asking it continuously, like a broken record.

5 Whys is an iterative interrogative technique used to explore the cause-and-effect relationships underlying a particular problem. The primary goal of the technique is to determine the root cause of a defect or problem by repeating the question "Why?" Each answer forms the basis of the next question. The "5" in the name derives from an anecdotal observation of the number of iterations needed to resolve the problem.

> **Note**
> Wikipedia, 5 Whys: https://en.wikipedia.org/wiki/5_Whys.

Figure 18.2: 5 Whys

Not all problems have a single root cause, so to uncover multiple root causes, you must repeat the method and ask a different sequence of questions each time. This method has no specific rules about what lines of questions to explore or how long to continue the search for additional root causes. Thus, even when the method is closely followed, the outcome still depends upon the knowledge and persistence of the people involved.

> **Note**
>
> Wikipedia, 5 Whys: https://en.wikipedia.org/wiki/5_Whys.

It is a critical component of problem-solving training, delivered as part of the induction into the Toyota Production System. The architect of the Toyota Production System, Taiichi Ohno, said that the 5 Whys were "the basis of Toyota's scientific approach" and that "by repeating why five times, the nature of the problem as well as its solution becomes clear." The tool has seen widespread use beyond Toyota, and is now used within Kaizen, Lean manufacturing and Six Sigma. In other companies, it appears in other forms. Under Ricardo Semler, Semco practices "three whys" and broadens the practice to cover goal setting and decision making."

> **Note**
>
> Taiichi Ohno, Toyota Production System: Beyond Large-Scale Production, https://www.goodreads.com/book/show/376237.Toyota_Production_System.

This technique has proved very useful for us in the past. Sometimes, well before the fifth why, something magical happens; the business domain expert, after a moment of reflection, answers, "That's a good question! I don't know it myself. Let me find out more..." That is the moment in which we contribute to knowledge crunching, and increasing shared understanding.

Impact Mapping

Another method very useful for going beyond traditional requirements and instead letting them emerge as a consequence of the business goals is impact mapping. It is a technique with a strong visual component since it uses a special kind of mind map diagram aimed at focusing on business information. The really effective point of mind mapping is that it is an interactive activity to perform collaboratively with the stakeholders, starting from the impact that the business is looking for (that is, from the strategic goal).

Let's see an example:

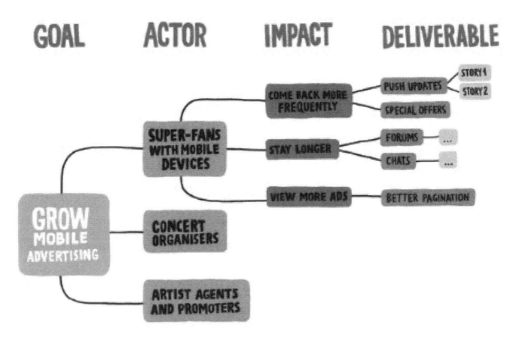

Figure 18.3: Impact mapping

It is a mind-map grown during a discussion facilitated by considering the following four aspects:

- **Goal**: The center of an impact map answers the most important question: *Why are we doing this?* This is the goal we are trying to achieve.

- **Actors**: The first branch of an impact map provides answers to the following questions: *Who can produce the desired effect? Who can obstruct it? Who are the consumers or users of our product? Who will be impacted by it?* These are the actors who can influence the outcome.

- **Impacts**: The second branch level of an impact map sets the actors in the perspective of our business goal. It answers the following questions: *How should our actors' behavior change? How can they help us to achieve the goal? How can they obstruct or prevent us from succeeding?* These are the impacts that we're trying to create.

- **Deliverables**: Once we have the first three questions answered, we can talk about scope. The third branch level of an impact map answers the following question: *What can we do, as an organization or a delivery team, to support the required impacts?* These are the deliverables, software features, and organizational activities.

Impact mapping helps to reduce waste by preventing scope creep and over-engineered solutions. It provides focus for delivery by putting deliverables in the context of impacts they are supposed to achieve. It enhances collaboration by creating a big-picture view that business sponsors and delivery teams can use for better prioritization and as a reference for more meaningful progress monitoring and reporting. Finally, it helps to ensure that the right business outcomes are achieved, or that unrealistic projects are stopped before they cost too much, by clearly communicating underlying assumptions and allowing teams to test them.

> **Note**
>
> Gojko Adzic, What is impact mapping? https://www.impactmapping.org/about.html.

On many software projects, the developers only get the lower tiers of an impact map – what the business thinks they need and how they think the developers should achieve it. With an impact map, though, you can unwind their assumptions and find out what they really want to achieve. And then you can use your technical expertise to suggest superior alternatives that they would never have thought of.

> **Note**
>
> Scott Millett and Nick Tune, Patterns, Principles, and Practices of Domain-Driven Design, https://www.goodreads.com/book/show/25531393-patterns-principles-and-practices-of-domain-driven-design.

PopcornFlow

Conway's Law states that "organizations which design systems [...] are constrained to produce designs which are copies of the communication structures of these organizations." So if we want to achieve the optimal design, it is often necessary to act first on those communication structures. The system should change first, otherwise our efforts would produce suboptimal solutions. But more often than not, human beings don't want to change. And neither do systems.

> **Note**
>
> Wikipedia, Conway's law: https://en.wikipedia.org/wiki/Conway%27s_law.

In our experience, one of the most evident consequences of this is the inability of organizations to evolve and adapt fast enough. This is another property of systems as defined by John Gall in his amazing book, The "Systems Bible:

IN ORDER TO REMAIN UNCHANGED, THE SYSTEM MUST CHANGE.

Specifically, the changes that must occur are changes in the patterns of changes (or strategies) previously employed to prevent drastic internal change.

– John Gall, The Systems Bible

> **Note**
>
> John Gall, The Systems Bible: The Beginner's Guide to Systems Large and Small (3rd ed.): https://www.goodreads.com/book/show/583785.The_Systems_Bible.

Fighting this natural tendency to inertia is also the goal of the 12th agile principle, if you think about it:

At regular intervals, the team reflects on how to become more effective, then tunes and adjusts its behavior accordingly.

– 12th Agile Principle

At an organizational level, one of the best ideas that we have seen recently on this topic is **PopcornFlow,** ideated by Claudio Perrone. The `PopcornFlow` method helps with the goal of embedding the change-enabling principle into your work habits.

`PopcornFlow` naturally supports the idea of the DevOps' Three Ways of effectiveness, using a visualization technique to support critical thinking and organizational learning via quick experimentation and feedback loops. You can read more about `PopcornFlow` in its own dedicated section at the end of the book.

User Story Mapping

Story maps solve one of the big problems with using user stories in agile development – that's losing sight of the big picture. Story maps look at a product or feature from the users' perspective. Building a story map asks the story mapper to think through the experience of using the product from their users' perspective.

> **Note**
>
> Jeff Patton, User Story Mapping: http://www.jpattonassociates.com/jeff-pattons-book-released-user-story-mapping/, http://www.jpattonassociates.com/user-story-mapping/.

User story mapping is a dead simple idea – talk about the user's journey through your product by building a simple model that tells your user's story as you do. It turns out this simple idea makes working with user stories in agile development a lot easier. More importantly, it'll keep your users, and what they're doing with your product front, and center in your development of these products. That's better than getting lost in feature arguments.

The technique is based on visualization of the backlog in a timeline in relation to someone doing something to reach a goal. To achieve that, the user stories are grouped in wider activities and tasks based on their contribution to a higher goal. They are then arranged in a narrative flow called *the backbone*. Smaller sub-tasks, user stories, details and variations hang down to form the ribs connected to the backbone.

Here is an example of how a user story map would look at the end of the conversation.

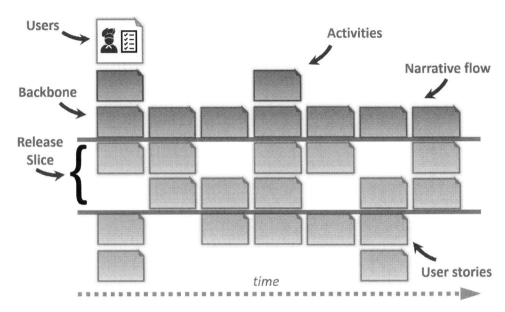

Figure 18.4: Example of a user story map

User story mapping is particularly useful in situations where there is a pre-existing backlog, but the overall understanding of it is lacking, unclear or scattered among several different actors in the business. It has been proven very effective in re-coordinating all the knowledge into a holistic understanding.

EventStorming

Unfortunately, most large companies are organized into sealed departments, and communication between them is often very difficult and ineffective. This makes it hard, and sometimes impossible, to reach an understanding of the business as whole.

Such a partial view of the system only encourages a greater degree of specialization because within the department, there is an unconscious bias to consider the department's needs as more important than the business as a whole. This situation is very risky because *systems tend to create goals of their own*, as John Gall explained. If the independent goals of the department are misaligned or in conflict with the main system's overall goal, the result is a huge amount of wasted resources that, in some cases, can threaten the life of the organization itself.

One of the best techniques that we have seen recently to help identify the optimal separation of bounded context and provide a real understanding of the organizational system and its value stream is EventStorming. Ideated by Alberto Brandolini, EventStorming uses the stream of domain events as the driver to discover all other components of the whole system. You can read more about event storming in its own dedicated section at the end of the book.

Business Model Canvas

Business Model Canvas is a strategic management and lean startup template for developing new or documenting existing business models. It is a visual chart with elements describing a firm's or product's value proposition, infrastructure, customers, and finances. It assists firms in aligning their activities by illustrating potential trade-offs.

The Business Model Canvas was initially proposed by Alexander Osterwalder based on his earlier work on Business Model Ontology. Since the release of Osterwalder's work in 2008, new canvases for specific niches have appeared.

> **Note**
>
> Wikipedia, Business Model Canvas: https://en.wikipedia.org/wiki/Business_Model_Canvas.

Among other canvases, the most significant is the **Lean Canvas** adapted by Ash Maurya.

The Lean Canvas is adapted from Alex Osterwalder's Business Model Canvas and optimized for the Lean Startup methodology with a big emphasis on finding customer problems worth solving.

> **Note**
>
> Lean Canvas: https://leanstack.com/leancanvas.

These templates offer a very focused way to see the whole business from an ever-higher perspective, basically providing a one-page snapshot of the organization's activities and their reason for being.

While the exercise of creating and updating a canvas is extremely useful for executives in order to keep activities and business goals aligned, the outcome of the exercise is also very effective for explaining the big picture of the organization to newcomers. The information presented is a great starting point for *asking meaningful questions of the domain experts* and participating in the evolution of the business with a deeper insight about the vision of its leading team.

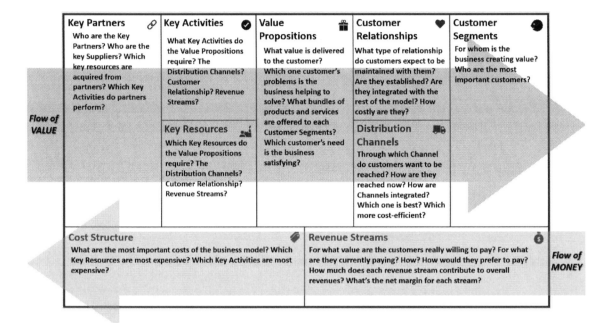

Figure 18.5: Business Model Canvas with questions, flow of money, and flow of value

The Business Model Canvas shows in its center the most important thing to identify for any business: *the value propositions*. It is basically the reason for the business to exist – the combination of products and services it provides to its customers and the core value that they supply. One way to identify this value is for an owner to specify what they want customers to remember about their interaction with the company.

The other parts of the canvas are related to the value proposition in a form of flow:

- On top, with a direction that goes from left to right, is the flow of value.

- At the top left are *partnerships*, *activities*, and *resources* involved in the *creation of the value*.

- At the top right are *customer relationships*, *channels*, and *customer segments*, focusing on the *delivery of the value*.

- On the bottom side is the flow of money that goes in the opposite direction: from the right with the *revenue structure* to the left with the *cost structure*.

Customers pay money for the value that the products or services of the company provide, which in turn pays money to other actors in order to perform activities that create that value. The difference between revenue and costs is the *margin* (that is, the net monetization of the value provided).

This template, in our opinion, is very useful because it shows in a very compact way the key components of any business, focusing on the most important aspect: the goal is providing value. It also shows that to create and deliver that value, the organization should be organized as a stream of activities: the cash flow is just a side effect of the effective alignment of these activities toward the goal. Hence, underlying every business is what is called a **value stream**.

Value Streams and Domain Events

"If you can't describe what you are doing as a process, you don't know what you're doing."

– William Edwards Deming

A value stream is a notion borrowed from lean manufacturing as the end-to-end sequence of value-adding activities that an organization undertakes in order to produce an overall result for a customer, stakeholder, or end-user, focused on both the production flow from raw material to end-product, and the design flow from concept to realization.

So we can think of it as a slightly more granular explanation of the *flow of value* of the Business Model Canvas, transposed in a temporal sequence of activities necessary to design, produce, and deliver the value propositions. An organization will usually have many of these values, and they will often have independent, changing pace.

There is a vast amount of literature about value streams and value stream mapping, but we feel that the key concepts to understand won't be enhanced with more detail. From this point of view, the idea of the lean value stream as a diagrammatic representation of the sequence of activities is the key starting point, as follows:

Value Stream

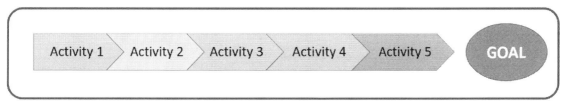

Figure 18.6: A high-level representation of a value stream as a sequence of activities

So, we now have a way to see the business as a sequence of key activities, and all of these activities would be supported by an information system. If this holistic view of the organization's activities is missing, what chance is there of creating systems that communicate in harmony with each other, smoothly mapping the flow of value with the flow of information?

If we look at software development from a value stream perspective, rather than simply looking at these activities as a process, we can emphasize the creation of customer value. As we have learned from Deming, it's all about improving the whole process, not just the parts – to minimize waste and ensure the customer gets exactly what they asked for.

The activities of the flow are independent, but interconnected; this is one of the properties of a Complex System. Each activity performs different tasks in autonomy, but feeds information back to other parts of the System that are needed for the chain of value to progress to the next stage.

For example, in an ecommerce company selling physical items online, the value stream activities include:

- Acquiring (physically or remotely) the items to be sold

- Describing their physical details (color, qualities, pictures and other information useful for their placement on the market)

- Assessing and interacting to handle the quantity in stock

- Creating and managing the mechanism for customers to browse the catalogue, place an order and pay, dispatch the items

In parallel, there's a marketing system to place advertisements, and after the sale is done, there will be some customer care functionality. This and all of the above are activities of the value stream. They can happen in parallel, and the stream might be somewhat complicated, but they can be carried on independently of one another. However, they have dependencies; for example, the system in charge of letting customers place an order obviously needs to know the stock of the available items—they are interconnected.

In order to keep the overall entropy of the information system of the whole organization under control, the business must correctly separate and group these activities into independent but interconnected subsystems and optimize their communication. This is a crucial point. In the world of **DDD**, these subsystems are called **bounded contexts**.

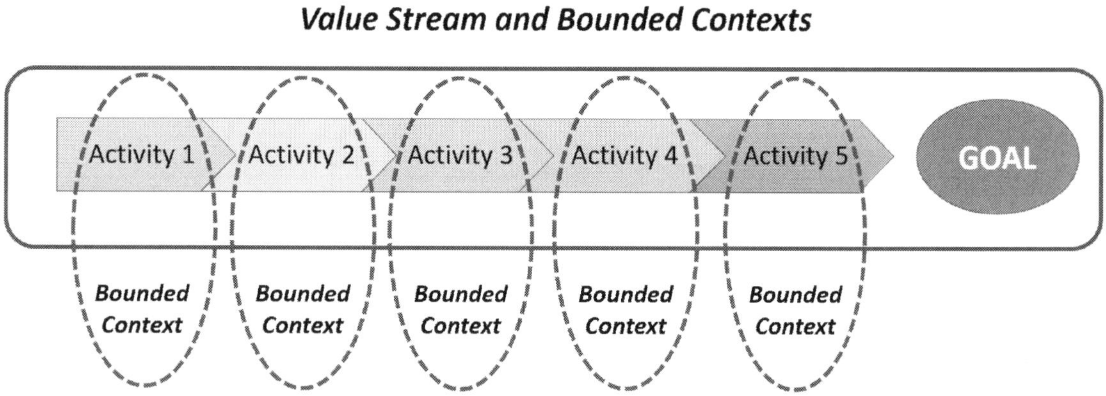

Value Stream and Bounded Contexts

Figure 18.7: Activities of the value stream mapped into bounded contexts

Each one of these activities produces data, be it newly created data or changed data (which, from an event-sourcing point of view, is just a special case of creating new data). However, not all of this huge amount of information is relevant to the whole business. Most is relevant just for a specific activity or task, while only some particular events would produce information relevant for the whole organization. These relevant events are the key information to focus on in order to optimize the communication between subsystems. In the world of DDD, they are called **domain events**.

For instance, in our previous example considering the activity of describing an item, there are many different aspects that must be considered: the brand, the name, the short description, and the technical details. Then pictures must be taken, edited, and linked to the item, and the available stock should be assessed. These subtasks generate and need data to be completed, but the completion of each one of them is not relevant outside the bounded context; therefore, its complexity should be completely encapsulated inside the bounded context.

What would be relevant for the next step of the value chain? To move forward in the next activity and place the item on the market, it's necessary that *all these subtasks have been completed* and the item has all the information needed to be ready for the next step. So, what this means is that *the required value has been added*. At this point, the bounded context needs to notify the other contexts about this event, which might be relevant for them and raise a domain event.

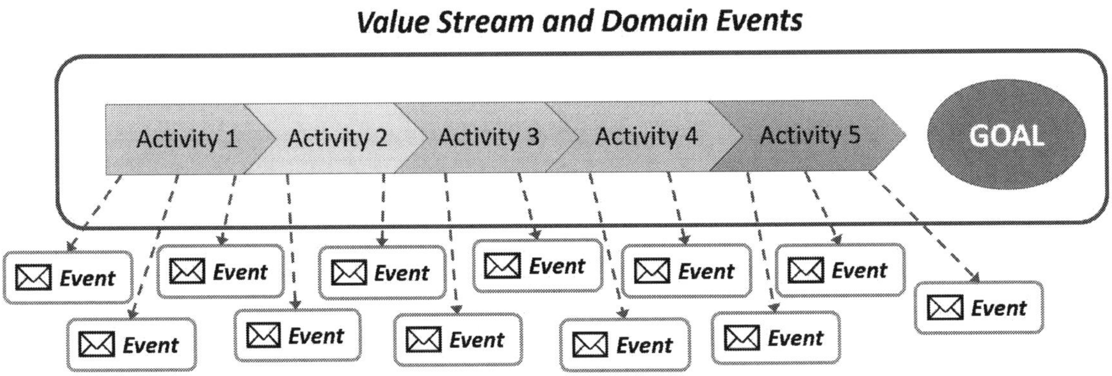

Value Stream and Domain Events

Figure 18.8: Activities of the value stream raising domain events

Bounded Contexts and Communication

If you remember the Alan Kay's quote in the previous lesson, the most important thing in making a great, growable system is designing how its modules communicate. The enabling factor here is *modularity*. Kay takes for granted that the system is fractally composed of modules, and says that how they communicate is the key point.

> **Note**
>
> The key in making great and growable systems is much more to design how its modules communicate rather than what their internal properties and behaviors should be.

From this point of view, since bounded contexts are high-level modules, there should also be a special focus on communication between them. Furthermore, given that to reach a good understanding, we should move the focal point to the external system (as noted previously by Russell Ackoff), this explains why it is important to understand the value stream in order to design the best interaction flow between the bounded contexts.

This logical, high-level view of the system is more important than the internals because it is the key to doing the right thing. And here, the crucial point is finding the perfect balance between their independence and their interrelations, determining how they should be split. What subtasks should be grouped together to form a bounded context, and what should be left on its own?

The answer is that it depends on the overall context—there is no silver bullet here either, sorry! But we have principles that can help with the inductive process of making decisions. For instance, we can see here the same forces in place that we have seen in cohesion and coupling:

- **Too much cohesion**: Keeping every task in one big bounded context would mean entangling the system, making it hard to change and scale, similar to the *god class* and *divergent change* code smells.

- **Too much coupling**: Splitting every task into its own bounded context would mean moving that complexity over the communication between them, generating an explosion of dependencies.

Furthermore, the way to achieving independence is not free in a **Service-Oriented Architecture (SOA)** environment; the infrastructural boundary must be created, deployed, maintained and monitored.

You have to choose where to pay the price of complexity. Because DDD is about reducing complexity in the software, the outcome is that you pay a price with respect to maintaining duplicate models, and possibly duplicate data.

> **Note**
>
> Eric Evans, Domain-Driven Design: Tackling Complexity in the Heart of Software, https://www.goodreads.com/book/show/179133.Domain_Driven_Design.

Here a good compromise can be to delay the implementation of the infrastructural boundary until the system requires scaling capabilities. Using the design principles explained in the previous section, it is possible to keep the logical separation between all the modules without forcing the infrastructure to follow. Additionally, a particular focus on the isolation of the data persistence and its access allows us to have a system easy to scale without paying the price of the infrastructural complexity until it is justified by business needs.

Bounded contexts are described in the book *Domain-Driven Design* by Eric J. Evans. The idea is that developers should be able to understand and update the code of a service without knowing anything about the internals of its peer services. Services interact with their peers strictly through APIs (and message queues) and thus don't share data structures, database schemata, or other internal representations of objects. Bounded contexts ensure that services are compartmentalized and have well-defined interfaces, which also enables easier testing.

> **Note**
>
> Gene Kim, et al., The DevOps Handbook: How to Create World-Class Agility, Reliability, and Security in Technology Organizations: https://www.goodreads.com/book/show/26083308-the-devops-handbook.

We agree with Nick Tune when he says that bounded contexts should show three core properties to be effective:

- **Isolation**: It must be possible to make changes to different contexts independently, without breaking other contexts.

- **Comprehensibility**: They must have an ubiquitous vocabulary and be named after it, enabling holistic conversations about them in relation with the business.

- **Parallelization**: They should be able to evolve in parallel with little or no coordination.

> **Note**
>
> Nick Tune, Strategic Domain Driven Design: What are the 3 virtues of modularity and how do you achieve them with Strategic DDD? http://www.ntcoding.co.uk/speaking/talks/strategic-domain-driven-design/agile-2018-san-diego-august-2018.

These three properties have the potential to minimize entropy and allow scalability.

Synchronous versus Asynchronous

With each bounded context having its own isolated access to low-level data storage, the biggest price to pay for this maintenance is not about data duplication because data storage is relatively cheap. The big price to pay is handling and designing the communication in order to achieve the optimal propagation of this data and enrich the value stream. There are a number of different ways to achieve this, but here, there are also a few principles that can help in our decisions.

In order to correctly make the choice of using one or the other, the most important thing to understand is the implications of synchronous and asynchronous communication.

As we have seen, instances of bounded context should have a high degree of independence, so it is important to minimize the number of dependencies among them. However, as we have seen with the concept of connascence, it is also important to understand their kind of dependency in order to maximize the autonomy of each single bounded context in a service-oriented scenario.

From this point of view, synchronous dependencies between services imply that the calling service blocks the execution and waits for a response from the called service before continuing. Very similar to the concepts of connascence of execution order and connascence of timing, this kind of dependency is very strong, tightly coupling the caller with the called. It does not scale very well, and the calling service may be impacted by errors in the called service. In systems with high availability as one of the non-functional requirements, this kind of communication is not desired.

A powerful alternative to the synchronous approach is asynchronous communication, using a publish/subscribe messaging system. In this scenario, the calling service simply publishes its message about a domain event occurring and continues with other work (unrelated to this request).

It is not blocking and waiting for a response after it sends a request, and this improves scalability. Problems in another service do not break this service, and when other services are temporarily broken, the calling service might not be able to complete a process completely, but the calling service is not broken itself. Thus, using asynchronous messaging, the services are more decoupled, preserving more autonomy.

The downside of the asynchronous messaging solution is that it increases the infrastructural complexity of the system because it requires mechanisms to send and handle messages. Furthermore, the design of the flow of domain events becomes essential when this pattern is used heavily, and this can move complexity into an area that is very difficult to monitor, opening the door for unwanted risks. We have seen scenarios where systems have been coupled to the internals of the messages so heavily that it was basically impossible to make a change to a bounded context without breaking another one. Remember, with great power comes great responsibility.

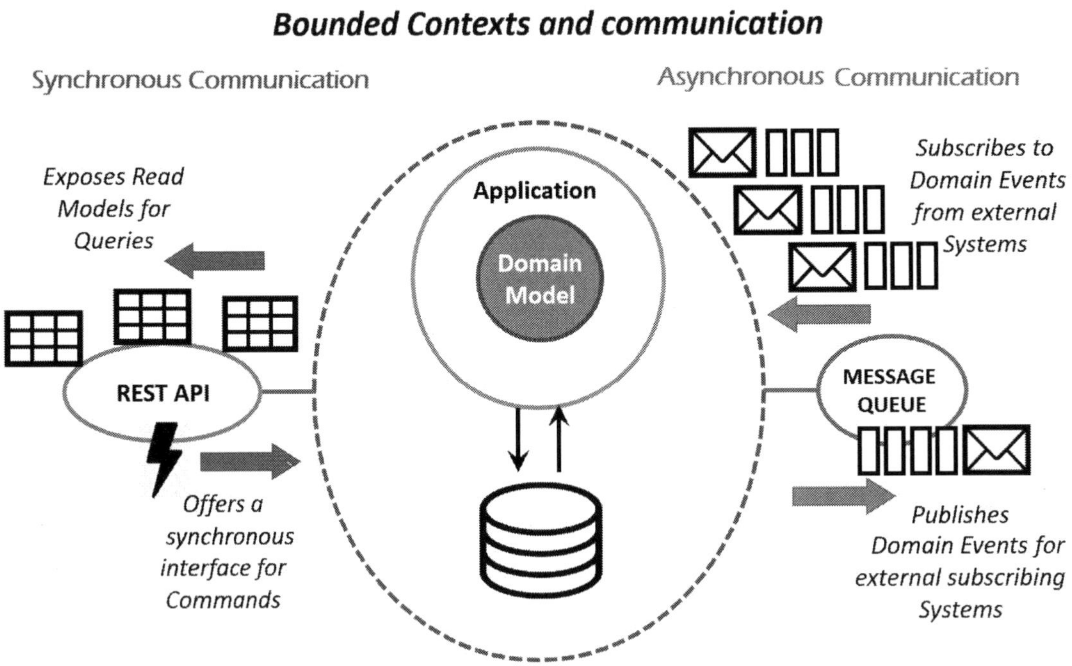

Figure 18.9: Bounded context communication

Command-Query Separation

From the point of view of communication, the separation concerns between commands and queries are also represented by the concept of bounded contexts. If we consider the different nature of commands and queries, we can see that they fit quite well with the synchronous and asynchronous ideas. Essentially, queries are a fit for synchronous communication since all they have to do is just expose data in a read-only mode, and ideally this operation is really fast and free of any race conditions.

Given the consequences of the CAP theorem, working in conditions of eventual consistency has been proven a key advantage in distributed systems in terms of resilience, scaling, and performance. This is an ideal situation for commands to happen inside asynchronous communication in a fire-and-forget mode. They might need more time to execute than queries and are often consequences of events, thus they are a very good fit.

> **Note**
>
> Wikipedia, [T]he CAP theorem implies that in the presence of a network partition, you have to choose between consistency and availability: https://en.wikipedia.org/wiki/CAP_theorem. The CAP theorem is relevant because the nature of the web is different from local networking and more similar to network partitioning, thus the choice between consistency and availability is something to consider in our web development.

Here it is important to pinpoint the difference between events and commands:

- The *event* is the trigger, the notification that *something relevant has happened at a systemic level*. It should contain the minimum information possible to identify itself (ideally, it is just a matter of its type and the IDs of the entities involved).

- The *command* is executed as the consequence of an event, and that which was responsible for raising the event might not even be aware of the command happening. If the command needs more data to execute, it can leverage synchronous communication and query the read model via an API to complete the information necessary. This is very important because it keeps the dependencies to the message itself to a minimum, which, in a publish/subscribe system, might be a one-to-many relationship. In this way, we move the dependency to the read models, which are much easier to change and expand and can have a greater granularity, breaking down the one-to-many relationship.

Business and DevOps

Once the bounded contexts are correctly defined and implemented, there is still one important aspect to consider for a complete and effective information system. The ability to make changes is meaningless if it doesn't include the ability to smoothly deploy them in production, because the value is delivered only when it is available to the end user. Furthermore, the systems must be monitored so that actions can be taken quickly when something doesn't work as expected. Finally, it must be possible to easily experiment in safe environments in order to find the best technical solutions based on empirical data gathered by experience. These are the ideas underlying DevOps as described in *The Phoenix Project* by Gene Kim, Kevin Behr, and George Spafford, and revisited in *The DevOps Handbook* by Gene Kim, Jez Humble, Patrick Debois, and John Willis.

Their work is essential to understanding how to maximize the value of DevOps, and it is particularly valuable because it has a business-oriented point of view, applying a systematic vision to it, which we have tried to apply to this book, and will share now, as well.

Essentially, what they say is that DevOps enables technology effectiveness in Three Ways.

The First Way

The First Way enables fast left-to-right flow of work from Development, to Operations, to the customer. In order to maximize flow, we need to make work visible, reduce our batch sizes and intervals of work, build in quality by preventing defects from being passed to downstream work centers, and constantly optimize for the global goals.

> **Note**
>
> Gene Kim, et al., The DevOps Handbook: How to Create World-Class Agility, Reliability, and Security in Technology Organizations: https://www.goodreads.com/book/show/26083308-the-devops-handbook.

This is in agreement with our systemic vision focused on delivering value to the customer, so only when the system is deployed and available to the customer is this value reached.

Figure 18.10: DevOps, the First Way

The Second Way

The Second Way enables the fast and constant flow of feedback from right to left at all stages of our value stream. It requires that we amplify feedback to prevent problems from happening again, or enable faster detection and recovery. By doing this, we create quality at the source and generate or embed knowledge where it is needed – this allows us to create ever-safer systems of work where problems are found and fixed long before a catastrophic failure occurs.

> **Note**
>
> Gene Kim, et al., The DevOps Handbook: How to Create World-Class Agility, Reliability, and Security in Technology Organizations: https://www.goodreads.com/book/show/26083308-the-devops-handbook.

This principle is about feedback loops, which are fundamental for the system to inspect and adapt. The quicker the feedback, the quicker the action. This is achieved with monitoring and alerting.

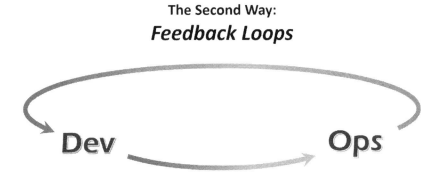

Figure 18.11: DevOps, the Second Way

The Third Way

The Third Way enables the creation of a generative, high-trust culture that supports a dynamic, disciplined, and scientific approach to experimentation and risk-taking, facilitating the creation of organizational learning, both from our successes and failures. Furthermore, by continually shortening and amplifying our feedback loops, we create ever-safer systems of work and are better able to take risks and perform experiments that help us learn faster than our competition and win in the marketplace.

As part of the Third Way, we also design our system of work so that we can multiply the effects of new knowledge, transforming local discoveries into global improvements. Regardless of where someone performs their work, they do so with the cumulative and collective experience of everyone in the organization.

> **Note**
>
> Gene Kim, et al., The DevOps Handbook: How to Create World-Class Agility, Reliability, and Security in Technology Organizations: https://www.goodreads.com/book/show/26083308-the-devops-handbook.

The last principle is about experimentation and knowledge sharing, so that breakthrough discoveries can quickly spread into the organization and improve the whole system.

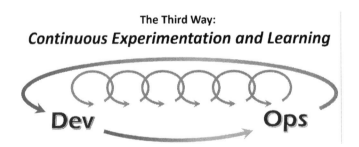

Figure 18.12: DevOps, the Third Way

Systems Thinking and Sociotechnical Organizations

We are almost at the end of our journey, and at this point, the attentive reader might have noticed a few patterns. The occurrences of concepts such as *feedback loops*, *communication*, *independence*, *value*, *entropy*, *whole*, and *effectiveness* are not a coincidence. All the subjects of this book have been viewed through the lens of Systems Thinking, hence the reason for focusing on these concepts.

Systems thinking, as "the capability to identify and understand systems, predicting their behavior and devising modifications to them in order to produce desired effects," gives an outstanding advantage, not only to understand the deep reasons behind the principles for writing good software, but also to understand the systemic problems arising in organizations. This is because Systems Thinking offers a generic set of principles applicable to every kind of system.

> **Note**
>
> Ross D. Arnold and Jon P. Wade, 2015 Conference on Systems Engineering Research.

Businesses, from this point of view, can be seen as sociotechnical systems, where the dynamics of deterministic systems (the software that we write) meet those of complex systems (the human beings interacting with the software and with each other), generating environments that display very defined properties that often are not understood. Deming said that "no amount of care or skill in workmanship can overcome fundamental faults of the system". We can change this to state, "no amount of *agile technical practices* can overcome the fundamental faults of the system."

> **Note**
>
> Edwards Deming, Out of the Crisis, https://www.goodreads.com/book/show/566574.Out_of_the_Crisis.

Human beings display non-linear behavior, so the difficult part of having them effectively work together doesn't reside on the technical side, but in the social side of the sociotechnical system that is the business. We have come to the conclusion that difficulties of a technical nature are more often than not just hiding problems of a social nature, and are merely the side effects of social consequences of these problems.

Resources

Web-based resources

- Everything You Need to Know About Theory of Constraints, Smartsheet: https://www.smartsheet.com/all-about-theory-of-constraints.

- From Mechanistic to Systemic thinking, Russell L. Ackoff: https://www.youtube.com/watch?v=yGN5DBpW93g.

- An introduction to user story mapping, Jim Bowes: https://manifesto.co.uk/user-story-mapping/.

- The Lean Canvas, Ash Maurya: https://leanstack.com/leancanvas.

- Microservices architecture principle #4: Asynchronous communication over synchronous communication, Gero Vermaas: https://xebia.com/blog/microservices-architecture-principle-4-asynchronous-communication-over-synchronous-communication/.

- Story Map Concepts, Jeff Patton: http://www.jpattonassociates.com/wp-content/uploads/2015/03/story_mapping.pdf.

- The Strategic Practices of Domain-Driven Design, Nick Tune: http://www.ntcoding.co.uk/workshops/strategic-ddd-practices.

- The True Difference Between Knowledge and Understanding, Colin Robertson: http://www.willpowered.co/learn/knowledge-understanding.

- User story mapping, Jeff Patton: http://www.jpattonassociates.com/user-story-mapping/.

- What is the Theory of Constraints? LeanProduction: https://www.leanproduction.com/theory-of-constraints.html.

- What is the Theory of Constraints, and How Does It Compare to Lean Thinking? LeanProduction: https://www.lean.org/common/display/?o=223.

Books

- Ackoff's Best: His Classic Writings on Management, Russell L. Ackoff: https://www.goodreads.com/book/show/1623149.Ackoff_s_Best.

- Agile Coaching, Rachel Davies, Liz Sedley: https://www.goodreads.com/book/show/6582184-agile-coaching.

- Agile Retrospectives: Making Good Teams Great, Esther Derby, et al.: https://www.goodreads.com/book/show/721338.Agile_Retrospectives.

- Business Model Generation, Alexander Osterwalder, Yves Pigneur: https://www.goodreads.com/book/show/7723797-business-model-generation.

- Critical Chain, Eliyahu M. Goldratt: https://www.goodreads.com/book/show/848514.Critical_Chain.

- The DevOps Handbook: How to Create World-Class Agility, Reliability, and Security in Technology Organizations, Gene Kim, Jez Humble, Patrick Debois, John Willis: https://www.goodreads.com/book/show/26083308-the-devops-handbook.

- Domain-Driven Design: Tackling Complexity in the Heart of Software, Eric Evans: https://www.goodreads.com/book/show/179133.Domain_Driven_Design.

- The Goal: A Process of Ongoing Improvement, Eliyahu M. Goldratt: https://www.goodreads.com/book/show/113934.The_Goal.

- Impact Mapping: Making a Big Impact with Software Products and Projects, Gojko Adzic: https://www.goodreads.com/book/show/16084015-impact-mapping.

- Implementing Domain-Driven Design, Vaughn Vernon: https://www.goodreads.com/book/show/15756865-implementing-domain-driven-design.

- Kanban: Successful Evolutionary Change for Your Technology Business, David J. Anderson: https://www.goodreads.com/book/show/8086552-kanban.

- The Mythical Man-Month: Essays on Software Engineering, Frederick P. Brooks Jr.: https://www.goodreads.com/book/show/13629.The_Mythical_Man_Month.

- Out of the Crisis, W. Edwards Deming: https://www.goodreads.com/book/show/566574.Out_of_the_Crisis.

- Patterns, Principles, and Practices of Domain-Driven Design, Scott Millett and Nick Tune: https://www.goodreads.com/book/show/25531393-patterns-principles-and-practices-of-domain-driven-design.

- The Phoenix Project: A Novel About IT, DevOps, and Helping Your Business Win, Gene Kim, Kevin Behr, George Spafford: https://www.goodreads.com/book/show/17255186-the-phoenix-project.

- Running Lean: Iterate from Plan A to a Plan That Works, Ash Maurya: https://www.goodreads.com/book/show/13078769-running-lean.

- The Systems Bible: The Beginner's Guide to Systems Large and Small: Being the Third Edition of Systemantics, John Gall: https://www.goodreads.com/book/show/583785.The_Systems_Bible.

- Theory of Constraints, Eliyahu M. Goldratt: https://www.goodreads.com/book/show/582174.Theory_of_Constraints.

- Theory of Constraints Handbook, F. Cox III, John G. Schleier Jr.: https://www.goodreads.com/book/show/8361069-theory-of-constraints-handbook.

- User Story Mapping: Discover the Whole Story, Build the Right Product, Jeff Patton: https://www.goodreads.com/book/show/22221112-user-story-mapping.

- Value Stream Mapping: How to Visualize Work and Align Leadership for Organizational Transformation, Karen Martin and Mike Osterling: https://www.goodreads.com/book/show/20456190-value-stream-mapping.

19
Story of Team C

You have your way. I have my way. As for the right way, the correct way, and the only way, it does not exist.

– Friedrich Nietzsche

Imagine you are in a big team, without a strong leadership everyone is going in a different direction. Just a few seem able to reach agreements, owning and sharing principles, and discussing how to apply them best for the collective benefit. They spend hours helping each other, often pairing together over the same code. But they are the minority and are largely outnumbered by egos and wannabe heroes.

Nevertheless, facts are with the few, which slowly over time conquer respect. But far from making the impact they want, the team as a whole is still delivering neither quality nor quantity, strangled by an unreachable consensus and inevitable, growing technical debt.

Then, imagine one day they told you, "If we don't deliver something significant in four months, our project will be dumped by the business. Pick who you want and build a new team to deliver a completely new piece of backlog. But you must do it quickly."

Desperation makes unthinkable things possible. What would you do? Would you accept the challenge? And how would you do it?

This is the story of what happened when Eldon and I (Marco) had the green light for starting "Team C," after we suggested our plan for saving the project when it was "red flagged."

> **Note**
>
> Team C and red flags are clues of the corporation environment we were working in. We didn't choose the name – we were a new micro-team created from the bones of the two main teams: Team A and Team B. Hence, we were Team C. This says a lot about the personalities not only inside the development teams, but in that overall corporate environment.

Terraforming

- **Eldon**: "They said yes, and we can even hire two new people!"
- **Me**: "You joking, mate?"
- **Eldon**: "Seriously. I already know someone who would fit with us perfectly and can come and join us. Do you know anyone yourself?"
- **Me**: "Actually, I do know an amazing guy, knowledgeable and humble, who worked with me in the past and is looking for something..."

Recruiting was sorted there and then – the essence of pragmatism. I am proud of having a good network of respectable and knowledgeable team players who enjoyed working with me and would love to do it again:

- **Eldon**: "But we must pick one tester and one business analyst as well; that's considered mandatory in a business team here."
- **Me**: "Let's take someone who would be happy to learn something new and make the team enjoyable."

- **Eldon**: "Definitely."

- **Me**: "I bet I can get them up to speed by writing the acceptance criteria directly in the code in a matter of weeks."

- **Eldon**: "I want to see that! It won't be easy, but it would be a winning shot. Let's try!"

Team Building

When we made the choice of **business analyst (BA)** and tester, we went to talk to them first to see whether they would like the idea of working with us. It was very humbling to feel they were genuinely excited about it, but also a bit scared:

- **BA**: "No one ever explained the backlog to me, and I've only been here a few months, so I can't say I really know the business. Are you really sure I can be of help? Maybe others more seasoned in the business will know more stuff!"

- **Me**: "I have the impression that no one here really understands the business. I feel that there are two kinds of people: those who pretend to know and those who express doubts. We prefer people of the second kind. We will dig into the business knowledge together as a team until we gain the understanding we need."

- **Tester**: "Guys, I have to let you know beforehand that I have never worked like that before. I am not sure if I am up to your expectations?"

- **Me**: "Don't worry, we are going to pair with you as long as you feel confident to try by yourself. We promise you will never be let alone, and you can grab one of us for help any time."

- **Tester**: "That makes me feel better, but I have never coded in my life."

- **Eldon**: "You are not required to really implement anything. It's just about learning a very easy, alternative way to write in plain English. I promise once I show it to you, everything will be less scary."

- **Tester**: "But, I mean, are you sure I can learn fast enough?"

- **Me**: "Listen, I learned to write code when I was 9. Do you know what that means?"

- **Tester**: "That you are really smart."

- **Me**: "Nope, wrong answer. It means it isn't so difficult! At least for the level required for your task. Trust me, in a few weeks time you will laugh about this fear."

> **Note**
>
> The thing I dislike the most of environments with a blaming culture is that it makes risk aversity spread and becomes entrenched in almost everybody. I remember when I was a young developer, I was often scared when performing some delicate task until I had an enlightening conversation with Matteo – the same guy mentioned in the *Design Patterns* lesson. Feeling my emotionally charged state when I had to do an update in the live database (let's skip the reasons for this), he told me: "Relax, mate, you're not a cardiac surgeon operating on someone's heart. No one is going to die if you make a mistake, chill out. This panic is not gonna help your performance, anyway. In the worst-case scenario, we just roll back." That was a pearl of wisdom I internalized with time, and when I see the same situation now, from the other side of the fence, I use the same joke.

The foundation for doing a great job was there: everyone in the team trusted each other, and we knew that these little fears were just an indication that they cared to be as effective as they could, and were focused on the common goal before anything else. With these premises, we could go far.

The Backlog: Crunching Knowledge for Breakfast

The first thing we did was obviously to start studying the backlog. We soon realized it was not worth it – it was completely indecipherable. We soon asked for help from BAs, but the more we talked to them, the more we realized they were parroting something that someone else said. Yes, that place was big. Loaded with people, procedures, middlemen, and constraints. We decided we had to dispose of the practices for normal duties and switch to the ones for systemic emergencies.

So, one morning we invited all the relevant stakeholders (users, BAs, and many others) in the same room with our team for an epic story map session. We had all the key people there ready to answer all of our questions. All BAs, including those from other teams, were also present so they could clarify their understanding too.

First, we identified our personas, because that was one of the most blurred concepts in our minds. That gave a new perspective to things and many "aha," "I see," and "that's why" moments followed up quickly. The discussions were very interesting, and it was great when, at a certain point, the conversation was hijacked from our facilitation and carried on independently by stakeholders and various business actors themselves. Everybody got excited about knowing more of how others worked and why they did things that way. What an amazing collective learning experience!

By 1 p.m. we had built our full, high-level domain knowledge with all of our questions answered. That allowed us to assemble the stories of the backlog into a logical order. Only implementation details remained buried in the old requirements, but there was time for the details. After half a day of user story mapping, we were ready to start!

Cracking On

We were just a team of four when we started, and we had to wait a few days before the two new members could jump on board. Eldon and I decided to split the job and tackle the two most critical tasks – one task each.

While he was setting up the walking skeleton and finding the best way to seamlessly integrate our new REST API with the legacy system that we were constrained to talk to for authentication and login purposes, I took the job of taking care of the requirements with the goal of building a proper acceptance test automation suite. That involved also coaching a BA and tester – this was the most delicate part of the job, in my point of view. I had already committed on it with them, and I couldn't let them down.

Typical discussions about **Behavior Driven Development** (BDD) frameworks arose, but the process to use a new framework for the team would have to go through bureaucracy and middle management – something we wanted to avoid because time wasn't on our side. Plus, we shared mixed feelings about existing frameworks, and we thought that the effort might not be worth the value.

I had been stewing on an idea for some time, and I shared it with Eldon: "Listen, give me a day to try something out, and let's see whether we like it enough." That's how EasyBdd was born. After a morning of work, we reviewed it together, we tweaked it a bit, and we fell in love with it. We were confident the BA and tester could work on it with a bit of practice.

From then on, I spent the next two weeks mob programming, tackling the initial stories of the backlog with the BA on the left of me and the tester on the right. We defined acceptance criteria, often going to talk to the business users, writing the criteria in code using EasyBdd.

Teaching by example is so powerful; after the second week, the BA and tester didn't need to ask us developers much anymore. They were pairing like seasoned XP practitioners, cracking on more requirements and acceptance criteria than we could handle, with a level of clarity and attention to detail I have hardly found again afterward.

The tester was writing the acceptance criteria in the solution and even learned to effectively use basic source control commands. We used to joke a lot together, and I told him, "You see, on your next job, you can change careers and apply for developer roles!"

Watching them working together like that after all their doubts was the chief picture of that experience that I want to keep in my heart.

From Forming to Performing

When there is team spirit in a group with a common goal, there is no storming phase. In Team C, we never had that experience. We knew exactly what we considered important and shared it with everyone from day one. After the initial coaching on the field, the other two team members arrived and, from then on, user stories began flying on the kanban board.

We had regular product demos with stakeholders, led every time by a different member of Team C. Those who weren't in the meeting were at their desks, working on the backlog.

The level of focus and commitment was outstanding. We had many discussions as a team, but decisions were always made by a consensus in a matter of minutes. We trusted the expertise that each member gave to the service of the team, always willing to try out something suggested by someone who knew more about the matter.

We also decided to take some risks that resulted in accidentally discovering a new, superfast way to work: Outside-In **Acceptance Test Driven Development (ATDD)** development with optional internal unit test cycles.

Outside-In ATDD with Optional Unit Tests

The idea behind my suggestion is very simple, and it relies heavily on the experience of the developers, which in this case was very high. To be effective, it requires the ability to write outside-in testable code naturally, without the need of a test to drive any class.

Basically, if we have a very good suite of acceptance tests like the one we were building in Team C, any bug in the code would be traceable to a few broken units and always at least one broken acceptance. So, acceptance tests would be the minimum number of tests we could write in order to have the safety network to refactor any part of our code.

So, I suggested, "Why don't we break the dogma of full test coverage and stop enforcing unit tests, as we already have the acceptance umbrella? If we write *testable* code, what's the problem? If at some point we feel like a class would benefit from a unit test, it will be easy to add. The advantage will be that we'll have much more freedom in the refactoring phase, with less moving parts in the test side to fix every time. We don't need many tests to develop outside-in approach; one is enough, after all. I do it all the time when I work on lone projects, and it allows me to be very quick. Why don't we try it?"

The resulting discussion was challenging, but not dogmatic. After all, we didn't have much time, we all knew exactly what we were doing, and this technique could reveal itself as a big win. We arrived quickly to the consensus of *unit tests at discretion of the developer*.

> **Note**
>
> We made the decision to try this experiment mostly because all four members of the team were very experienced and, in any situation, would naturally write code outside in without the need of tests. Furthermore, their maturity was high enough to decide to add tests when they felt there was value in them. Be very careful in trying this technique as a team without mastering outside-in development.

The Green Flag

The technique revealed itself to be very successful. After the first month and a half, our system was already in great shape. The business stakeholders couldn't believe their eyes. Finally, after years, something was deployed that actually worked, and it steadily grew, feature after feature, and without defects. After a few more months (in record times by the standard of the old team), we had successfully implemented the whole backlog we were in charge of.

A few weeks later, the news no one would have bet a dime on arrived: the project had been green flagged. We had ensured the budget for the whole team to be available for another year. We made possible what a few months before seemed impossible.

The technical skills that we applied, along with the experience and the principles described in this book, were of great importance. We balanced risk mitigation and development speed using a superior acceptance test suite and a maniacal focus on clean code, SOLID principles, and a simple design.

Working on that code was pure joy, and the direct result was a truly collective code ownership. Anyone could easily find out where to act in the code to get the desired result. Curious members of the other teams often asked if they could see it, like it was some sort of attraction: "Wow, it's so *simple and easy to understand!*"

The Moral of the Story

The real reason we achieved a considerable goal that time, however, goes beyond the mere technical aspect. The full exploitation of the great potential of the single individuals was possible only because we set up a fully functional team where everyone was trying to meet each other's needs.

We never grew tired of explaining things to one another, trying someone's new ideas that resonated with others, and generally helping each other every time someone needed it. We were a team of servant leaders where trust, support, and empathy felt natural. We never blamed each other, and together we reviewed improvement points several times without anyone ever feeling personally attached to a piece of code. What a childish concept; it wasn't my code or his code – it was ours.

Creating an environment of truly selfless collaboration allowed everyone to freely try out ideas with the consequence of attaining awesome knowledge and technical implementation breakthroughs. It also enabled the team to surpass the limits of the individual by sharing abilities when it was needed, as no one was ever afraid to ask questions, reveal they were stuck, or didn't know something. Such an environment enabled everyone to effectively use the knowledge of the whole team in every situation because everyone knew that the best solution was always just a quick question away.

That was the real ingredient missing in other teams, where too many egos clashed, competing for doing things their way instead of being open to trusting each other without caring about who suggested this idea or that solution.

We built a fully functional, highly effective, sociotechnical system, which surpassed, by far, the sum of the skills of the individuals. If you think about it, that is one of the main general properties of systems. As we learned from Deming, 95% of our performances depended on that. That was the real secret of Team C.

> **Note**
>
> William Edwards Deming, "The fact is that the system that people work in and the interaction with people may account for 90 or 95 percent of performance."

20
Conclusion

Information, knowledge and understanding enable us to do things right, to be efficient, but wisdom enables us to do the right things, to be effective. Science pursues data, information, knowledge and understanding: what is truth; but the humanities pursue wisdom: what is right.

– Russell Lincoln Ackoff

One of the great things about working in smaller companies – especially in growing startups – is that you can have deep, human contact with everybody in the business, including key leaders driving the vision into execution. These people usually have extensive experience and knowledge. When they are also servant leaders, it's a real pleasure hanging out with them because there is always something to learn, even from unexpected situations.

For example, a few days after joining one of the most exciting Italian startups at the time, I was invited for lunch by Max, who was an important man on the Board. We had already exchanged some words before, and I was pleasantly surprised to see how down-to-earth he was. The dialogue was enjoyable, and I immediately had good feelings about him.

Over some pasta, the dialogue moved to sports – an Italian classic.

"I do like football," I said.

"What football team do you support?"

"Fiorentina."

That didn't go down too well, since he was for Juventus – historically the worst rival of Fiorentina. But we were laughing about it.

He suddenly asked me a tricky question, "Since you love football as much as I do, let's see whether you know this: what's the lineup of the last Italian World Cup winning team?"

Without hesitation, I began, "Zoff, Gentile, Cabrini, Scirea, Collovati, Oriali..."

> **Note**
>
> This story occurred before 2006 when Italy won the last World Cup. The previous one referred to in the story is the one of 1982.

He couldn't believe his ears and joked, "Are you sure you're a developer? The CTO must have missed something! Do you know that I have never yet found a developer claiming he loves football and even knows about it?"

We laughed again. Then, he asked me, "Do you play or have played any sport?"

I explained a bit of my story: "When I was a kid, I played roller hockey semiprofessionally for 12 years for the junior team in my town, which happens to be in the major Italian league. We even won the Italian championship in 1986. I gave it up only when I enrolled at the university...."

I could sense he was intrigued and had a reason for the odd questions. He said, "You know, this is something I often ask to my interviewees because I believe that the key quality for the people I hire is being a good team player. In my experience, I have observed that those who have played team sports and love them also tend to have an outstanding approach with regard to professional teams."

I was amazed. Being young, that was the first time I had heard someone senior talking about team play. It resonated a lot with me and, as you can see, I still remember that conversation. I loved working there, and that spirit was the key to their success. Unfortunately, as the years have gone by, I've realized that executives with such a mindset are not so common.

The Human Factor

An excellent distillation of the elixir for building software effectively would be missing an essential flavor if we didn't touch on the topic of people. Even when building software as a single developer, there are always interactions with other people in the form of clients, stakeholders, and end users. Closed systems exist only in the academic world of theories and live only inside books.

Any model – technical, methodological, or psychological – has very little relationship to reality when the human and social aspects are not considered. This is ultimately the greatest strength of the 12 agile principles.

> **Note**
>
> Kent Beck, et al., Principles behind the Agile Manifesto: http://agilemanifesto.org/principles.html.

Despite the general, diffused disillusion we sense over the Agile hype, we still don't agree with what we've heard, that is "Agile is dead." Maybe it's the hype that is about to die, and that might even be a good thing. Agile, before anything else, is an idea based on a set of 12 principles. And you cannot kill ideas or principles – that's their ultimate strength.

However, ideas can be misunderstood and resisted, either unconsciously or wickedly planned – you decide. The original Agile idea has been twisted until it has become a mockery of itself. Replaced by a set of ceremonies, methodologies, and self-referential facilitation techniques that, despite being easy to brand (and, hence, to certify), have very little to do with the original 12 principles.

We suggest the reader to go beyond the agile manifesto and read over the 12 principles to better understand them. They are unfortunately relegated to "page 2" of the agile manifesto website, so we have reproduced them at the end of this book.

When someone says that "Agile is dead," we suggest that (after reading the principles) they should ask whether Agile was ever "born" in the first place. As clothes do not make the man, "Agile methodologies" in job specifications, some tests in the code, a whiteboard with colored post-its, and a stand-up/scrum at 9:00 in the morning doesn't make a team Agile.

A much better starting point is the high regard for the human nature of the individuals who work inside teams and companies, which is proven by attending to their needs and appreciating their professionality.

That's the reason why Toyota allowed competitors to walk through their factories and production plants. When others asked Toyota whether they feared they would be copied, they replied that the strength of the Toyota production system wasn't about the methodologies they used, but the principles underlying them: the team spirit, the passion, and the continuous improvement of the skills of their people. You can't grasp that simply by looking at a kanban board.

It's the fifth principle, after all:

Build projects around motivated individuals.

Give them the environment and support they need, and trust them to get the job done.

– Fifth Agile Principle

Team Play

Teamwork requires some sacrifice up front; people who work as a team have to put the collective needs of the group ahead of their individual interests.

– Patrick Lencioni

The best team players all have one very distinguishable characteristic in common: they put the common goal of the team before any personal one. In that context, they are selfless – because they are able to merge their ego with the collective consciousness of the team.

This single aspect is the most significant for the success of any team, and is well beyond technicalities or methodologies. In an environment composed of selfless personalities, a few experienced leaders are enough to rapidly spread knowledge and common understanding because everyone is constantly focused on *giving*, not on receiving. This enables the most wonderful feedback loop of all, that is, everybody acquiring the missing skills and insights of others, allowing the team to grow constantly and steadily every day. Not only do individuals become better, but the positive form of collaboration and the collective exploration of new ways give the enthusiasm and the motivation necessary to achieve what would be unachievable by the individual working alone:

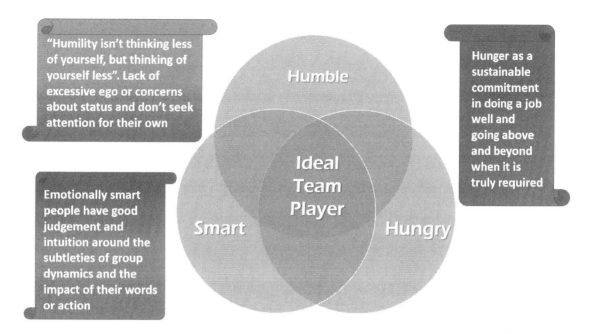

Figure 20.1: The three essential virtues of the "ideal team player" by Patrick Lencioni

That's exactly the reason we were motivated to write this book with six hands; we have enjoyed working together so much as a team of coaches and developers in the past that sharing this vision and experiencing this magic was a no-brainer, despite having to move out of our coding comfort zone as a team.

The best part of the experience of crafting this book has been getting together for remote mob writing sessions. We were always pleasantly surprised by the chain reaction of ideas (and motivation) coming out of it. We discussed a lot, sometimes very deeply and from different positions. But there was always the belief and trust in each other and the opportunities to change our mind when new relevant elements arose in matters.

When team members trust each other and know that everyone is capable of admitting when they're wrong, then conflict becomes nothing more than the pursuit of truth or the best possible answer.

— Patrick Lencioni

Bounded Rationality and Knowledge Sharing

Bounded rationality is the idea that, in decision making, the rationality of individuals is limited by the information they have, the cognitive limitations of their minds, and the finite amount of time they have to make a decision. The term was coined in the 1950s by Herbert A. Simon, and a lot has been written about its implications from an economic perspective. This simple concept plays a very important role in how we make decisions as a group.

Essentially, deductive rationality in a complex system tends to break down. The obvious reason is that beyond a certain level of complexity, the human mind reaches its natural limit to cope; hence, human rationality is *bounded*.

This is why it is easier to have an effective, small team rather than a large one. This is why we keep our classes small, we break user stories down into the smallest deliverable units, and we strive to reduce the responsibility of our bounded contexts. In turn, this limits the size of our services. Limiting the complexity of the system, which means striving for low entropy, also maximizes the potential use of deductive rationality.

The problem is that, as W. Brian Arthur has noted, once we reach those boundaries in interactive situations of complexity, which are somewhat inevitable when human beings are involved, "agents cannot rely anymore upon the other agents […] to behave under perfect rationality, and so are forced to guess their behavior. This lands them in a world of subjective beliefs, and subjective beliefs about subjective beliefs."

So, if we have to rely on inductive rationality using subjective beliefs as Arthur said, we should share as a team (and as an organization) a set of principles and values. These should be simple enough to be widely understood, but strong enough to allow us to work out decisions limiting the subjectivity. In this way, the decisions have a better chance of being correct and reaching a consensus becomes simpler.

In our experience with development teams, sharing knowledge with the goal of reaching a common understanding of the principles and values we presented in this book has always had a tremendous positive impact in limiting friction about consensuses. In fact, we also wrote this book with the intent of having a reference manual for recalling and reviewing principles to support our personal activities of coaches and mentors, hoping that we can help everyone in the same situation and share the same values.

The activity of teaching we have been doing recently has been a real game changer for us, and we highly suggest readers to try it. Nothing in our profession has been more humanly rewarding than sharing our knowledge and our understanding with less experienced, eager-to-learn young professionals and seeing them improving by the day. Their gratitude for what they have learned has been humbling and represents the real proof that we have been helping them with something they feel is important.

Furthermore, the challenging discussions with them have led us to clarify our own thoughts. We've also acquired more insight about the concepts we have always understood, and the new ideas that have come along the way have been priceless.

In the end, we are not just part of a team or an organization. As IT professionals, we are all part of a wider community connected by general knowledge and understanding. If you think about it, our profession is based on the knowledge and understanding of the people of the past who were kind enough to share it.

Think, for example, about the work of Alan Turing, Von Neumann, Claude Shannon, and many others. If they didn't share their ideas at first (which became general knowledge after), our jobs would be very different. But their ideas came after they studied other materials with the knowledge and the ideas of the people who came before them. We could carry this concept back to prehistory. Sharing knowledge, understanding, and ideas has been the real enabling point for the holistic progress of human civilization.

That's why we think that knowledge is one of the most precious collective things we have as social beings. So, foster it, share it, and expand it with new ideas. It's one of the highest purposes we can think of. Being able to genuinely enjoy this process of appreciating and sharing immaterial things is what makes the real difference in software development, in organizations, and in life.

It is only with the heart that one can see rightly; what is essential is invisible to the eye.

– Antoine de Saint-Exupery, The Little Prince

Resources

Web

- Inductive Reasoning and Bounded Rationality, *Complexity and the Economy*, W. Brian Arthur: http://tuvalu.santafe.edu/~wbarthur/Papers/El_Farol.pdf.

Books

- *Drive: The Surprising Truth About What Motivates Us*, Daniel H. Pink : https://www.goodreads.com/book/show/6452796-drive.

- *The Five Dysfunctions of a Team: A Leadership Fable*, Patrick Lencioni : https://www.goodreads.com/book/show/21343.The_Five_Dysfunctions_of_a_Team.

- *Hearts over Diamonds*, Bob Marshall : https://leanpub.com/heartsoverdiamonds.

- *The Ideal Team Player: How to Recognize and Cultivate the Three Essential Virtues*, Patrick Lencioni : https://www.goodreads.com/book/show/28930640-the-ideal-team-player.

21
The 12 Agile Principles

1. Our highest priority is to satisfy the customer through early and continuous delivery of valuable software.

2. Welcome changing requirements, even late in development. Agile processes harness change for the customer's competitive advantage.

3. Deliver working software frequently, from a couple of weeks to a couple of months, with a preference for the shorter timescale.

4. Businesspeople and developers must work together daily throughout the project.

5. Build projects around motivated individuals. Give them the environment and support they need and trust them to get the job done.

6. The most efficient and effective method of conveying information to and within a development team is a face-to-face conversation.

7. Working software is the primary measure of progress.

8. Agile processes promote sustainable development. The sponsors, developers, and users should be able to maintain a constant pace indefinitely.

9. Continuous attention to technical excellence and good design enhances agility.

10. Simplicity – the art of maximizing the amount of work not done – is essential.

11. The best architectures, requirements, and designs emerge from self-organizing teams.

12. At regular intervals, the team reflects on how to become more productive, and then tunes and adjusts its behavior accordingly.

22

PopcornFlow by Claudio Perrone

Inertia is your enemy.

– *Claudio Perrone*

We have seen that the teams and the organizations we work in are Sociotechnical Systems that naturally tend to inertia. Let's read the quote from John Gall again and try to understand it better. "*In order to remain unchanged, the system must change. Specifically, the changes that must occur are changes in the patterns of changes (or strategies) previously employed to prevent drastic internal change.*"

What John says here is that inertia it is not absolute. The system actually has changing patterns, but they are naturally, and mostly unconsciously, used to prevent drastic internal change. They are often just effects of decisions taken without the goal of changing.

The concept of PopcornFlow, created by Claudio Perrone exploits these changing patterns, essentially making the collective consciousness of the system aware of them through visualization. This consciousness empowers the folks working in the system with these changes so they can actively make conscious decisions about them through experimentation and learning. Coupled with an iterative way of feedback, this results in experiments that enable collective learning, triggering a chain reaction of initiatives and ideas because teams feel that they own their destiny and can objectively view the consequences of their willingness to move in a specific direction.

From this point of view, PopcornFlow introduces, sustains, and accelerates continuous innovation and change, promoting ultra-rapid experimentation to help support the decision-making process under uncertainty. It consists of two parts: an iterative decision cycle based on seven visualizable steps, and a set of principles:

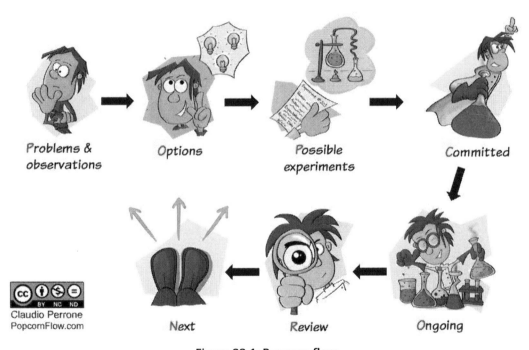

Figure 22.1: Popcorn flow

The 7-Steps Decision Cycle

The iteration cycle consists of seven steps, each mapped to a column, which is essential to give visibility about the state of the learning activities. The initial letter of each step forms the word **POPCORN**.

- Problems and observations
- Options
- Possible experiments
- Committed
- Ongoing
- Review
- Next

Teams and individuals focus on and discuss the problems they face, options to solve or reduce the impact of those problems, and possible experiments to explore one or more of those options. Either just in time or on a regular, but fast-paced basis, they describe the details on sticky notes and place them on the board. They then execute the experiments, making the notes flow through the board, creating what Claudio calls "a learning stream."

The Principles

PopcornFlow is a principle-based, antifragile philosophy, and these are its guiding principles:

- **If change is hard, make it continuous.**
- (*The Virus Principle*)
- **It's not only what you do, but also what you learn by doing it, that matters.**
- (*The Ladder Principle*)
- **Everybody is entitled to their own opinion, but a shared opinion is a fact.**
- (*The Freedom Principle*)

- **It's not "fail fast, fail often", it's "learn fast, learn often."**

- (*The Skateboarder Principle*)

- **Small bets, big win..**

- (We like to call this *The Venture Principle*)

> **Note**
> Nassim Nicholas Taleb, Antifragile: Things That Gain from Disorder: <u>https://www.goodreads.com/book/show/13530973-antifragile</u>.
>
> The wording of this principle is still a work in progress, but it's based on Nassim Taleb's concept of "option asymmetry." In a nutshell: it's not about how frequently we meet or exceed our expectations, but rather about how to limit the cost of each experiment and how much we gain when we are right, even if only occasionally. We like to call this "the Venture principle" because it is the same idea of venture capital for start-ups; most of it gets lost in ideas that will fail, but the few successful ones will pay off way more than what is lost.

Who Can Benefit from PopcornFlow

Accordingly to Claudio, PopcornFlow performs best in complex domains where the problems are, essentially, system probes. To a great extent, what the method does is use uncontrolled parallel experiments to explore options and change the system dynamics.

It is particularly useful in any organization that wants to innovate, especially if it doesn't know how. It has already found its way into start-ups, large financial institutions, well-known technology companies, and many more different environments. For example, last year, a group in the Canadian public sector won two prestigious national innovation awards by using it.

PopcornFlow, born as Claudio's idea while working in Agile and Lean environments, is obviously well fit to coach Agile teams with and facilitate highly effective retrospectives. Teams can trade options outside their immediate circle, too – a crucial mechanism to reduce the inevitable bias. Combined with jobs-to-be-done theory, it also works well for product and service innovation, and can help even sales and marketing teams.

Resources

Web-based resources:

- PopcornFlow: Continuous Evolution Through Ultra-Rapid Experimentation, Claudio Perrone: https://popcornflow.com/.

Books:

- Antifragile: Things That Gain from Disorder,Nassim Nicholas Taleb: https://www.goodreads.com/book/show/13530973-antifragile.

23

EventStorming by Alberto Brandolini

Everybody is a master in his own silo.

– *Alberto Brandolini*

We have seen that building a software system is an activity with the goal of automating the information flow to support a business's value stream. This means that a software system should exist to support the business processes and should be shaped around them, be at their service, optimize them, and make them more effective.

It is definitely easier said than done for several reasons. One of the main reasons that we've repeatedly seen in past clients is the lack of a shared understanding of their value stream. Only a few select people have an idea (usually not up to date) of the whole high-level picture, while others are hermetically separated into departments where they can be productive with the minimum amount of knowledge possible.

This overview of EventStorming (and the diagrams) borrows from Alebrto Brandolini's book, *Introducing EventStorming: An Act of Deliberate Collective Learning*, with his permission. To learn more, see the *Resources* section at the end of this *Appendix*.

Silos and Value Streams

An alternative word for department is **silo**, to use a common metaphor. Brandolini says that "Silos do excel in one thing: they minimize the amount of learning needed for newcomers," or, expressed in the reverse way, they "Maximize the overall ignorance within an organization." Every organization is made up of silos to some extent, degrading its effectiveness, eroding its margins, or – in the worst cases – dooming it to fail. "The really nasty trait of silos is their asymmetry; they're easy to establish, and really hard to remove."

> **Note**
>
> All the quotes in this appendix are from Alberto Brandolini's book. Alberto Brandolini is an entrepreneur, consultant, developer, teacher, public speaker, and author. He has been coding since 1982, and his skillset encompasses topics such as Agile, Domain-Driven Design, Lean, Complexity, Management 3.0, and "everything needed in order to solve the problem." He is the CEO and Founder of Avanscoperta (https://www.avanscoperta.it/en/), he writes a blog (http://ziobrando.blogspot.com/), and he is a very active public speaker (https://www.slideshare.net/ziobrando).

Figure 23.1: EventStorming by Alberto Brandolini

In complex environments, the key factor in minimizing the effects of bounded rationality is access to the right information for making decisions. Basically, silos serve as boundaries, limiting the spread of knowledge in organizations, and preventing holistic understanding. This makes different departments behave more like different entities than parts within the same organization. In consequence, this promotes what Brandolini calls the *uneven distribution of expertise.* "Usually we'll have to deal with different knowledges and expertise, and the information we'll achieve can only be locally consistent: nobody holds the whole truth."

> **Note**
>
> Bounded rationality is a concept defined by Herbert Simon, winner of the Nobel Prize in Economics in 1978 and the Turing Award in 1975. It states, "Human beings make quite reasonable decisions, but only based on the information they have." The idea is that when individuals make decisions, their rationality is limited by the tractability of the decision problem, the cognitive limitations of their minds, and the time available to make the decision (https://en.wikipedia.org/wiki/Bounded_rationality and https://en.wikiquote.org/wiki/Bounded_rationality).

The main problem becomes evident when we consider that the value stream of an organization crosses all its silos; often the output of one department is the input for the next one downstream. "The obvious evidence of the problem is that one single source of knowledge won't be enough to solve problems that are spanning across multiple areas."

The Importance of Learning

Software development is a learning process, working code is a side effect.

– Alberto Brandolini

Dividing organizations in sealed departments without effective communication generates several problems, the main one being the lack of understanding of the business as a whole system by the people inside the single departments. The good thing is that the problem can potentially be resolved – or at least improved – with the right dose of learning. In this context, EventStorming becomes an amazing tool for enabling rapidly shared learning at an organizational level.

"It allows learning to happen across the silo boundaries. It's not an initiative to transform the organization, but a tool to understand what's going on, at a wider scale. We'll see how asking stakeholders to model a complex business flow together will expose many of the conflicts and contradictions happening at the boundaries between silos. It will also help to look for system-optimal solutions, which is hard, because the system is really hard to see, instead of a local, sub-optimal solution and a lot of useless politics to justify them."

The EventStorming Approach

EventStorming is a learning activity about the business's value stream delivered in the form of workshop. At a very high level, it can be seen as a process composed of several steps:

1. See the system as a whole.

2. Find a problem worth solving.

3. Gather the best, immediately available information.

4. Start implementing a solution from the best possible starting point.

This is what Alberto does with EventStorming: he gathers the people with the best available knowledge for the job and collaboratively builds a holistic model of the problem space, which usually is very complex.

In a changing world, everything is evolving: technology, people, the organization itself, the surrounding business, and the job market too. Assuming that one of these ingredients will be immutable during a nontrivial change initiative is not a legitimate simplification: it's just plain naive. But there is one thing that we can do: we can take a snapshot of the current reality and ensure that all the key players are looking at the same thing.

Whether the goal is to write a piece of critical software for the organization, or to design the next implementation of a business flow for a startup, or to redesign a key business process for an existing line of business, this means having a clear, shared understanding of the problem landscape and of the possible solutions.

The Workshop: A Quick Overview

The workshop requires a big enough space where a long paper roll (minimum of 8 meters) can be attached to the wall, where there is enough room for the people involved to walk up and down near the wall, but also at distance for a better holistic view. Seats should not be easily available, in order to stimulate participation and focus:

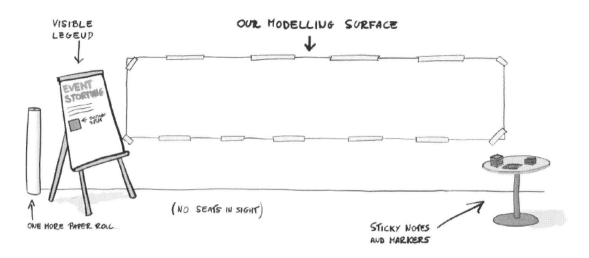

Figure 23.2: The room setup before the workshop

The workshop consists of using domain events and their temporal flow to build a model of the current shared understanding of the business. Each actor contributes to the part of the system he knows the most, which is always interrelated with other parts. At the end of the workshop, everything will be organized together in a coherent timeline stream, providing a detailed model of the current system.

After sorting out the logistics, the most important thing for a successful workshop is having the right people involved. Essentially, there are two kinds of people that are particularly interesting to have in the room: the ones who care and will ask questions, and the ones who know and will provide answers.

Caring about the problems, diversity in background, and a positive, inquisitive attitude are crucial. In fact, EventStorming provides a solid background for meaningful conversations across silo boundaries and an adaptable format that allows collaboration across multiple disciplines. This means that business experts, Lean experts, service designers, and software developers could all be part of the same conversation.

The goal of the workshop is set in the beginning: "**We are going to explore the business process as a whole by placing all the relevant events along a timeline. We'll highlight ideas, risks, and opportunities along the way**. Consider the following diagram:

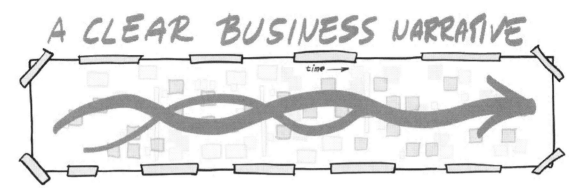

Figure 23.3: Building the narrative of the business

The process starts with the identification of the flow of domain events, represented by orange post-its and a name. Events are written in past tense (the order submitted, payment taken, and so on). This temporal flow forms the narrative of the business, and the events will be the building blocks of the business-related storytelling.

The model then gets enriched with the source of the events (user interactions triggering commands, external systems, and temporal triggers or automatic ones as a consequence of other events), the read models helping user decisions, and the policies describing the "aftermath" of an event, under the form of other commands to be triggered. Then, the discovery carries on, letting aggregates emerge as the central entities responsible for executing some of the commands and raising the relevant events. Any of these different elements of the model will have a different color to better identify the different concepts and to highlight them on the timeline:

Figure 23.4: The result of enabling shared understanding

Different Flavors of EventStorming

There are several levels of depth corresponding to several flavors of EventStorming, each one appropriate for a different context. Alberto says that he likes to think about it as "pizzas," with a common base but different toppings.

Here are the different flavors of EventStorming:

- **Big picture EventStorming**: The method used to kick off a project, with every stakeholder involved.

- **Design-level EventStorming**: Digs into possible implementation, often in DDD-CQRS/ES7 style.

- **Value-driven EventStorming**: A quick way to get into value-stream mapping, using storytelling as a possible platform.

- **UX-driven EventStorming**: Similar to Value-Driven EventStorming, focusing on the user/customer journey in the quest for usability and flawless execution.

- **EventStorming as a retrospective**: Using domain events to baseline a flow and expand the scope in order to look for improvement opportunities.

- **EventStorming as a learning tool**: Perfect to maximize learning for new hires.

360 | EventStorming by Alberto Brandolini

Complex Systems and Proven Solutions

In complex systems, context becomes the driving force; strategies and solutions are not safely repeatable. There are no silver bullets, and what worked before might not work tomorrow for a different situation since the new contextual information will be different.

We agree with Alberto when he says, "Conservative organizations are usually reluctant to fully embrace the consequences of complexity. Risk-adverse culture manifests itself in the pursuit of proven solutions rather than adventurous experimental ones in controlled environments or forms."

Unfortunately, in complex domains, there is no such thing as a "proven solution." Like in football, hiring the best coach with the longest winning streak does not guarantee that your team will win the championship next year.

In practice, being dogmatically risk-averse turns out to be a very risky strategy in a complex domain. And, we might add, incredibly wasteful.

Resources

Web

- Alberto Brandolini's blog: https://medium.com/@ziobrando.

Books

- Introducing EventStorming, An Act of Deliberate Collective Learning, Alberto Brandolini: https://leanpub.com/introducing_eventstorming.

License: CyberDojo

About CyberDojo Foundation Exercises

Most of the exercises used in this book are from the CyberDojo Foundation. We used these exercises since many developers are already familiar with them.

Web Resources

- CyberDojo exercises: https://github.com/cyber-dojo-retired/start-points-exercises.

Sample Solutions

Sample Solutions: FizzBuzz in Clojure

For the kata associated with this solution, see FizzBuzz by CyberDojo:

```clojure
(ns clojure-katas.fizzbuzz)


(defn fizzBuzz [n]
  (let [divisible-by? #(= 0 (rem %2 %1))
        divisible-by-three? (divisible-by? 3 n)
        divisible-by-five? (divisible-by? 5 n)
        divisible-by-three-and-five? (divisible-by? 15 n)]
    (cond
      divisible-by-three-and-five? "fizzbuzz"
      divisible-by-three? "fizz"
      divisible-by-five? "buzz"
```

```
        :else (str n))))
```

```
  (ns clojure-katas.fizzbuzz-test
    (:require [clojure.test :refer :all]
              [clojure-katas.fizzbuzz :refer :all]))
```

```
(deftest should-fizzbuzz-number
  (are [number expected] (= expected (fizzBuzz number))
    1  "1"
    2  "2"
    3  "fizz"
    6  "fizz"
    9  "fizz"
    5  "buzz"
    10 "buzz"
    20 "buzz"
    15 "fizzbuzz"
    30 "fizzbuzz"
    45 "fizzbuzz"))
```

Sample Solutions: Fibonacci Sequence in C++

For the exercise associated with this solution, see Nth Fibonacci section by CyberDojo:

```
#ifndef CPPKATAS_SRC_FIBONACCI_H
#define CPPKATAS_SRC_FIBONACCI_H

constexpr auto Fibonacci(const unsigned short index)
{
    if(index == 0) { return 0;}
    if(index == 1) { return 1;}
```

```
        return Fibonacci(index - 1) + Fibonacci(index - 2);
}


#endif


#define CATCH_CONFIG_MAIN


#include "catch.hpp"
#include "../src/Fibonacci.hpp"


TEST_CASE("Calculate fibonacci number for index", "[Fibonacci]")
{
    REQUIRE(Fibonacci(0) == 0);
    REQUIRE(Fibonacci(1) == 1);
    REQUIRE(Fibonacci(2) == 1);
    REQUIRE(Fibonacci(3) == 2);
    REQUIRE(Fibonacci(3) == 2);
    REQUIRE(Fibonacci(4) == 3);
    REQUIRE(Fibonacci(5) == 5);
    REQUIRE(Fibonacci(6) == 8);
    REQUIRE(Fibonacci(7) == 13);
}
```

Sample Solutions: Roman Numerals in C#

For the kata associated with this solution, see Roman Numerals by cyber-dojo:

We start by writing the simplest unit test we can think of:

```
[TestFixture]
public class RomanConverterShould
{
    [TestCase(1, "I")]
```

```
    public void ConvertNumberToRoman(int number, string expected)
    {
        var romanNumeral = new RomanConverter().Convert(number);
        Assert.That(romanNumeral, Is.EqualTo(expected));
    }
}
```

We start the implementation using the first transformation, that is, no code to nil:

```
// 1 nil
public class RomanConverter
{
    public string Convert(int number)
    {
        return null;
    }
}
```

The first transformation is not enough to make the test pass, so we apply the second transformation: nil to constant. This is enough to make the test pass, so we stop evolving the code until we have a failing test:

```
// 2 nil -> constant
public class RomanConverter
{
    public string Convert(int number)
    {
        return "I";
    }
}
```

We add a new failing test:

```
[TestFixture]
public class RomanConverterShould
{
    [TestCase(1, "I")]
    [TestCase(2, "II")]
```

```
        public void ConvertNumberToRoman(int number, string expected)
        {
            var romanNumeral = new RomanConverter().Convert(number);
            Assert.That(romanNumeral, Is.EqualTo(expected));
        }
    }
```

The next transformation, constant to variable, is not sufficient to make the test pass. The next transformation, statement to statements, is also not sufficient to make the test pass.

> **Note**
>
> This is not strictly true; there is a constructor of a string that repeats a char. We could have used it here, but we decided not to. Applying the next transformation, unconditional to conditional, is sufficient to make the test pass.

```
// 6 unconditional -> conditional
public class RomanConverter
{
    public string Convert(int number)
    {
        var result = "I";

        if (number >= 1)
        {
            result += "I";
        }

        return result;
    }
}
```

We add a new failing test:

```
 [TestFixture]
 public class RomanConverterShould
 {
     [TestCase(1, "I")]
     [TestCase(2, "II")]
     [TestCase(3, "III")]
     public void ConvertNumberToRoman(int number, string expected)
     {
         var romanNumeral = new RomanConverter().Convert(number);
         Assert.That(romanNumeral, Is.EqualTo(expected));
     }
 }
```

Adding another conditional will make the test pass, but cause duplication:

```
 public class RomanConverter
 {
     public string Convert(int number)
     {
         var result = "I";
         if (number > 1)
         {
             result += "I";
         }

         if (number > 2)
         {
             result += "I";
         }

         return result;
     }
 }
```

Applying the next transformation, variable to array, removes the duplication:

```
// 7 variable -> array
public class RomanConverter
{
    public static readonly string[] Results = { "I", "II", "III" };

    public string Convert(int number)
    {
        return Results[number - 1];
    }
}
```

We add a new failing test:

```
[TestFixture]
public class RomanConverterShould
{
    [TestCase(1, "I")]
    [TestCase(2, "II")]
    [TestCase(3, "III")]
    [TestCase(4, "IV")]
    public void ConvertNumberToRoman(int number, string expected)
    {
        var romanNumeral = new RomanConverter().Convert(number);
        Assert.That(romanNumeral, Is.EqualTo(expected));
    }
}
```

To make the test pass, we don't need to apply the next transformation. We can make the test pass by adding a new element to the array:

```
// no transformation
public class RomanConverter
{
    public static readonly string[] Results = { "I", "II", "III", "IV" };
```

```
    public string Convert(int number)

    {

        return Results[number - 1];

    }

}
```

While adding a new element to the array was enough to make the test pass, we now spot some duplication on character I. By applying the next transformation, statement to tail recursion, we can get rid of this duplication. Since we are trying to follow the transformation table, we applied the array to the container (in this case, we used a collection container) transformation before the tail recursion:

```
// 8 array -> collection
public class RomanConverter

{

    public static readonly IDictionary<int, string> Results =

        new Dictionary<int, string>

        {

            {1, "I"},
            {2, "II"},
            {3, "III"},
            {4, "IV"},

        };


    public string Convert(int number)

    {

        return Results[number];

    }

}
```

```
// 9 statement -> tail recursion
public class RomanConverter

{

    public static readonly IDictionary<int, string> Results = new
    Dictionary<int, string>
```

```
{
    {1, "I"},
    {4, "IV"},
};

public string Convert(int number)
{
    if (Results.ContainsKey(number))
    {
        return Results[number];
    }

    return Results[1] + Convert(number - 1);
}
}
```

We add a few more failing tests, but as the last transformation was still allowing us to make tests pass, we waited until we had a duplication to refactor:

```
[TestFixture]
public class RomanConverterShould
{
    [TestCase(1, "I")]
    [TestCase(2, "II")]
    [TestCase(3, "III")]
    [TestCase(4, "IV")]
    [TestCase(5, "V")]
    [TestCase(6, "VI")]
    [TestCase(7, "VII")]
    [TestCase(8, "VIII")]
    public void ConvertNumberToRoman(int number, string expected)
    {
```

```
        var romanNumeral = new RomanConverter().Convert(number);

        Assert.That(romanNumeral, Is.EqualTo(expected));

    }

}
```

No other transformations are required. Simply adding new values to the dictionary allowed us to make the tests pass, but we can now spot the duplication, which is again around character I:

```
public class RomanConverter

{

    public static readonly IDictionary<int, string> Results =

    new Dictionary<int, string>

    {

        {1, "I"},

        {4, "IV"},

        {5, "V"},

        {6, "VI"},

        {7, "VII"},

        {8, "VIII"},

    };

    public string Convert(int number)

    {

        if (Results.ContainsKey(number))

        {

            return Results[number];

        }

        return Results[1] + Convert(number - 1);

    }

}
```

To fix the duplication, we again apply the transformation statement to tail recursion. We don't yet need to move to the next transformation:

```
// 9 statement -> tail recursion
public class RomanConverter
{
    public static readonly IDictionary<int, string> Results =
    new Dictionary<int, string>
    {
        {1, "I"},
        {4, "IV"},
        {5, "V"},
    };

    public string Convert(int number)
    {
        if (Results.ContainsKey(number))
        {
            return Results[number];
        }

        if (number > 5)
        {
            const string result = "V";
            return result + Convert(number - 5);
        }

        return Results[1] + Convert(number - 1);
    }
}
```

Again, we add more failing tests, and again the last transformation is still making tests pass:

```
[TestFixture]
public class RomanConverterShould
{
    [TestCase(1, "I")]
    [TestCase(2, "II")]
    [TestCase(3, "III")]
    [TestCase(4, "IV")]
    [TestCase(5, "V")]
    [TestCase(6, "VI")]
    [TestCase(7, "VII")]
    [TestCase(8, "VIII")]
    [TestCase(9, "IX")]
    [TestCase(10, "X")]
    [TestCase(40, "XL")]
    [TestCase(44, "XLIV")]
    public void ConvertNumberToRoman(int number, string expected)
    {
        var romanNumeral = new RomanConverter().Convert(number);
        Assert.That(romanNumeral, Is.EqualTo(expected));
    }
}

// Wait for patterns to emerge
public class RomanConverter
{
    public static readonly IDictionary<int, string> Results =
        new Dictionary<int, string>
        {
            {1, "I"},
            {4, "IV"},
```

```
                {5, "V"},
                {9, "IX"},
                {10, "X"},
                {40, "XL"},
        };

public string Convert(int number)
{
    if (Results.ContainsKey(number))
    {
        return Results[number];
    }

    if (number > 40)
    {
        const string result = "XL";
        return result + Convert(number - 40);
    }

    if (number > 10)
    {
        const string result = "X";
        return result + Convert(number - 10);
    }

    if (number > 5)
    {
        const string result = "V";
        return result + Convert(number - 5);
    }
```

```
            return Results[1] + Convert(number - 1);

    }

}
```

We spot duplication around **if** statements, so we refactor the code to the next transformation. **if** to **while**. This gets rid of the **if** statement duplication, but we now have the **while** statement duplication:

```
// 10 if -> while

public class RomanConverter

{

    public static readonly IDictionary<int, string> Results =

        new Dictionary<int, string>

        {

            {1, "I"},

            {4, "IV"},

            {5, "V"},

            {9, "IX"},

            {10, "X"},

            {40, "XL"},

        };


    public string Convert(int number)

    {

        if (Results.ContainsKey(number))

        {

            return Results[number];

        }


        string result = string.Empty;


        while (number >= 40)

        {
```

```
        result += "XL";
        number -= 40;
    }

    while (number >= 10)
    {
        result += "X";
        number -= 10;
    }

    while (number >= 5)
    {
        result += "V";
        number -= 5;
    }

    while (number >= 4)
    {
        result += "IV";
        number -= 4;
    }

    while (number >= 1)
    {
        result += "I";
        number -= 1;
    }

    return result;
    }
}
```

We apply the same **if** to **while** transformation to the remaining **if** statement, and this allows us to get rid of the duplicated **while** statements. In order for this to work, it's more convenient to have the dictionary reversed, so we also do this:

```csharp
// 10 if -> while. We used a foreach in place of a while loop since it is a
simpler contruct in C#
public class RomanConverter
{
    public static readonly IDictionary<int, string> mappings =
        new Dictionary<int, string>
        {
            {40, "XL"},
            {10, "X"},
            {9, "IX"},
            {5, "V"},
            {4, "IV"},
            {1, "I"},
        };

    public string Convert(int number)
    {
        string result = string.Empty;

        foreach(var mapping in mappings)
        {
            while (number >= mapping.Key)
            {
                result += mapping.Value;
                number -= mapping.Key;
            }
        }
    }
```

```
        return result;
    }
}
```

We add more failing tests, but the last transformation is sufficient to make all new tests pass. We cannot think of any more failing tests, and this implies we are done. We refactor the code to make it more readable, and we are done. We decided to refactor the outer **while** loop to a **foreach** loop since it simplifies the code.

This is an example of where you can start changing the table to better fit the language you work with. In this case, you replace the **while** loop transformation with a **foreach** transformation:

```
// final solution

[TestFixture]

public class RomanConverterShould

{
    [TestCase(1, "I")]
    [TestCase(2, "II")]
    [TestCase(3, "III")]
    [TestCase(4, "IV")]
    [TestCase(5, "V")]
    [TestCase(6, "VI")]
    [TestCase(7, "VII")]
    [TestCase(8, "VIII")]
    [TestCase(9, "IX")]
    [TestCase(10, "X")]
    [TestCase(40, "XL")]
    [TestCase(50, "L")]
    [TestCase(90, "XC")]
    [TestCase(100, "C")]
    [TestCase(400, "CD")]
    [TestCase(500, "D")]
    [TestCase(900, "CM")]
```

```
[TestCase(1000, "M")]
[TestCase(846, "DCCCXLVI")]
[TestCase(1999, "MCMXCIX")]
[TestCase(2008, "MMVIII")]
public void ConvertNumberToRoman(int number, string expected)
{
    var romanNumeral = new RomanConverter().Convert(number);
    Assert.That(romanNumeral, Is.EqualTo(expected));
}
}


public class RomanConverter
{
    public static readonly IDictionary<int, string> arabicsToRomans =
            new Dictionary<int, string>
            {
                {1000, "M"},
                {900, "CM"},
                {500, "D"},
                {400, "CD"},
                {100, "C"},
                {90, "XC"},
                {50, "XL"},
                {40, "XL"},
                {10, "X"},
                {9, "IX"},
                {5, "V"},
                {4, "IV"},
                {1, "I"},
            };
```

```
        public string Convert(int number)
        {
            var result = string.Empty;

            foreach(var arabicToRoman in arabicsToRomans)
            {
                while (number >= arabicToRoman.Key)
                {
                    result += arabicToRoman.Value;
                    number -= arabicToRoman.Key;
                }
            }

            return result;
        }
    }
}
```

Sample Solutions: Tic-Tac-Toe in Swift (Partial Solution)

For the exercise associated with this sample solution, see Smelly Tic-Tac-Toe:

```
import XCTest

enum TicTacToeError: Error {
    case invalidPlayer
    case invalidPosition
}

enum Player {
    case o
    case x
}
```

```swift
enum Position {
    case topLeft
    case topMiddle
}


class Board {
    var playedPositions: [Position] = []

    func append(position: Position) throws {
        if playedPositions.contains(position) {
            throw TicTacToeError.invalidPosition
        }

        playedPositions.append(position)
    }
}


class Game {
    var lastPlayer: Player = .o
    let board: Board = Board()

    func play(player: Player, position: Position) throws {
        if lastPlayer == player {
            throw TicTacToeError.invalidPlayer
        }

        lastPlayer = player
        try board.append(position: position)
    }
}
```

```swift
class TicTacToeTests: XCTestCase {

    let game: Game = Game()


    func test_thatGameDoesNotAllowPlayerOToPlayFirst() {
        XCTAssertThrowsError(try game.play(player: .o, position: .topLeft))
{ error in
            XCTAssertEqual(error as? TicTacToeError, .invalidPlayer)
        }
    }


    func test_thatGameDoesNotAllowPlayerXToPlayTwice() {
        XCTAssertNoThrow(try game.play(player: .x, position: .topLeft))
        XCTAssertThrowsError(try game.play(player: .x, position: .topMiddle))
{ error in
            XCTAssertEqual(error as? TicTacToeError, .invalidPlayer)
        }
    }


    func test_thatGameDoesNotAllowPlayersToPlayInPreviousPlayedPosition() {
        XCTAssertNoThrow(try game.play(player: .x, position: .topLeft))
        XCTAssertThrowsError(try game.play(player: .o, position: .topLeft))
{ error in
            XCTAssertEqual(error as? TicTacToeError, .invalidPosition)
        }
    }


    func test_thatGameDoesNotAllowPlayersToPlayInAnyPreviousPlayedPosition()
{
        XCTAssertNoThrow(try game.play(player: .x, position: .topLeft))
        XCTAssertNoThrow(try game.play(player: .o, position: .topMiddle))
        XCTAssertThrowsError(try game.play(player: .x, position: .topLeft))
{ error in
            XCTAssertEqual(error as? TicTacToeError, .invalidPosition)
```

```
        }
    }
}
```

Sample Solutions: Connecting Code Smells with Cohesion/Coupling

For the kata associated with this solution, see the Connecting Code Smells with Cohesion/Coupling section:

Code smells	Indication of Cohesion/Coupling problem
Alternative Classes with Different Interfaces	Too low Coupling – The class hierarchy is probably wrong.
Comments	Too low Cohesion
Data Class	Too low Cohesion – Class misses behavior.
Data Clumps	Too low Cohesion – Duplication instead of encapsulation.
Dead Code	Too low Cohesion
Divergent Change	Cohesion/Coupling
Duplicated Code	Cohesion/Coupling
Feature Envy	Too high Coupling and too low Cohesion – Data and behavior in separate places.
Inappropriate Intimacy	Too high Coupling and too low Cohesion – Data and behavior in separate places.
Large Class	Too high Cohesion – The class is probably doing too much.
Lazy Class	Too low Cohesion – Class misses state or behavior.
Long Method	Too high Cohesion – The method is probably doing too much.
Long Parameter List	Too high Cohesion – The method is probably doing too much.
Message Chains	Too high Coupling – A class knows too much about non-immediate neighbors.
Middle Man	Too low Cohesion – Class just delegates behavior and has no behavior or state.
Parallel Inheritance Hierarchies	Too low Coupling – The class hierarchy is probably wrong.
Primitive Obsession	Too low Cohesion – Behavior that should be in a type is scattered.
Refused Bequest	Too high Coupling – The class hierarchy is probably wrong.
Shotgun Surgery	Cohesion/Coupling
Speculative Generality	Too low Cohesion
Switch Statements	Too low Cohesion – If switch statements are duplicated.
Temporary Field	Too low Cohesion – Field is not really part of the state of a class.

Figure 25.1: Connecting code smells with cohesion/coupling

Sample Solutions: Connecting Object Calisthenics with Code Smells and Cohesion/Coupling

For the kata associated with this solution, see Connecting object calisthenics with code smells and Cohesion/Coupling:

Object calisthenics	Code smell	Cohesion / Coupling
Only one level of indentation per method.	Long Method	Cohesion
Don't use the ELSE keyword.	Long Method / Duplicated Code	Cohesion
Wrap all primitives and strings.	Primitive Obsession	Cohesion
First class collections.	Divergent Change	Cohesion
One dot per line.	Message Chains	Coupling
Don't abbreviate.	NA	Cohesion
Keep all entities small.	Large Class / Long Method / Long Parameter List	Cohesion
No classes with more than two instance variables.	Large Class	Cohesion
No getters / setters / properties.	NA	Coupling
All classes must have state, no static methods, no utility classes.	Lazy class / Middle Man	Cohesion

Figure 25.2 : Connecting object calisthenics with code smells and cohesion/coupling

Sample Solutions: Connecting Cohesion/Coupling and SOLID Principles

For the kata associated with this solution, see the Connecting Cohesion/Coupling and SOLID Principles section:

Solid Principle	Cohesion / Coupling	Reason
Single Responsibility Principle	Cohesion	Functional Cohesion
Open/Closed Principle	Coupling	Coupling and Cohesion by change
Liskov Substitution Principle	Coupling	Coupling at inheritance tree level
Interface Segregation Principle	Cohesion	Functional Cohesion
Dependency inversion Principle	Coupling	Reduce Coupling by not having dependencies internally

Figure 25.3: Connecting cohesion/coupling and SOLID principles

Feedback

Personalized Coaching

Sometimes just reading a book on your own is not enough. If you want to get feedback on your progress, discuss the ideas presented in the book, get help on a specific topic, or have one of us coach you or your team, we are more than happy to help. We have multiple options available targeted to organizations and individuals.

Individuals

If you want to have feedback or give feedback or just watch the discussions about the single topics presented, please join our free community at Agile Tech Praxis https://discourse.agiletechpraxis.com/.

Organizations

All authors have multiple years of experience coaching developers in a wide range of organizations. If you would like to discuss coaching services for your organizations, contact us at **info@agiletechpraxis.com** or on Twitter **@agiletechpraxis**. We can provide onsite or online coaching of software developers and teams.

We are based in London, UK, but we can travel or alternatively use remote technology for coaching sessions.

Feedback Please

We can't just sit back and wait for feedback to be offered, particularly when we're in a leadership role. If we want feedback to take root in the culture, we need to explicitly ask for it.

– Ed Batista

Following up to this quote, we would love to hear your feedback about this book:

- What you liked

- What inspired you

- What you learned

- What we missed

- What we could have explained better

- What you disagree with

We value your opinions and feelings about this work, and we will be always thankful if you decide to share them with us. You can go to our Quick Feedback Form at http://www.agiletechpraxis.com/feedback or send us an email at **info@agiletechpraxis.com**.

When we make progress and get better at something, it is inherently motivating. In order for people to make progress, they have to get feedback and information on how they're doing. Daniel H. Pink

Index

About

All major keywords used in this book are captured alphabetically in this section. Each one is accompanied by the page number of where they appear.

Printed in Great Britain
by Amazon